Perfect D

AMSTERDAM

Travel with
Insider
Tips

www.marco-polo.com

MARCO ⊕ POLO

Contents

 TOP 10   4

That Amsterdam Feeling   6

For chapters: see inside front cover

TOP 10

Not to be missed!

Our TOP 10 hits – from the absolute No. 1 to No. 10 – help you plan your tour of the most important sights.

⭐ CANAL TOURS ➤ 88
Hundreds of canals, lined with old trees and magnificent merchant mansions, traverse the old city. Amsterdam seems to have been made to be enjoyed from the water.

⭐ RIJKSMUSEUM ➤ 120
Rembrandt, Vermeer, et al. – the Rijksmuseum is one of Europe's greatest art centres. It reopened in 2013 after ten years of renovation and once again shines in all its original glory.

⭐ VAN GOGH MUSEUM ➤ 124
It was almost impossible to sell Vincent van Gogh's works during his lifetime but today his art is sold for record sums. The world's finest collection of his works can be found in Amsterdam.

⭐ JORDAAN ➤ 92
Atmospheric architecture, a village ambiance and picturesque views set the scene in the former working-class Jordaan district. Top tip: the hidden *hofjes*.

⭐ ANNE FRANK HUIS ➤ 96
From the outside, it is hard to imagine the drama that took place behind the facade of this merchant house on Prinsengracht. Today this impressive place is a sobering reminder of the fate of Anne Frank, who lived here in hiding for two years.

⭐ DE WALLEN ➤ 56
Prostitutes, coffeeshops and the oldest buildings in the city: every city has its red-light district where the normal rules of society no longer apply – but nowhere else is it quite like Amsterdam.

⭐ STEDELIJK MUSEUM ➤ 128
With the fascinating, sophisticated works on display, the Stedelijk – the city's museum of modern art – makes sure that lovers of art are kept up to date. A futuristic new extension was opened in 2013.

⭐ VONDELPARK ➤ 130
Locals and tourists alike flock to the city's green lung to enjoy all of its attractive recreational facilities, including theatre performances, a rose garden, fountains and cafés.

⭐ HET SCHEEPVAARTMUSEUM ➤ 146
The 17th and 18th centuries were the golden age of Amsterdam's merchant fleet and its history is brought to life in the exhibits of this maritime museum. A tall ship replica is also moored outside the museum.

⭐ WESTERKERK ➤ 101
This is one of the city's first Protestant churches and is also Rembrandt's final resting place. The tower houses Amsterdam's heaviest bell and also offers wonderful panoramic views.

THAT

AMSTERDAM

Find out what makes the city tick, experience its unique flair – just like the Amsterdammers themselves.

CYCLE THROUGH THE CITY ON A *FIETS*

Rent a **bicycle** (➤ 28) and peddle through the Grachtenring, the narrow streets in the Jordaan district, across the Dam or along the banks of the IJ at your own pace. Do as the locals: cyclists are allowed to ride side by side and the wrong way down one-way streets here. You will find a café where you can stop for a break wherever you go. Those who don't want to be alone can take part in one of the **guided tours** that many bicycle rental companies offer (such as the two-hour tour with Yellow Bike, daily 1:30pm, Nieuwezijds Kolk 29).

MULTICULTURAL LIFE AT THE MARKET

Especially on Saturday, it seems that half of Amsterdam is out shopping for fish and vegetables at the street markets – or to eat some fresh syrup waffles or crispy *loempia* spring rolls. The largest market with the greatest cultural mix is the **Albert Cuypmarkt** (➤ 165); things are somewhat more tranquil at **Noordermarkt** (➤ 113) and on neighbouring **Lindengracht**. It is part of the market tradition to end the visit with a slice of apple pie and a *koffie verkeerd* in **Café Winkel** (➤ 47).

TEMPTING CHIPS

Crispy, hot chips with a decent portion of creamy mayonnaise wrapped in a paper cone: the very thought is enough to make your mouth start to water. The best chips in Amsterdam are served at small street stalls at the markets or at established locations. The popular **Vleminckx** chip shop on Voetboog-straat (➤ 47) even offers 20 varieties of mayonnaise. As an alternative, the locals sometimes eat their *frietjes* with Indonesian peanut sauce but never with tomato ketchup.

AND NOW, LET'S CROSS THE IJ...

When Amsterdammers feel the need to escape from the hustle and bustle of the inner city, they just take the ferry **across the IJ**. The five-minute boat trip to the shore on the other side is free of charge and you are sure to enjoy the wonderful view across the water. There, you will be able to choose between a visit to the futuristic Film Museum and **EYE Film Instituut** (➤ 132; ferry to Buiksloterweg, IJpromenade 1, daily 10am–1am) or a cycle tour through **Nieuwendammerdijk** (✚ 207 northeast of the F5); what was formerly a dike village is now a piece of picture-book Holland

FEELING

The laid-back atmosphere of the street cafés on the Lindegracht in the Jordaan

That Amsterdam Feeling

The EYE Film Instituut

on the outskirts of town. You can pause for refreshments at the idyllic harbour café **'t Sluisje** (daily from midday, Nieuwendammerdijk 297, www.cafehetsluisje.nl).

PROOST!

The literal translation of *borreluur* is "cocktail hour" and describes the period after office hours when colleagues like to get together in one of the "brown cafés" just around the corner. There, those in the convivial groups drink a beer accompanied by a couple of *bitterballen* – round croquettes. Quite a few of the pubs are completely full at that time and people just have to take their beer and stand outside. The **Café Brandon** (Keizersgracht 157, ✚ 203 D2) is one of the most popular watering holes because it even has its own landing stage on the canal.

CREATIVE SCENE AT THE SHIPYARDS

Amsterdam is famous for its liberal creative scene and you can im-

merse yourself in it when you take the twenty-minute free ferry trip from the main railway station to the **NDSM-Werft**. An art community has now settled where ship hulls used to be welded. There are several cafés, an urban beach and artists' studios, and a gigantic flea market is held once a month in an old wharf warehouse. The dates of the flea market vary. (TT Neveritaweg 15, www. ijhallen.nl, ✚ 203 north of the E5).

AN EVENING SPENT STROLLING AROUND THE CANALS

The canals, with their picturesque bridges and magnificent mansions, are very beautiful during the day. But an **evening stroll** also offers many rewards: hardly any of the houses have curtains and it is therefore possible to see into the well lit rooms on the lower floors. The people living there are aware of this and they have their best furniture on display there. You will see designer furnishings or high-quality antiques beneath stucco ceilings and centuries-old beams and get an insight into life along the canals.

LONG LIVE THE KING!

Collective madness is de rigueur at the annual **King's Day** celebrations. Until recently Queen Beatrix was honoured but now attention is officially focused on her son Willem-Alexander on 27 April. In reality, it is all about the typical Dutch party spirit coupled with business acumen: the entire city is turned into an enormous flea market in the morning and bands perform everywhere in the afternoon. Make sure you have some cash with you to buy some trinkets and head off to the Jordaan district where the festivities are the most social.

The Magazine

Cultural Capital

In the family of great European cities, Amsterdam is the younger sibling. In recent years, though, the city has really come of age.

Cultural Centres

After an extensive renovation the Stedelijk Museum of Modern Art (➤ 128) was reopened in 2013 and once again features influential exhibitions. Amsterdam also hosts world-class theatre and dance, but is, above all, musical. Bells ring out from its centuries-old carillons and the city boasts a rich programme of musical events. The Royal Concertgebouw Orchestra, along with visiting companies from jazz to world music, perform at the Concertgebouw (Concert Hall) (➤ 129–130). The city's cultural scene is all-inclusive as well as a thriving street art scene. Amsterdam can never be accused of being elitist.

Golden Age

A millennium ago, the city was nothing but a marsh, a short way inland from where the Rhine spills into the North Sea. The first inhabitants set about modifying the swampy surroundings, establishing the pattern for the growth of the city. Adaptability and change are the watchwords of the Dutch – virtues that enabled them to survive against considerable natural and man-made adversity, then use the upsurge in world trade to fund the Golden Age of the 17th century. The profit centre then, as now, was Amsterdam, the city that lives by its wits.

Building Bridges

The city's articulate, animated community resides on the banks of a network of canals. The inky waters reflect a thousand bridges, and many thousands of handsome houses overlooking cobbled streets.

WHERE'S THE PARLIAMENT?

Even though Amsterdam is the Dutch capital, the country's elected represent-
atives meet at a much smaller city. The Hague owes its position as seat of the
Dutch government to its choice as the residence of Count Willem II of Holland
in the 13th century; the official name, s-Gravenhage, means "the count's
hedge". Later, the States-General of Holland was established there. Parliament
still deliberates well away from the many temptations of Amsterdam – partly
through tradition, but also because many Dutch people fret about the concentration of power in Amsterdam, a city that dominates commercially and
culturally, yet is home to just one in 20 of the nation's population.

Compact Centre

In many ways, the city still resembles the village that the original inhabitants
created by damming the Amstel River. Yet, despite its size, it is one of the
most cosmopolitan cities on the Continent, with large communities from
Indonesia, the Caribbean and North Africa. Compared with other European
capitals, Amsterdam is tiny – just three-quarters of a million people packed
into not quite enough space. Nevertheless, the city boasts one of the highest
concentrations of art and culture in the world and is an undisputed cultural
capital, as civilized as it is diverse.

A Civilized Approach

The famous tolerance of its inhabitants has helped make Amsterdam
superlative in terms of art, architecture and culture. Deeply democratic,
its all-embracing attitude has acted as a magnet for artists from all over
the world, while its practical, open approach towards drugs and prostitution,
in many ways means a more civilized city for all.

Prostitutes are regularly health screened and pay the highest rate of taxes,
while the distinction between hard and soft drugs and the emphasis on
education has resulted in one of the lowest rates of drug use in the world.

Magere Brug allowing water traffic through on the Amstel River

RECLAIMED
FROM THE SEA

Flying into Schiphol airport is an interesting experience. The North Sea ends abruptly at a sturdy line of dunes and the pilot has to land his plane 3.35m (11ft) below sea level.

In theory, much of the Netherlands is unfit for human habitation. Just north of Rotterdam, it hits an all-time low: the land is 6.76m (22.1ft) below sea level. This is a country where, extraordinarily, one third of the nation, including a substantial proportion of Amsterdam, lies beneath a line over which the North Sea would naturally flow were there no barrier. Sixty per cent of the Dutch population, in a band between the Schelde estuary near Belgium and the German border, lives beneath NAP – Normaal Amsterdams Peil, or Standard Amsterdam Level.

Shore Foundations
It was not always like this. In 500BC, the sea level was lower and much of the coastline intact. By the end of the first millennium, the North Sea had encroached on large parts of what is now the Netherlands, with broad

Around 3,000km (1,865 miles) of dykes protect the land from flooding

The IJsselmeer, a popular sailing area, was created in its present form in 1932

estuaries interspersed with precariously marshy land. The first settlers in Amsterdam started to make the terrain habitable using a method that has served the Dutch well ever since: digging earth from the swamp to build up artificial islands, which gradually grew and became linked as human activity increased. The construction of robust dykes meant that the enclosed area, once drained, could be populated or farmed. Two great technological developments accelerated the process: the use of windmills to drive screw pumps, enabling larger areas to be drained and kept free of water; and the arrival of steam-powered pumps at the end of the 18th century. These added more muscle, and enabled the large-scale reclamation most notable in the former Zuiderzee ("South Sea", north of Amsterdam), now the IJsselmeer.

Statue of the final block being laid on the Afsluitdijk

Restless Tides

There have been disastrous floods along the way, though, and the water that helped Amsterdam make its fortune is treated with great respect. Its significance and destructive potential was acknowledged more than three centuries ago, long before London became the location for the world's prime meridian: in 1684,

The Magazine

Standard Amsterdam Level was established. The zero-point from which altitude is calibrated in much of northern Europe was located in the city, which, at the time, was connected with the North Sea, as the average high water mark of the Zuiderzee. Today, you can visit a replica of the original bronze marker in the Stopera. It is beneath ground level at that point, but not by very much. Alongside it are water columns that give a graphic representation of the problem. A digital link from the North Sea shows the current level of the tide at IJmuiden (the closest North Sea port to Amsterdam) and Vlissingen, in the far southwest. A third column shows the level reached by the sea in the most recent catastrophic floods: in 1953, much of it was inundated by a tide that reached 4.5m (14.7ft) above sea level in Amsterdam.

Piles of Piles

Every Dutch schoolchild knows that the Royal Palace is supported on 13,659 wooden piles, to keep it from sinking into the swamp on which Amsterdam stands unsteadily. The technique of driving round wooden

piles down to the first solid layer of sand, 12m (39ft) below ground level, was widely employed during the building of the city – but not universally, as several dangerously teetering houses will testify. The most notable is De Sluyswacht, at the south end of Oudeschans, just opposite the Rembrandthuis (➤ 70). It was built, not particularly well, in 1695 and soon acquired its amusing

> "One aesthetic benefit of the challenge to builders is that Amsterdam's sky-line has few skyscrapers"

lop-sidedness. It is now a café (➤ 76). As long as the wooden piles are completely surrounded by water, they remain intact. However, if air comes into contact with them they can start to rot, with unhappy consequences. Modern building techniques use square concrete piles, driven down to the second layer of sand at 20m (65ft), or even lower. One aesthetic benefit of the challenge to builders is that Amsterdam's skyline has few skyscrapers.

An Italian Connection?

Amsterdam is often described by travel writers short of a cliché as "The Venice of the North". Numerically, there are clear similarities: both cities were built on around 100 islands, crossed by about 150 canals and linked by several hundred bridges. Both used their maritime connections to develop economic and cultural links that placed them well ahead of rival cities, and each is now heavily reliant upon tourism. But the comparison stops there. Venice may slowly be sinking, but at least the first settlers enjoyed terra firma to start with. The Italians have not filled in many of their canals, as they have in Amsterdam; and Venice is unsullied by the cars that clog the narrow streets of the Dutch city. It could be some time before Venice finds itself described as "The Amsterdam of the South".

De Sluyswacht café enjoys a prime position

GABLE
VISION

Amsterdam is coy about architecture. There are few extravagant flourishes; nothing to match the dramatic structures of London, Paris or Berlin. So, instead of a single icon, the defining image of Amsterdam is on a much smaller scale: the ornate gables that top many canalside buildings.

Ornamental Origins

To cope with the all too frequent rain, roofs need to be sharply raked. Elsewhere in northern Europe, these steep roofs are unadorned, but in

The Prinsengracht has many beautiful and historic gabled houses

JAN PIETERSZ· HUIS

KNOWN AT THIS ADDRESS

"Gable stones" are the often beautifully designed tablets that embellish many old houses. In the days when many people could not read or write, these signified the owner or purpose of the premises. The best collection is on a wall in the southwest corner of the Begijnhof (▶ 61), where gable stones from a number of demolished properties are embedded.

Amsterdam, during the 17th-century Golden Age, it became de rigueur to decorate and hide their inverted "V" shape. In keeping with the city's spirit of diversity, gables are individual and distinctive. Most, though, fall into one of four categories. The most basic version is a spout gable, like an upside-down funnel, which adheres closely to the shape of the roof, and is only a modest embellishment to the form of the front wall. There are lots of examples among the warehouses in the Jordaan area (▶ 92) of Amsterdam. Next is the step gable, like two staircases meeting at the top; the best examples are on Bartolotti House on Herengracht (▶ 181).

The neck gable signified a more classical design, with a tall rectangular screen perching on the cornice like a head on shoulders; the elevated neck gable involved an intermediate step. There are plenty of examples around the canals of Prinsengracht, Keizersgracht and Herengracht.

Most visually appealing of all is the bell gable, where delicate arcs sweep up to a narrow summit. This style can be found in profusion throughout the city. All gables are ornamented to a greater or lesser degree, and the elaborate and imaginative designs, each seeking to outdo the neighbours, are among the greatest visual delights in Amsterdam.

The Leaning Houses of Amsterdam

Many houses in the city are inclined at angles other than 90 degrees to the horizontal. When the house leans to the left or right, the reason is structural weakness, usually caused by rotting piles. As the foundations decay, the building may start to sag to one side, often causing its neighbour to slant as well. A forward lean, however, is usually a deliberate policy. Before proper drainage became common, the upper floors of a housefront were often intended to project outwards, so that water thrown from the windows fell on to the street (and passing pedestrians), not on to lower floors. And there's another good reason: the steep, narrow staircases in canal houses don't lend themselves to the movement of bulky pieces of furniture. Removable windows and a pulley looped through the beam projecting from the top of the house allow the furniture to be hoisted up from the outside. Tilting the facade forwards reduces the risk of damage to the housefront should the load start to sway.

Trading **Places**

On paper, Dutch economic prospects appear bleak. Europe's most densely populated major country possesses modest natural gas reserves, dwindling fishery potential and a small agricultural sector. Yet the Dutch enjoy wealth out of all proportion to their natural resources. The Netherlands is among the richest countries in the world, and Amsterdam is one of the wealthiest cities in Europe.

The Dutch secret is to match supply with demand and to take a cut in the process. Politically, technologically and commercially they've become the warehouse of the world.

The neutrality of the Netherlands in a turbulent continent allowed early traders to link Germany and Scandinavia with southern Europe. Cheap timber from the Baltics was used to build large cargo ships that carried much more than those from rival countries. Also the financial institutions, from banks to the stock exchange, became established early enough to facilitate commerce during the expansionism of the 17th century – the Golden Age, economically as well as culturally. Amsterdam came to dominate the global economy by devising corporatism, a model established by the Dutch East India Company (VOC – Vereenigde Oost-Indische Compagnie), formed in the early 17th century to exploit Asia.

The First Multinational

This first multinational brought together backers from Amsterdam and other Dutch towns to spread the heavy risks – and share the bumper profits – of trading with territories from Java to Japan. The VOC's great strength was its focus on commerce alone. Unlike the Spanish and Portuguese, the Dutch had no interest in converting locals to Christianity, making them more acceptable to foreign rulers.

The same model was used by the Dutch West India Company (WIC – Weit-Indische Compagnie), which traded with the Caribbean and South America and played a major part in the slave trade. The Noordsche Compagnie exploited the northern seas. By 1800, 4,000 vessels were trading with over 600 ports around the world.

Protectionism and military incursions by more powerful nations eventually sent the Dutch economy into decline, but the spirit of enterprise continued – Amsterdam made the first loan to the new US government after the American War of Independence.

Rotterdam gives the Netherlands one of the most important ports in the world

The Profit Principle

The principles of global wheeling and dealing remain intact. Although somewhat overtaken by the ports of Asia, Rotterdam is still one of the busiest ports in the world. KLM still carries more passengers each year than the entire population of the Netherlands, even though it's now part of Air France. Today, the service sector accounts for two-thirds of the national economy. Other countries make goods; the Dutch buy, sell and move them. Amsterdam is racing forwards in the 21st century with a massive building project south of the city. Just eight minutes from Schiphol airport, Zuidas is positioning itself as a major international business district, attracting more foreign companies than anywhere else in the country.

NOTABLE CURRENCY

The first single European currency originated in Amsterdam. In the 17th century, bankers in the city would accept any currency and exchange it for the gulden *florijn* (golden florin). That's why the former national currency was Anglicised to "guilder", a corruption of *gulden*, yet was written Fl – short for *florijn*.

The change to the euro in 2002 robbed Europe of some of its most colourful currency. In the 1960s, De Nederlandsche Bank revolutionized graphic design for bank notes. Images of cultural figures were imposed on strong, simple typography. The culmination was the 10-guilder note in 1997. On one side, imagery from electronic circuitry was used to remarkable effect, while on the reverse was an underwater masterpiece complete with figurative fish and the poem, *IJsvogel*, by Arie van den Berg.

JEWISH AMSTERDAM

A HISTORY OF REPRESSION AND SURVIVAL

"One day this terrible war will be over," wrote Anne Frank in her diary in April 1944. "The time will come when we will be people again and not just Jews! We can never be just Dutch, or just English, or whatever, we will always be Jews as well. But then, we'll want to be."

The First Jewish Community

From the 16th century, Amsterdam has been a place of sanctuary for thousands of Jewish people, forced from their homes in eastern and southern Europe. Sephardic Jews were expelled from Spain and Portugal, while Ashkenazic Jews faced persecution in Poland and Germany. Even in liberal, tolerant Amsterdam, they faced restrictions for 200 years – forbidden from owning shops and barred from many skilled trades. At the end of the 18th century, in a tide of egalitarianism following the French Revolution, the Act of Civil Equality ended such discrimination.

Fascism and War

When Adolf Hitler's National Socialist Party seized power in Germany in 1933, the Netherlands was a natural refuge for Jewish people – among them the family of Otto Frank, a merchant living in Frankfurt, where his

daughter Anne was born on 12 June 1929.

War broke out in Europe on 1 September 1939. In May 1940, the Nazis occupied the Netherlands, and the persecution of Jewish people began. By October, Dutch civil servants had to sign a declaration of Aryan (non-Jewish) descent, and Jewish people faced compulsory registration. The Jewish community formed a self-protection force. During a clash in February 1941, a member of the Dutch Nazi party died. In retribution, the Germans rounded up 400 Jewish people. This, in turn, triggered a call from the Dutch trades union movement for a general strike in protest. From 3 May 1942, Jewish people had to wear a yellow star. Jewish-owned businesses were requisitioned by the occupiers. By 1943, Jewish people were being rounded up in their thousands and sent east to take part in "work projects" in Germany. Of the 140,000 Jewish people in the Netherlands at the time of the Nazi invasion, 107,000 were deported to concentration camps. Only a very few survived the experience.

> **"MY BICYCLE BACK"**
> Dutch antipathy towards Germany has not entirely disappeared. When the former Queen Beatrix married the German Claus von Arnsberg in 1966, a huge crowd gathered outside the wedding in the Westerkerk, many demanding: "My bicycle back". This stems from the last few months of the war, when German troops took thousands of bicycles from the locals, either as scrap for the war effort, or as a form of transport to accelerate their retreat.

Going Underground

The Frank family were among many Jewish people who went underground, which often involved hiding in an attic or basement. Some Dutch people performed heroic acts to protect them; but half the 16,000 who hid were captured and sent to death camps. Most were betrayed by informers, who received a reward of seven guilders for each Jewish person arrested. No one is sure how the Frank family was found, but when the Nazis and their Dutch collaborators raided the house at Prinsengracht 263 (▶96) they went straight to the bookshelf that hid the entrance to the secret annexe. Only Otto Frank survived the Nazi death camps to which his family was sent. He published Anne's diary in 1947, and nowadays the Anne Frank House is a museum open to the public.

Jewish Connections

There are several other pockets of Jewish history. **Ets Haim** is the oldest Jewish library in the world and has a UNESCO-listed collection; visits are by appointment only (Mr. Visserplein 3, www.etshaim.org). The **Portuguese Synagogue** (▶157) has survived in good shape, while four other synagogues form the **Jewish Historical Museum** (▶152). The **Resistance Museum** (▶158) is an important complement to these sites.

A statue of Anne Frank stands outside the Westerkerk

The Magazine

PORTRAIT OF THE
ARTIST
AS AN OLD MAN

The city's favourite painter, Rembrandt Harmenszoon van Rijn died in 1669 a penniless outcast, shunned by the wealthy Amsterdammers who had previously bankrolled him.

Syndics of the Cloth Guild, a masterpiece dating back to 1662

Rembrandt was born in 1606 in Leiden (➤ 176), where he lived for 25 years. His father, a miller, had big plans for his son. Aged 14, Rembrandt won a place at Leiden's university, but left to study painting. At the time, the world of art was dazzled by the Italian baroque – notably the work of Caravaggio, itself influenced by early Flemish art. Rembrandt found a teacher, Jacob van Swanenburgh, and studied in Amsterdam for six months under Pieter Lastman. Under this tutelage, Rembrandt strengthened the intense humanity that characterizes so much of his work. He returned to Leiden, and began to give lessons, but the city soon proved insufficiently dynamic to satisfy his ambition.

To Amsterdam

In 1631, Rembrandt moved to Amsterdam. Thanks in no small part to the mercantile adventures of the Dutch East India Company (► 18), the economy was booming, and rich merchants were commissioning biblical paintings and portraits. Always pragmatic, Rembrandt used members of his family as models: his depiction of his mother as the Prophetess Anna hangs in the Rijksmuseum (► 120).

A year after his arrival in Amsterdam, he won the contract for *The Anatomy Lesson of Dr Nicolaes Tulp* (*c.*1632), a group portrait of seven surgeons and a physician which hangs in the Mauritshuis in The Hague. Rembrandt also became adept at etching; most of his detailed works are on display in the Rembrandthuis (► 70).

Fame and Fortune

Besides his own creative work, which broke new ground in combining dynamism with rationalist restraint, Rembrandt traded in the efforts of others. As an art dealer, he made a healthy profit of 100 guilders buying and selling *Hero and Leander* (*c.*1605) by Rubens.

Rembrandt wed very much for love, but his marriage in 1634 to Saskia van Uylenburgh was commercially fortuitous.

> "Rembrandt wed…
> for love, but his marriage…
> was commercially
> fortuitous"

She was from a well-to-do family, and was the cousin of a leading art dealer. By means of such networking, Rembrandt built up a profitable portfolio of commissions. Many of his works used Saskia as a model. In the 1630s, he produced some of his most expressive self-portraits.

Rembrandt became sought-after as a teacher, and his pupils helped keep pace with the demand for portraits, religious paintings and secular landscapes. Even today there is dispute over the authorship of some of the works attributed to him.

In 1639, the young couple moved into a fine house in the heart of the Jewish quarter (now maintained as the Rembrandthuis museum, ► 70). It cost the huge sum of 13,000 guilders – for which he had to take out a mortgage – and financing the mortgage later caused him financial difficulties that ended in bankruptcy.

The Night Watch, one of Rembrandt's most famous works, was painted in 1642

Birth, Death and Success

During the 1630s, Rembrandt and Saskia had three children who tragically died in infancy. In 1641, Saskia gave birth to a son, Titus, who survived – but she died a year later. She left her fortune to Titus, but entrusted its management to Rembrandt – as long as he did not remarry. The following year Rembrandt completed his most celebrated work. *The Shooting Company of Captain Frans Banning Cocq* (*c.*1642) shows a band of civil guardsmen, looking casual and cocksure. Darkened with age, it became known as *The Night Watch*, and now hangs in the Rijksmuseum.

Rembrandt was not a great traveller, though to see some of the landscapes he created at this time you would imagine that he had seen much of Europe and the Bible lands. He used some of his income to buy all manner of exotic artefacts from Asia and the Americas, which are displayed at the Rembrandthuis.

INSIDER INFO

The outstanding **Hermitage Amsterdam** (▶ 150) is an arm of the St Petersburg's State Hermitage Museum. Two of Amsterdam's other leading art museums are the **Rijksmuseum** (▶ 120) and the **Van Gogh Museum** (▶ 124), just a few minutes' walk apart. The **Stedelijk Museum's** (▶ 128) collection of modern art rivals that of the MoMa of New York with a concentration on Bauhaus, De Stijl and Pop Art, among others. For 21st-century art, the place to go is the **Westergasfabriek** (▶ 106), the reclaimed gasworks where varied temporary installations are on display. For those who want to buy as well as look, there are dozens of commercial galleries, the greatest number in the **Jordaan** (▶ 92).

Insider Tip

INSIDER INFO

Reminders of Rembrandt are dotted throughout the city. Visitors can admire the large collection of his masterpieces in the **Rijksmuseum** (➤ 120), and wander around the rooms of his former residence, the **Rembrandthuis** (➤ 70) and see the studio where he worked and taught his students. Dominated by a statue of the artist, the bustling **Rembrandtplein** (➤ 188) is the square named in his honour. A number of specialist tours – on foot and also by bike – (see www.iamsterdam.com for more details) take in these key spots, including the 14th-century **Oude Kerk** (➤ 57), where his wife Saskia is buried, and **Westerkerk** (➤ 101), where Rembrandt's remains lie, although no one is sure exactly where. In an upper room in **De Waag**, Rembrandt painted *The Anatomy Lesson of Dr Nicolaes Tulp* (*c*.1632). This bulky gatehouse is now home to a restaurant and café (In de Waag, ➤ 75), the perfect spot to end any Rembrandt tour.

Decline and Fall

In 1649, the artist hired a housekeeper, Hendrickje Stoffels, who soon became his lover. Amsterdam society gossiped about Rembrandt's mistress, but most tolerated his affair. He continued to produce some fine work, much of which, such as *Nathan Admonishing David* (*c*.1652–53), hangs in overseas galleries.

Rembrandt's extravagant lifestyle, and increasing disdain for deadlines, proved his financial downfall. In 1656, he was bankrupt, and his collection of art and antiquities auctioned to pay his creditors. Not entirely through choice, he continued to work. His 1661 depiction of *The Syndics of the Cloth Guild* (1662), in the Rijksmuseum, shows his talents undimmed.

In 1663, Hendrickje died, and then his beloved son, Titus, aged 17. Less than a year later, poor and alone, Rembrandt died on 4 October 1669. Rembrandt may be buried in an unknown grave, but his legacy is outstanding.

Statue of the artist on Rembrandtplein

Drinking in Amsterdam:
steeped in
TRADITION

In medieval times, the Count of Holland decided to boost the fledgling city's coffers. In 1323, he designated Amsterdam one of only two ports in his province allowed to import beer from Hamburg, the most important ale-producing town in northern Europe. At that time, beer was far safer to drink than water.

The Heineken Story

Heineken started brewing lager in Amsterdam in 1864, and is now one of the largest brewery companies in the world, selling beer in 170 countries. The firm attributes much of its success to the cultivation of the Heineken A-Yeast in 1886: every month the yeast cell is still flown out from its main brewery near Amsterdam to its 100 breweries abroad. Though its Amsterdam brewery stopped production in 1988 and is now a tourist attraction (➤ 148), Heineken's presence in the city is still unavoidable. The famous De L'Europe hotel (➤ 44) is home to Freddy's Bar, named after Freddy Heineken. The

There is a party atmosphere in the popular Heineken Experience Tasting Bar

Heineken empire also includes a number of other brands such as Amstel and Murphy's Irish Stout.

For Good Measure
Beer is usually served in a 25cl flowerpot-shaped glass, and will be presented with a two-finger-thick head. The bartender usually makes a point of skimming off the extra froth with a plastic spatula). In brown cafés (► 31), you usually need to order at the bar, and can either pay on the spot, or, if you're staying for a few, ask for a tab.

Dutch Spirit
Gin – known locally as *jenever* (► 45), the Dutch word for juniper – originated in the Netherlands in the 17th century before being exported to England. It is still produced in distilleries around the country that date back from this time and can be sampled in a number of traditional tasting houses (► 31). At the House of Bols (Paulus Potterstraat 14, tel: 020 5 70 85 75, www.house ofbols.com, Sun–Thu noon–6:30, Fri noon–10, Sat noon–8) visitors can learn about the history and traditions of both the company and the spirit.

Heineken on tap is the freshest and tastes the best

INSIDER INFO

For the most satisfying beer-drinking, visit one of the independent outfits, such as **Brouwerij 't IJ** (► 161), with its own in-house brewery. Several cafés, like **In de Wildeman** (► 72), sell an extraordinarily wide range, including some Belgian varieties. **Café 't Arendsnest**, (Herengracht 90, www.arendsnest.nl, Sun–Thu 2–midnight, Fri–Sat 2–2), stocking only specialist Dutch beers, aims to represent every Dutch brewery and also features guest brews. You can also learn about it from the well-informed barman. Amsterdam's best retail outlet for beer is **De Bierkoning** (Paleisstraat 125, near Dam Square: bierkoning.nl, tel: 020 6 25 23 36, Mon–Sat 11–7, Sun 1–6). It sells 1,200 varieties, including beer in champagne bottles, Belgian Trappist beers and the original Czech Pilsner.

Insider Tip

CYCLE CITY

The bicycle mirrors Amsterdam perfectly: it is human-scaled, often elegant and mostly gentle. It's also the best way to get around. The city is flat and compact, while narrow streets and bridges give cyclists an edge on motorized transport, which is practically non-existent. In Amsterdam, there are more bikes than people – and even the royal family cycles.

Rewarding Rides

The city is made for cyclists. Tourists can join commuters, shoppers, and even police on two wheels. Bike lanes are almost everywhere, often separated from traffic and pedestrians, with cycle parking facilities taking precedence over parking for cars. The flat terrain means that the only effort required is to cross one or two of the steeper bridges.

Positive Policy

Apart from being environmentally friendly, the widespread use of two wheels is just one of the reasons why Amsterdam is such a pleasant city to visit. It simply doesn't have the level of pollution and traffic that dog other cities. Since the 1970s, Amsterdam has had a highly progressive policy of actively promoting cycling and safety whilst discouraging car use that other cities around the world are only now looking at emulating. On top of this, despite having one ofthe highest numbers of cyclists in the world, bike fatalities in Amsterdam are among the lowest recorded.

Cycling Style

Bike riders in Amsterdam are quite a spectacle. Business men in suits, women with small children,

RENTING A BICYCLE

Bike City
✉ Bloemgracht 68–70, Jordaan
☎ 020 6 26 37 21; www.bikecity.nl
🚊 13, 14, 17 to Westermarkt

Damstraat Rent-a-Bike
✉ Damstraat 20–22, south-east corner of Dam Square ☎ 020 6 25 50 29; www.rent abike.nl 🚊 4, 9, 14, 16, 24, 25 to Damrak

Orange Bike
✉ Singel 233
☎ 020 5 28 99 90; www.orangebike.nl
🚊 2, 4, 9, 16, 24, 25 to Dam Square

Holland Rent-a-Bike Beursstalling
✉ Damrak 247
☎ 020 6 22 32 07 🚊 4, 9, 16, 24, 25

Mac Bike
✉ Waterlooplein 199
☎ 020 4 28 70 05; www.macbike.nl 🚊 14
✉ Weteringschans 2, close to Leidseplein
☎ 020 528 7688 🚊 1, 2, 5, 7, 10).

octogenarians and dogs all travel by pedal power – often on the same bike. Even if you decide to hail a cab, it doesn't mean you have to get in a car – in Amsterdam you can catch a bike taxi (tel: 06 28 24 75 50; www.wielertaxi.nl), or even take to the water on a canal pedal boat.

On Your Bike

When renting a bicycle, check the brakes before you set off, and make sure the seat and handlebars are firm. If you want to ride with a helmet you should bring your own

at tourist offices and book shops. The rental companies Orange Bike and Mac Bike (listed left) also offer tours with a guide.

Keep wheels from getting caught in tram tracks by crossing them at a wide angle, and take special care around Dam Square and Centraal Station, where there is a profusion of tracks.

You'll notice that most of the bikes in the city look beaten up and scratched. This is partly because bike theft is such a serious problem in the city. If you bring your own bike (many airlines let

Amsterdam is one of the most cycle-friendly cities in the world. It claims that 60 per cent of all inner-city journeys are done by bike

as hardly any of the bike rentals in Amsterdam supply them. 🚼 Child seats and child bikes can usually be rented. Most bike hire places will require you to leave a deposit (some prefer cash to credit cards), and sometimes a passport too.

Maps that show all the cycle routes in the city can be purchased

you take them for free), use a good lock, preferably two.

The Netherlands is small and it is straightforward to take bikes on the trains (with a purchase of the Dagkaart Fiets pass, €6), except during peak hours, so you may want to explore beyond Amsterdam on two wheels.

CAFÉ
SOCIETY

Eetcafé interior (left); De Drie Fleschjes (right)

Amsterdammers regard their cafés almost as second living-rooms – places to meet up with friends, or just to chill out reading the newspapers. Amsterdam is mercifully free of chain coffee shops; here the independent café rules. The best examples epitomize *gezelligheid,* which loosely translates as an infectiously cosy and sociable atmosphere. This concept is almost part of the national psyche.

The Dutch use of the term "café" is confusing for foreigners. It describes not only a place where you might have a cup of coffee or snack, but also where drinking is the focus of activity – in other words, what Americans would call a bar, and the British a pub. Even establishments that are virtually restaurants can, in Dutch parlance, be called cafés. To complicate matters further, many cafés perform a number or all of these roles.

Brown Cafés

These are the archetypal Amsterdam cafés: the oldest, dating from the 1600s, look as if they could be lifted from a Rembrandt or Vermeer painting. They are rather like old-fashioned British pubs, but have a more intimate, parlour-like feel. The "brown" in the title comes from the tobacco-stained ceilings and walls (more mustard-coloured, in fact), and the wood panelling and floorboards. You may also find little Persian

Coffeeshop Johnny, Elandsgracht (left); Cosy coffeeshop interior (right)

rugs on tables, frilly net curtains on windows, newspapers on racks, flickering candles and gleaming brass taps on a worn old bar, and a cat snoozing on a tatty chair. Usually, the barman is deep in conversation with a local, and the male customers outnumber the women.

Brown cafés are perfect bolt-holes to escape from the biting Amsterdam winter, but many put a bench or table or two outside during fine weather. As well as alcohol, they always serve coffee. In terms of food, basic sandwiches, croquettes, nuts, cheese, boiled eggs (displayed in a stand on the bar) and perhaps apple pie may be on offer.

■ **Best brown cafés:** Café Papeneiland (➤ 107), Café 't Smalle (➤ 108), Café de Dokter (➤ 74), Oosterling (➤ 162), In de Wildeman (➤ 76).

Tasting Houses

In previous centuries, customers visiting *jenever-* (Dutch gin) and liqueur-distillers were given free samples before buying. Only a handful of *proeflokaalen*, or tasting houses, still exist, and now they charge for drinks (➤ 47). Even so, a visit is highly recommended as they are

The Magazine

some of Amsterdam's most civilized and atmospheric bars, decorated with old wooden casks and stone bottles. Amsterdammers often pop in for a quick *jenever* or three (few have anywhere to sit) before heading home.

■ **Best tasting houses:** De Drie Fleschjes (➤ 75), Wynand Fockink (➤ 76).

Eetcafés

These encompass both brown and more modern cafés where, even though people can just drink, the emphasis is on the food (some call themselves *petits restaurants*). They used to focus on cheap traditional

Café Papeneiland on Prinsengracht

Dutch dishes, but many now offer more adventurous, high-quality fare. With most of the city's restaurants only open in the evening, *eetcafés* make good lunchtime options.

■ **Best *eetcafés*:** Café de Prins (➤ 108), Spanjer & Van Twist (➤ 108), 't Gasthuys (➤ 75), Walem Café (➤ 109).

Tea Rooms

Amsterdam has plenty of cafés that might also be called tea rooms – daytime venues serving sandwiches, cakes, pastries, tea and coffee. Some are attached to department stores, others are at the back of *pâtisseries*.

■ **Best tea rooms:** Pompadour (➤ 112), Villa Zeezicht (➤ 76).

Coffeeshops

Since the mid-1970s, the Dutch authorities have tolerated the sale and consumption of small amounts of hashish and marijuana, arguing that this keeps users apart from the criminal underworld. Soft drug use is on a par with other EU members and the US, while the use of hard drugs is significantly lower. In recent years, however, the conservative government has been bowing to challenges of this liberal attitude from the international community. While you can still get stoned in Amsterdam in one of the 200 or so establishments that euphemistically call themselves "coffeeshops", some 30 per cent have shut over the last few years, with more set to close due to crackdowns. Coffeeshops now cannot sell alcohol and smoking tobacco is illegal, which means you can be fined and even arrested for having a joint because of its tobacco, but not its marijuana content.

To find a coffeeshop, just look for the green-and-white sticker in the window. In a typical Dutch compromise, while these are officially licensed to sell soft drugs, the deliveries they receive from suppliers are technically illegal. Small coffeeshops keep the drugs menu on or behind the bar, while larger ones sell the drugs from a separate booth. You can buy a bag (5 grams/one-sixth of an ounce) maximum or a ready-rolled joint. You can smoke on the premises or, as most Dutch people do, take your purchase away (though not, of course, out of the country). They may also sell space-cakes – their effect is delayed but stronger than that of smoking cannabis, so if you want to remember anything about your weekend treat them with caution.

These places vary enormously in atmosphere. Those in the city centre are often grungy, psychedelic dives, while outlets of the Bulldog chain are brash and commercial.

■ **Best coffeeshops: Rusland**, said to be the oldest in town (Rusland 16), **Barney's**, which serves snacks all day (Haarlemmerstraat 102), **La Tertulia**, an innocent-looking daytime corner café (Prinsengracht 312), **De Rokerij** (Lange Leidsedwarsstraat 41), an exotic, candlelit den with a party atmosphere in the evenings.

INSIDER INFO

Airier, brighter, modern alternatives to brown-café nostalgia began appearing in the 1980s. In contrast to the nostalgic little "bruin cafés", they are often located in hall-like rooms with minimalist style furnishings. In the evening they are popular late-night haunts and meeting places before and after cinema or theatre performances. But the so-called "grand cafés" have a wider appeal, attracting everyone from businesspeople to shoppers and students. While some fail to live up to their name, the best, with their lofty ceilings, striking bar displays and library-style reading tables piled high with magazines and newspapers, capture something of the style of Viennese coffee houses and more fashionable Parisian cafés. Most offer meals, ranging from lunchtime snacks to three-course dinners.

Best grand cafés: Café Américain (▶ 101), Café de Jaren (▶ 70), Café Luxembourg (▶ 70–71), De Kroon (▶ 155–156).

A Taste of
AMSTERDAM

Van Gogh's famous painting, *The Potato Eaters* (1885), which hangs in the Van Gogh Museum (▶ 124–127), depicts the earthy eating habits of the Dutch. While *stamppot* – potato mashed with other vegetables, and sometimes bacon – may still be a traditional national staple, cuisine in the capital has moved way beyond these modest origins.

Star Quality

Gourmets have a choice of ten Michelin-starred restaurants in Amsterdam. Three fine choices include: the French-Mediterranean Restaurant La Rive, (www.restaurantlarive.nl), which boasts its own wine room within the Amstel Intercontinental Hotel; **Yamazato** (www.yamazato.nl, ▶ 164), at the Okura Hotel, the only traditional Japanese restaurant in Europe to boast a Michelin star; in the same hotel is the

French-inspired **Ciel Bleu** (► 163), the only one in town to have
achieved two stars and to top that off it also offers fantastic views from
its position on the 23rd floor.

A Culinary Calendar

Taste (www.tasteofamsterdam.com) is a relatively new addition to
Amsterdam's foodie celebrations. In June, visitors can sample signature dishes from prestigious restaurants, mingle with top chefs, and
browse the stalls of a gourmet food market. Another newcomer is

Above: Edam cheeses, one of the Netherland's most popular exports

Left: Leidseplein is a popular meeting place with plenty of outdoor cafés

INSIDER INFO

Edam and Gouda are probably the first types to come to mind at the mention
of Dutch cheese. These mild, semi-hard cheeses make up the bulk of cheeses
sold outside of the Netherlands, which is one of the biggest cheese exporters
in the world. Look too for Maasdammer, which has large holes and a nutty
taste, artisan cheeses like Boerenkaas, made from unpasteurised milk, and
the award-winning Old Amsterdam, an aged Gouda savoured by epicureans.
In Amsterdam, pop into **De Kaaskamer**, "The Cheese Room" (► 112),
and perhaps pick up some cumin-flavoured Komijnenkaas or join locals at
Fa. H. Wegewijs (Rozengracht 32, tel: 020 6 24 40 93, www.wegewijs.nl),
the city's 100-year-old cheese shop.

Insider Tip

the fun Weekend of the **Rollende Keukens** ("Rolling Kitchens"; www.rollendekeukens.nl) with mobile music and entertainment at the Westergasfabriek (▶ 106) in the first weekend of June. Parts of Amsterdam are turned into a huge open-air restaurant, allowing visitors to experiment with local dishes during the **New Food Fair** (www.caulils.com/newfoodfair) in September.

Silver from the Sea

Gone are the days when Amsterdam cuisine was defined by its herring, although this dish did play a significant role in the city's road to prosperity. In medieval times, its fishermen improved the way the ubiquitous herring was cured, by gutting the fish before treating it with salt. This meant that it could be transported on long sea voyages. "The silver from the sea gave the Dutch the Golden Age", is how Holland's pre-eminent food writer, Johannes van Dam, poetically puts it.

Going Dutch

Despite the phrase, "As American as apple pie", the dish originated in the Netherlands. Almost every café in Amsterdam features apple pie on its menu, embellished with either cinnamon, raisins, icing or cream. Dutch pancakes are a speciality all of their own; you don't have to go far in Amsterdam before you run into a pancake house. Completely different from French or Belgian crepes, Dutch pancakes may be savoury or sweet and are so thick they can be served as a meal – either breakfast, lunch or dinner – on their own.

Zeeuwse mussels from Zeeland are world-famous, and during the season (from September to March), may be served fried as fast food or a starter, but more traditionally with fries and mayonnaise.

In the Netherlands, Indonesian food is practically regarded as indigenous. The Dutch invented the *rijsttafel* (rice table), a feast made up of anything from six to 60 Indonesian dishes all served with rice.

INSIDER INFO

Amsterdam's eateries offer vibrant, quirky and eclectic experiences. Diners eat in the dark at **Ctaste** (www.ctaste.nl), or enjoy an organic lunch inside a functioning greenhouse at **De Kas** (www.restaurantdekas.nl). Fair trade food is on offer at **UMOJA** (www.umojafood.nl), whose name is Swahili for "unity".

Edel (www.edelamsterdam.nl) is a jewel of a café-restaurant housed in an old silversmiths college where French and Italian classics are served on the delightful waterfront terrace. Those after an altogether more quintessentially Dutch meal should visit **Moeders** (www.moeders.com, ▶ 110).

At **Haesje Claes** (www.haesjeclaes.nl), local specialities such as mussels and *stamppot* are served in a series of traditional dining rooms.

Finding Your Feet

First Two Hours

Amsterdam deserves the prize as Europe's most accessible city. It is easy to reach by train, boat and plane.

Schiphol Airport

Amsterdam's airport has become one of the most important air travel hubs in Europe.

■ **Schiphol** (www.schiphol.nl), 14km (9 miles) southwest of the city, is certainly the most passenger-friendly of Europe's large airports, with effectively a single terminal and easy public transport to the city centre. It is worth arriving early at the airport on your return, as there is an express spa, casino, play areas, panoramic viewing terrace and an annexe of the Rijksmuseum (► 120, behind passport control, daily 7–8, free admission), with a permanent collection of ten works by Dutch Masters, as well as changing exhibitions.

■ The tourism information office (7am–10pm) is in **Arrivals Hall 2.**

Airport Transfers

By Train

■ The **quickest and cheapest way** into Amsterdam (other than cycling) is by rail, less than €5 each way from the station under the airport concourse.

■ There are at least five trains an hour between 6am and midnight, with hourly departures through the night. **Slow trains** to Amsterdam's Centraal Station take 20 minutes; non-stop expresses are a few minutes faster.

■ You must **buy your ticket in advance** or face a big fine on the train.

■ **Be careful with your bags** – the run from Schiphol to the city centre and back is a favourite with petty thieves and con artists.

By Bus

■ **Connexxion airport buses** (tel: 03 83 39 47 41, www.airporthotelshuttle.nl) run from the airport to over 100 hotels for €16.50 one way or €26.50 return.

■ There are departures **twice each hour** between around 6am and 9pm.

■ Some hotels are easily accessed by bus, but many are not; check before you board. The **journey to and from the airport** takes between 20 and 50 minutes depending on where your hotel is located on the bus circuit of the city.

By Taxi

■ **Fares to the city centre** are around €50.

■ It's **usually faster** to go by train to Centraal Station and then take a taxi.

By Bike

A specially constructed cycle path allows you to cycle from the airport into the centre of town. There is also a bike route right around the airport.

Centraal Station

Whether you arrive by air and take the train to town, travel by rail from elsewhere in Europe, or take the sea-rail connection from Harwich via Hoek of Holland, you end up in a station that is an historical monument (► 72) – but it is best enjoyed when you are unencumbered by luggage.

- You descend from the platforms **to the main concourse**, basically a shopping centre.
- The station is the **most popular venue in Amsterdam among pickpockets and hustlers,** who target tourists assiduously.
- If you're using one of the automatic ticket machines, you may be **approached by someone trying to sell you a ticket**. Decline any such offer; at best you will end up with a dud or overpriced ticket, at worst you'll be robbed during the transaction.
- Most people head straight out of the main (south) entrance, to be confronted by a confusion of taxis, trams, vendors and bicycles. The main **taxi rank is to the right of the main entrance**, as are the **stands for trams 1, 2, 5, 13 and 17**. To the left you will find the **stands for trams 4, 9, 16, 24, 25 and 26**, and the **entrance to the Metro** (underground railway).
- The **city's main tourist office** (Mon–Sat 9–5, Sun 10–5, closed 1 Jan, 25 Dec), which was once a tram station, lies beyond the Metro entrance in an imposing white-painted wooden building on Stationsplein. To the left is the **GVB (public transport) office** (Mon–Fri 7–9, Sat, Sun 8–9), where you can buy travel passes, such as the 24-, 48- and 72-hour cards.

Tourist Offices

The information service in the Netherlands is known as the **VVV (Vereniging Voor Vreemdelingenverkeer)**. It is a commercial organisation, making money from commission on accommodation bookings and selling tours, maps, etc.

If you have specific questions, they will be answered, but queues are long and responses brisk. **Offices may close their doors** for up to half an hour if there are more customers than the staff can cope with.

There are two offices on Centraal Station (see above). Also, **Leidseplein** (in the Stadsschouwburg, daily 10–5, closed 1 Jan, 25 Dec). In addition, a **telephone information service** (tel: 020 7 02 60 00) offers advice Mon–Fri 8–5. See also www.iamsterdam.nl.

Getting Around

Amsterdam's layout still follows the basic pattern from 1609. The centre, with most places of interest, is a collection of islands, divided by canals and connected by bridges. It forms a semicircle, with the IJ River as the straight side, and the major canals extending concentrically, like ripples in a pond.

Orientating Yourself

- The main canals (going outwards) are Singel, Herengracht, Keizersgracht and Prinsengracht; *gracht* **means canal**. A number of lesser canals have been added to these, they radiate out from the centre or cut across the others.
- To confuse matters, the most important post-1609 additions are Singelgracht (beyond Prinsengracht) and Singel (without the *gracht),* inside Herengracht.
- To the east, the system is disrupted by the broad Amstel River.

Finding Your Feet

Areas

Besides the divisions used in this book, there are a few smaller areas you should know about, again running clockwise from the IJ River:

- **De Wallen** – literally "the walls", which used to enclose the river: now Amsterdam's main red-light district.
- **De Pijp** – due south of the centre, a multicultural area with many immigrants an students.
- **Spiegelkwartier** – a stylish art and antiques shopping area, centred on Nieuwe Spiegelstraat.
- **Spuikwartier** – the lively area around the southern half of Spuistraat, merging into the square named Spui.
- **9 Straatjes** – the three-block square just west of Spuistraat, literally "nine streets" (➤ 111).
- **Jordaan** – west again, the city's most upwardly mobile quarter.

Streets

Going clockwise from the station, the most important streets are as follows:

- **Prins Hendrikkade** – running southeast to the docks area.
- **Zeedijk** – curving south past the red-light district to Nieuwmarkt.
- **Damrak** – running directly southwest to the city's main square, Dam.
- **Nieuwendijk** – shadowing Damrak, just to the west, and one of Amsterdam's main shopping streets.
- **Nieuwezijds Voorburgwal** – another street parallel to Damrak, and carrying the bulk of trams. It leads to many of the areas most popular with tourists.
- **Leidsestraat** – across Herengracht, the old road to Leiden leading to the busy tourist area of Leidseplein.
- **Haarlemmerstraat** – the old road to Haarlem, running west and dividing Jordaan from the Western Isles.

Public Transport

Distances in the city centre are short, and many visitors never step on to a tram, bus or metro train. On a bad day though, you may be grateful for them – and a tram trip is an attraction in its own right. Amsterdam has great public transport; for full details, including timetables, visit www.gvb.nl.

Trams

- Most services **radiate out from Centraal Station**.
- **Tram stops are usually easily identifiable**, and the busier ones have indicator boards showing when the next three services are due.
- **Ring the bell** a little ahead of the stop to ensure that the driver will stop.
- Take care when getting off, many stops are **in the middle of the road**.

Buses

- Trams, buses and trains run from around 6am to 12:30am. Between around midnight and 6:30am, **night buses** run on a dozen routes to and from Centraal Station. GVB 1-hour tickets are not valid on night buses.
- Always enter at the front and exit using the rear door.

Metro

- Running both over and underground, there are **four metro lines** – 51 (to Westwijk), 53 (to Gaasperplas) and 54 (to Gein) all terminate at Centraal Station (CS); route 50 serves the more suburban west side of the city.

■ The new **Noord/Zuidlijn line**, running through central Amsterdam to connect the north of the city with the south, is only due to be completed in 2017.

The OV-chipkaart

■ The **OV-chipkaart** is now used on city public transport. This is an electronic card that can be used to cover single or multiple journeys, as well as weekly and monthly travel passes.

■ There are three types of card: **anonymous** *(anonieme)*, **personal** *(persoonlijke)* and **disposable** *(wegwerp)*. As a visitor you're likely to use the disposable card (the latter options carry a one-off fee for the cards themselves and are aimed at residents).

■ **Disposable OV-chipkaarts** work for a single trip or for a short number of days, for example a 3-day ticket, for use on all public transport in the city. They can be purchased from station ticket machines, bus and tram drivers, tourist information centres and some hotels.

■ It's vital that when using your OV-chipkaart that you **check in** at the beginning of your journey and **check out** at the end, including if you transfer from one mode of transport to another. To do this, hold the card to the reader until a green light is visible and a bleep indicates that your card has been registered. If you forget to do this, disposable cards will stop working and on anonymous and personal cards you'll be charged the full boarding rate rather than the actual cost of your journey.

Discount Tickets and Passes

■ The **I amsterdam City Card** is ideal for anyone who plans to pack a large amount of sightseeing into a few days. The card includes unlimited travel on public transport, a canal cruise, plus admission to many major museums and discounts on numerous other attractions, bars and restaurants. Visit the website www.iamsterdam.com. The price is €42 for 24 hours, €52 for 48 hours and €72 for 72 hours.

■ The *Museumkaart* (www.museumkaart.nl) is a good-value annual pass (€39.95) offering free admission to over 400 museums around the Netherlands. Even with this pass and the I amsterdam City Card, you may have to queue up at the cash desk for your visit to be registered; ask about the card at major museums.

Taxis

■ Do not count on being able to hail a taxi in the street: **most Amsterdammers summon one by telephone** (tel: 020 677 7777) or walk to a rank.

■ Taxi ranks tend to be found at major intersections or outside big hotels.

■ Most passengers **round up the fare**, but rarely give a more substantial tip.

Cycling

Amsterdam is **well designed for cycling**; there are plenty of cycle lanes, no hills, and distances are short. For details of where to rent a bicycle, ►28.

Boats

Besides the regular canal tours operating on fixed routes (►88), there are three more ways of getting around the city on water.

■ Behind Centraal Station there are **free ferries** that leave throughout the day for locations in **Amsterdam-Noord**. The shortest trip goes to

Finding Your Feet

the EYE Film Instituut and takes just three minutes; the longest is to the NDSM-Werft and takes 20 minutes.

- **For the Canal Bus** (www.canal.nl), buy a ticket valid all day (a slightly more expensive version includes other forms of transport). There are four main routes, plus two more operated by new small, silent, eco-friendly electrical boats called Canal Hoppers.
- The **Museumboot/City(s)hopper** (www.lovers.nl) operates from Centraal Station and stops at: Anne Frank Huis, the Museum Quarter, the Flower Market, Waterlooplein and NEMO. A day ticket allows you unlimited rides all day and gives discounts on admission to numerous museums. Boats run to a regular schedule.
- **Water taxis** must be booked in advance and fares are high (tel: 020 535 6363, www.water-taxi.nl).

Car

Driving is **not an ideal way of getting about**, because of the scarcity and high cost of public parking, and the Byzantine system of one-way streets. If you decide to drive, check out the latest advice for driving overseas at: www.theaa.com/motoring_advice/overseas.

- **Look out for cyclists**, many of whom ignore all known traffic rules, and beware of trams that do not hesitate to assert their priority.
- To **park** on a street in central Amsterdam you will need to pay for a parking ticket at a vending machine. You enter your vehicle registration plate details and pay by credit card.
- **Park and Ride locations** ring the city, connecting with (sometimes free) public transport to the centre. Tickets are €7 for 24 hours. Holders of the I amsterdam City Card (➤ 41) receive a 50 per cent discount.
- During the annual **King's Day celebrations around 26 April**, many of the city's roads are closed to all motor traffic.

Car Rental

The biggest range of companies is available at **Schiphol airport**. Information: on www.schiphol.nl.

Accommodation

Virtually any hotel you might consider will be within walking distance of all the city's major attractions. The most appealing area to stay in is the Canal Ring, where the old gabled buildings house dozens of hotels. The medieval centre has some of both the grandest and the seediest establishments, while the Museum Quarter is convenient for culture-lovers, though the canal-free streets and the buildings have less character than those on the Canal Ring.

What to Expect

- **Most canalfront hotels are small** and offer only bed and breakfast. Stairs may be improbably steep (and there may be no lift); bedrooms come in all shapes and sizes, and the cheapest may not have private bathrooms.
- Breakfast – **usually a buffet of breads, fruit, meats and cheeses** – and the 5 per cent city tax are normally included in rates at inexpensive establishments, but charged as extras at luxury hotels.

Booking

Book as far in advance as possible! Hotels, especially the most characterful ones recommended on the following pages, are booked solid, particularly at weekends and May to September. Even in low season (November to March, when rates drop by around a quarter), try to make plans well ahead.

■ You can make bookings, daily 9–5, through the **Amsterdam Tourist Board** (tel: 020 7 02 60 00), for a fee of €15, or online at www.iamsterdam.com for free.

■ Tourist offices (➤ 39) also make **on-the-spot bookings** for a small fee.

Hostels

Amsterdam's many hostels are important in the accommodation scene.

■ One of the best is **Stayokay Amsterdam Vondelpark** (Zandpad 5, tel: 020 5 89 89 96, www.stayokay.com). It is set on the eastern edge of Vondelpark (close to the big museums and the nightlife around Leidseplein), and has a bar, bicycles to rent and some rooms with private bathrooms, as well as dormitory accommodation.

■ If it's full, consider **Shelter Jordaan** (Bloemstraat 179, tel: 020 6 24 47 17, www.shelter.nl), a Christian youth hostel which is smoke- and alcohol-free, and has a recommended upper age limit of 40.

■ Another option is **Hans Brinker** (Kerkstraat 138; tel: 020 6 22 06 87; www.hansbrinker.com), spartan but with a prime location near Leidseplein.

Apartments, Home Stays and Hotels

■ **Amsterdam House** ('s Gravelandseveer 7, tel: 020 6 26 25 77, www.amsterdamhouse.com) has apartments, most on canals, and hotel rooms. There is usually a minimum stay of four nights across weekends.

■ **Apartments Houseboats Amsterdam** (tel: 06 4671 6676, www.apartments-houseboats-amsterdam.nl) offers apartments and houseboats in Amsterdam. Its website allows you to search for accommodation from a room to a house, ranging from basic to luxury.

Accommodation prices

Hotel rates fluctuate wildly in Amsterdam, and can go sky-high on weekends. The following is only a guide to what you may expect to pay per standard double room per night:

€ under €150 **€€** €150–€300 **€€€** over €300

Ambassade €€

Old-fashioned elegance is the name of the game in this hotel, which spreads through ten 17th-century canal houses. The Louis XVI-style furniture creates a refined air in the bedrooms. The most characterful, with vaulted, beamed ceilings, are under the gables.

✚ 204 C4 ✉ Herengracht 341, 1016 AZ

☎ 020 5 55 02 22; www.ambassade-hotel.nl

Bed & Breakfast La Festa €

Four cool, clean and contemporary rooms at reasonable prices in the Jordaan district. There's free WiFi, and rooms come with coffee and tea-making facilities and a mini fridge. Two of the studio rooms have full kitchenettes. On the ground floor of the B&B is their La Festa Italian restaurant, which offers a variety of generously sized portions of fresh pastas and cheesy pizzas.

🏠 204 B4 ✉ Hazenstraat 64, 1016 SR
☎ 6 17 73 88 85; www.bb-lafesta.com

Brouwer €

The building (1625) is a grand old sea captain's house. Inside, the reception, which doubles as the breakfast room, has antique Delft tiles and paintings of Amsterdam scenes on the walls. Bedrooms, all of which face the Singel Canal, are simple but attractive, with wood floors, beams and Dutch art prints. One room, called Mondrian, has a wooden gutter (no longer in use) running through it.

Insider Tip

🏠 203 E2 ✉ Singel 83, 1012 VE
☎ 020 6 24 63 58; www.hotelbrouwer.nl

Canal House €€

This pair of 17th-century canal houses has been converted into a civilized hotel with grand, comfortable features. Its centrepiece is a stately breakfast room, overlooking a pretty garden. Antique bric-a-brac – such as hats, lamps, mirrors, clocks – decorates corridors and bedrooms.

🏠 197 D2 ✉ Keizersgracht 148, 1015 CX
☎ 020 6 22 51 82; www.canalhouse.nl

The Dylan €€€

Housed in what was originally a 17th-century theatre, The Dylan has just 41 bedrooms (and a delightful courtyard) and is the city's most sumptuous boutique hotel. The dramatic, oriental-influenced decor is the creation of designer Anouska Hempel. Choose from a spacious "loft", a decadent "Kimono" or a peaceful "Zen" room.

🏠 204 C4 ✉ Keizersgracht 384, 1016 GB
☎ 020 5 30 20 10; www.dylanamsterdam.com

Estheréa €€

A comfortable, central canal-front hotel with some character. Occupying several 17th-century red-brick houses, for three generations it has been in the Esselaar family, who are much in evidence. The de luxe bedrooms are worth the extra cost: they have canal views.

🏠 204 C4 ✉ Singel 303–309, 1012 WJ
☎ 020 6 24 51 46; www.estherea.nl

De L'Europe €€€

Fin de siècle opulence rules at this landmark luxury hotel dating from the late 19th century, in the form of chandeliers and frescoed ceilings in the public areas, acres of drapes over beds in bedrooms, and floor-to-ceiling marble in the bathrooms. Its location on the Amstel River could hardly be better. Many bedrooms have private balconies overlooking the river, and there is a waterside dining terrace, weather permitting.

🏠 205 D4 ✉ Nieuwe Doelenstraat 2–14, 1012 CP ☎ 020 5 31 17 77; www.leurope.nl

De Filosoof €

Although part of a chain, this is a more interesting offering than most as a philosophical theme runs throughout the decor. Murals of Plato and Aristotle line the entrance of the 19th-century house and text from famous works cover tablemats in the breakfast room. Bedrooms are themed after thinkers, and, instead of the usual Bible, each comes with philosophical works. The hotel has a pleasant garden and Vondelpark is on the doorstep.

🏠 208 C1 ✉ Anna van den Vondelstraat 6, 1054 GZ ☎ 020 6 83 30 13; www.hotelfilosoof.nl

Grand Hotel Amrâth €€€

The historic Scheepvaarthuis (Shipping House, ➤ 72) has been sensitively converted into a luxury hotel, with furnishings in keeping with the Amsterdam School architecture and fittings. Exceedingly comfortable bedrooms come with widescreen TVs, electronically controlled curtains and free mini-bars. Rooms on the Binnenkant side are the quietest and have the best views. Down in the basement, there's a rarity in Amsterdam – a swimming pool and a fully equipped spa.

➕ 206 B4 ✉ Prins Hendrikkade 108, 1011 AK
☎ 020 5 52 00 00; www.amrathamsterdam.com

't Hotel €€

This B&B couldn't be better placed, occupying a 17th-century house on one of the prettiest side canals. Bedrooms are under-stated, with art deco lamps, brown armchairs and grey-and-white bathrooms. Those with a canal view cost a little extra. As with many canalside establish-ments, the stairs are steep and there is no elevator.

➕ 203 D2 ✉ Leliegracht 18, 1015 DE
☎ 020 4 22 27 41; www.thotel.nl

The Lloyd €/€€€

A 1921 office block in the formerly forlorn eastern docks has been transformed into a distinctive hotel with inspiration from some of Amsterdam's best designers. From the bright ground-floor restaurant to the individually designed rooms, with innovative furniture, the place feels a world away from more traditional locations. Apart from its unique design, The Lloyd also boasts a unique concept. Rooms are available from one (with shared bathroom) to five stars. All guests enjoy the same service and facili-ties, but prices range from €95 to €450. The hotel is located in a new residential district that is ten minutes from the main station on tram 26.

➕ 207 off F4
✉ Oostelijke Handelskade 34, 1019 BN
☎ 020 5 61 36 36; www.lloydhotel.com

Orlando € Insider Tip

This stately, canal-facing, 17th-century house has just seven bedrooms but they're absolutely delightful. Expect bare oak floors, silk curtains, sophisticated lighting and big, bold modern paintings –

and fantastic value. Utrechtsestraat, which is full of restaurants, is just round the corner.

➕ 205 E2 ✉ Prinsengracht 1099, 1017 JH
☎ 020 6 38 69 15; www.hotelorlando.nl

Pulitzer €€€

A first-rate conversion of 25 17th- and 18th-century canal houses, all interconnected or linked via covered walkways through the hotel's large courtyard garden. Though a chain hotel, it doesn't feel like it. Quality art and tasteful modern furniture offset original features in bedrooms, such as painted beams. The restaurant, with an iconoclastic version of a Frans Hals painting, is distinctly upmarket.

➕ 204 B5 ✉ Prinsengracht 315–331, 1016 GZ
☎ 020 5 23 52 35; www.pulitzeramsterdam.com

Rho €

The 165-room Rho is close to Dam square down a quiet side street so has a great central location. Bedrooms are plain, but the lobby, once a theatre, is a vast, vaulted, art nouveau wonder. A breakfast buffet is included in the price.

➕ 205 D4 ✉ Nes 5–23, 1012 KC
☎ 020 6 20 73 71; www.rhohotel.com

Seven Bridges €

Located in an old house on the city's prettiest canal, this is every-one's favourite B&B. The 11 bedrooms are furnished with eclectic pieces, such as Louis XVI cupboards and art deco lamps. Breakfast is served in the bed-rooms, so you may want to pay extra for a big room.

➕ 205 E2 ✉ Reguliersgracht 31, 1017 LK
☎ 020 6 23 13 29; www.sevenbridgeshotel.nl

Seven One Seven €€€

Dutch fashion designer and interior decorator Kees van der Valk has turned this early 19th-century canal house into a discreet, luxury guesthouse. Most of the nine

Finding Your Feet

bedrooms, themed after painters, authors and composers, are spacious suites. All are treasure troves of art – from African masks and Murano glass to modern paintings – and have indulgent features such as colossal sofas and deep, sunken baths. Rates include afternoon tea and drinks.

✚ 205 D2 ✉ Prinsengracht 717, 1017 JW
☎ 020 4 27 07 17; www.717hotel.nl

Sofitel Amsterdam The Grand €€€

Built in the 16th century for the Admiralty, this "classic baroque" building served as the city hall until 1988. Now it is the most understated and peaceful of the city's luxury hotels, despite being just south of the red-light district. The plush bedrooms overlook two beautiful courtyards and serene canals.
The in-house Bridges restaurant specializes in seafood, and guests can relax and pamper themselves in the spa.

✚ 205 D4 ✉ Oudezijds Voorburgwal 197, 1012 EX ☎ 020 5 55 31 11; www.accorhotels.com

stayokay €

This branch of the modern Dutch chain of hostels has more than 500 rooms. It is ideally located near Vondelpark. All of the two-, four- and six-bed rooms have their own shower and toilet and there are also eight- and ten-bed dorms. Breakfast is included, and there is a TV room, laundry and facilities for children. Note: if you have kids under 12 you will need to book a private room.

✚ 204 B2 ✉ Zandpad 5, 1054 GA
☎ 020 5 89 89 96; www.stayokay.com

Vondel €€

Occupying four houses on a quiet, early 20th-century street a short walk from Leidseplein and the big museums, the Vondel has been given a slick, minimalist revamp. Bedroom walls, bedspreads, curtains, sofas and armchairs are all white or cream. The bar and lobby, with big bold sofas and stripped floorboards, look equally stylish.

✚ 204 A2 ✉ Vondelstraat 26, 1054 GE
☎ 020 612 0120; www.vondelhotels.com

Food and Drink

Like any vibrant city eating scene, Amsterdam's is changing all the time (► 34). Visitors can dine on fine, Michelin-starred cuisine, chow down in cheap and cheerful cafés, or tuck into contemporary fusion fare in modern eateries.

Ethnic Cuisine

Amsterdam's multicultural population is reflected in its range of ethnic restaurants: there are said to be 40 types of cuisine on offer.

■ The most common ethnic restaurants are **Indonesian and Chinese,** but you'll also come across Surinamese cafés, Spanish tapas bars, Argentinian steak houses and an increasing number of Thai and

---

Restaurant Prices

Expect to pay per person for a three-course meal, excluding drinks and service:

€ under €20 €€ €20–€40 €€€ over €40

Japanese establishments as well, of course, as the ubiquitous Italian restaurants.

■ **The Dutch consider Indonesian food,** introduced to the Netherlands by the Dutch East India Company in the 17th century, to be virtually part of their own culinary culture. Indonesian restaurants offer *rijsttafels* – literally "rice tables", from the Dutch *rijst* (rice) and *tafel* (table). The table is laden with a large bowl of rice, and anything from six to 60 dishes, to share with your dining companions. Some sauces, such as *sambal*, are hot enough to blow your head off. Note that you don't have to order such a feast; the Dutch often go *à la carte* instead.

Traditional Dishes

Though there is a trend towards "New Dutch" cooking, with lighter dishes and sauces, a number of atmospheric, old-fashioned restaurants still specialize in traditional Dutch food. Depending on your point of view, it's either simple and nourishing or bland and rather stodgy, with an emphasis on quantity as much as quality. Traditional main courses are, for example, *stamppot met rookworst* (mashed potatoes mixed with vegetables and smoked sausage) or various types of *stoofpot* (stew). A typical dessert is *hangop met stoofpeertjes*: thick yogurt with pears poached in red wine.

Snacks

■ Arguably, Dutch food is ideal for snacking. Street vendors offer raw herring (►36), and, less of an acquired taste, chips, which the Dutch traditionally eat with a dollop of mayonnaise. **Vleminckx**, at Voetboogstraat 33, serves Amsterdam's best chips (crispy on the outside, fluffy on the inside). Other vendors sell pancakes and *poffertjes*; several cafés, such as the **Pancake Bakery** (►110), serve pancakes and little else.

■ If you're feeling brave or ravenous, you might want to try a meat or cheese-filled croquette deep fried in breadcrumbs from **Febo's** coin-operated hatches: there are outlets all over town.

■ **At lunchtime**, most Amsterdammers make do with a *broodje* (sandwich), either in a café or from one of the many take-away sandwich shops. Cafés also traditionally serve *kroketten* (meat or shrimp croquettes), *uitsmijter* (fried eggs on ham and cheese and bread), and often home-made *appeltaart* (apple pie, ►36), served with a dollop of *slagroom* (whipped cream). The pie at the **Café Winkel** (Noordermarkt 43), heavily flavoured with cinnamon and with the flakiest of crusts, may be the culinary highlight of your stay.

What to Drink

■ Apart from beer (►26), **the favourite Dutch tipple** is *jenever* (Dutch gin), made from molasses and flavoured with juniper berries. Whether *oud* (old – and mellow and a little yellow), or *jong* (young – and sharp and transparent), *jenever* has a stronger taste than English gin but is less potent. *Jenever* is drunk neat and served in tulip-shaped glasses filled to the brim. You're expected to leave the glass on the bar and bend down for the first sip. Serious drinkers order a *kopstoot* (a knock on the head) – a beer with a *jenever* chaser.

■ **Tasting houses** (►31) also specialize in fruity liqueurs with delightful names.

■ The Dutch are very partial to coffee. **It is traditionally served black**. If you want a coffee with milk, ask for a *koffie verkeerd* (literally "coffee wrong").

Practicalities

- Most restaurants open only in the evening. The Dutch tend to **eat dinner early,** so they are busiest between 7 and 8pm. The sign *keuken tot:...* gives the time the kitchen closes; few places take orders after 10pm.
- **Cafés usually open** some time in the morning (but drinking-orientated ones tend to open in the afternoon), and close at 1am Sun–Thu, 2am Fri–Sat, but stop serving food around 10 or 11pm.
- More often than not, **a menu is available in English,** and you can invariably rely on the staff to speak English.
- At stylish restaurants: **book ahead.**
- Only the most **formal restaurants** in luxury hotels **have a dress code**.
- The custom is to **round up the bill or tip 10 per cent** of the amount.

Shopping

Amsterdam excels in its dozens of little specialist shops, some dedicated to selling one item such as old spectacles, toothbrushes or olive oil; and in its many and varied markets. It's also refreshingly free of shopping malls.

Best Shopping Areas and Streets

- In the city centre, pedestrianised **Kalverstraat** (www.kalverstraat.nl) (➤ 79) has the greatest concentration of mainstream high-street shops and department stores.
- The **9 Straatjes** (www.theninestreets.com, ➤ 111), the Nine Streets on the western canal ring, are crammed full of tiny, often offbeat stores. The nearby backstreets of the Jordaan offer more of the same.
- The **Spiegelkwartier** (www.spiegelkwartier.nl, ➤ 164) has more than 100 classy art galleries and antiques shops.
- **PC Hooftstraat** (➤ 139), in the Museum Quarter, amounts to a roll-call of famous names in the world of international fashion.

Best Markets

- **Albert Cuypmarkt** (➤ 159): general street market.
- **Bloemenmarkt** (➤ 159): flower market.
- **Noordermarkt** (➤ 112): Saturday flea market and organic market.
- **Waterlooplein** (➤ 81): flea market.

What to Buy

- Art and antiques: in the **Spiegelkwartier** (➤ 164), **De Looier** indoor market (➤ 113) and along **Prinsengracht** (➤ 112), you can pick up anything from old Delftware tiles to city prints, toys, clocks and medical instruments.
- **Bulbs:** tulips, narcissi and hyacinths are on sale at the **Bloemenmarkt** (➤ 165). There are no restrictions for exports to the UK, but US buyers should ask market traders about certification before buying.
- **Chocolates:** best from places such as **Pompadour** (➤ 112) and **Holtkamp** (➤ 165), which make their own.
- **Cheeses:** *jonge* (young) and *oude* (old), and factory-produced or farm-produced, the latter unpasteurized and stamped *boerenkaas*. Specialist cheese shops such as **De Kaaskamer** (➤ 112) let you taste before buying, and vacuum-pack your purchase.

- **Delftware:** the genuine article, only made by De Porceleyne Fles, is sold in shops such as **Galleria d'Arte Rinascimento** (▶ 112) and **Aronson Antiquairs** (▶ 164).
- **Diamonds:** Factories such as **Coster Diamonds** (▶ 134) offer free tours to attract customers into their salerooms.

Smart Shops

Amsterdam's liberal policy towards drugs is evident not only in the presence of coffeeshops (▶ 32), but also in the many "smart shops" peddling "smart drugs" that have sprouted in the last few years. Although the sale of hallucinogenic "magic" mushrooms was banned, these shops still sell mind enhancers, as well cannabis paraphernalia. Also on display are kits that test for impurities in Ecstasy tablets and cocaine, and less contentious products such as herbs claiming aphrodisiac properties.

Opening Hours

Though **opening hours are gradually becoming more flexible,** they are still restricted. On the main shopping streets in the city centre, stores typically open (although timings may vary) Mon noon–6, Tue, Wed and Fri 10–6, Thu 10–9, Sat 9–5 and Sun noon–5. Specialist stores, however, generally do not open on Sundays, and can even sometimes be closed on Mondays.

Taxes

Tax **is included in advertised prices.** If you live outside the European Union, you are entitled to a refund on the value-added tax (21 per cent) minus a commission at shops displaying a "Tax Free Shopping" sign, as long as you spend €50 or more in the shop in a single day. For more information, go to www.global-blue.com.

Airport Shopping

If all you want is a typical Dutch souvenir, you could leave your shopping until just before you leave the country. The **shops after passport control** at Schiphol airport sell chocolates, Gouda, Edam, smoked herring and smoked eel, as well as bulbs, clogs, *jenever* and diamonds. Note that for journeys within the European Union, there are no longer any tax benefits on purchases made at the airport.

Entertainment

For after-dark entertainment, it's hard to improve on the simple pleasures of a stroll along the canals and a beer or two in one of the many atmospheric cafés.

The liveliest areas at night – worth either seeking out or avoiding, depending on what you're looking for – are the **red-light district** (▶ 56), **Spuikwartier** (▶ 76), **Leidseplein** (▶ 113) and **Rembrandtplein** (▶ 166). Cafés stay open to a late hour: until around 1am or 2am on Fri and Sat.

Information Sources

A calendar of events can be found at www.iamsterdam.com, in English magazines such as *A-mag* and *Timeout* or in the free *Uitkrant* (in Dutch).

Finding Your Feet

Booking Tickets

The best place to book tickets is the **AUB Ticketshop** in the Stadsschouwburg (tel: 020 7 95 99 50, Mon–Fri 10–7, Sat 10–6, Sun noon–5). It stocks every possible cultural leaflet and the staff are both helpful and knowledgeable. You can also buy tickets online: www.aub.nl. Another option is the www.lastminuteticketshop.nl website which sells same day tickets at a 50 per cent discount; they come on sale daily from 10am.

Nightclubs

- Most clubs open only Thu–Sun, and **don't get going until around midnight**.
- **Entry is normally inexpensive** (€5–€10), but may be dependent on dressing to impress the bouncers.
- Some clubs allow dope to be smoked, but the **sale of drugs is strictly prohibited**.

Gay Amsterdam

Ultra-tolerant Amsterdam has one of the most vibrant gay scenes in Europe, www.amsterdam4gays.com and www.gayamsterdam.com are **useful starting points for venues and events**.

- Many gay bars and clubs can be found on **Reguliersdwarsstraat** (➤ 166), **Warmoesstraat** (➤ 82) and on **Kerkstraat,** around the intersection with Leidsestraat.
- Several bars and clubs stock **free publications** and flyers listing gay-orientated venues.

Cinema

- Amsterdam has some highly individual cinemas such as the **Tuschinski Theater** (➤ 166).
- Cinemas screen the vast majority of films in their **original language with Dutch subtitles**. The exception to this is children's films.

Live Music

- The bastions of high culture are the **Muziektheater** (➤ 82), **Concertgebouw** (➤ 136) and the new **Muziekgebouw aan 't IJ** (➤ 166).
- Many churches regularly lay on classical concerts, baroque chamber music and organ recitals. The **Engelse Kerk,** in the Begijnhof (➤ 62), normally has the fullest programme. Other venues include: **Oude Kerk** (➤ 58); **Nieuwe Kerk** (➤ 68); **Westerkerk** (➤ 92–93), carillon concerts noon–1pm on Tue; **Amstelkerk** (➤ 188); and **Waalse Kerk** (Walenpleintje 157).
- The **Amsterdam ArenA (www.amsterdamarena.nl)**, Ajax's futuristic football stadium, holds large-scale rock concerts.
- The more intimate **Melkweg** and **Paradiso** (➤ 113) host up-and-coming bands, as well as megastars such as the Rolling Stones, who would never normally choose to play to such relatively small audiences.

Summer Entertainment

- Most cultural events **take place in summer**. They include the **Holland Festival** (www.hollandfestival.nl), in June, and the **Grachtenfestival** (www.grachtenfestival.nl) in August, with classical music events.
- **Amsterdam Gay Pride festival** (www.amsterdamgaypride.nl), held in late July/early August, includes a large procession of boats along the canal.
- **In late August**, organizations advertise their shows by performing excerpts free of charge at the **Uitmarkt** (www.amsterdamsuitburo.nl).
- See also ➤ 130 for the **Vondelpark open-air theatre**.

Medieval Amsterdam

 Little Treats

Exclusive cigars
The art deco interior of **Hajenius** (➤80) creates the perfect ambiance for you to purchase some quality cigars.

Art for free
The covered alley between the **Amsterdam Museum** (➤63) and Begijnensteeg is the Schuttersgalerij with dozens of paintings.

Sint Annenstraat
In the **alleyways of the red-light district** (➤57) sleazy meets design: to the left are scantily clad ladies, to the right are boutiques.

Getting Your Bearings

The old heart of Amsterdam feels like two distinct cities. The more obvious of the pair comprises the sort of brash tourist trappings that you find in any major European city, in this particular case augmented by the unabashed indulgence of the main red-light district, De Wallen. Yet alongside such excess you can find oases of calm and solitude, plus some charming little places to eat, drink and shop.

De Dam, the main square, is not the most beautiful plaza in Europe, but it serves as a good hub for exploring the rest of the area. Everything in medieval Amsterdam is a short walk from here, including the main shopping streets and the rejuvenated Amsterdam Museum – a user-friendly introduction to the story of this extraordinary city. Almost next door, the Begijnhof, a cloister for the support and protection of women, maintains its principles and decorum. Even in the middle of the red-light district (often also known as Rosse Buurt), there are strikingly beautiful structures, steeped in history. Medieval Amsterdam forms the perfect introduction to the city, whatever your interests are.

Herengracht
Singel
Spuistraat
Nieuwezijds
Raadhuisstraat
Koninklijk Paleis
De Dam 13
Madame Tussauds 16
Rokin
Amsterdam Museum 12
Begijnhof 11
Rokin
Munt-plein

Statue of Christ on the lawn of the Begijnhof

0   250 m
0   200 yd

De Ruijterkade

Het IJ

18 Centraal Station

Stations-plein

IJ-tunnel

Prins Hendrikkade

Voorburgwal

Damrak

15 Ons' Lieve Heer op Solder

17 Beurs van Berlage

NEMO **20**

19 Scheepvaarthuis

Oosterdok

Geldersekade

⭐ De Wallen

Nieuw-markt

CENTRUM

Prins Hendrikkade

Kloveniersburgwal

St. Antoniesbreestr.

Oudeschans

Rembrandthuis **14**

Jodenbreestr.

Valkenburgerstr.

universiteit

Stadhuis

Mr. Visserplein

Muziek-theater

Waterlooplein

Amstel

The Perfect Day

If you're not quite sure how to structure your day in Amsterdam, this itinerary recommends a practical and enjoyable day out exploring the medieval quarter of Amsterdam, taking in some of the best places. For more information see the main entries (➤ 56–73).

🕘 9:00am

This is the earliest you can visit the ⑪ **Begijnhof** (chapel, below, ➤ 54–55), the serene heart of the city; arrive promptly to dodge the worst of the crowds, then have a coffee at the grand Café Luxembourg (➤ 74) on Spui, the square just to the south.

🕘 11:30am

A few minutes' walk north takes you to the ⑫ **Amsterdam Museum** (➤ 63), where you can brush up on the background of the medieval city.

🕘 1:00pm

Wander east to combine lunch with people-watching at **In de Waag** (➤ 75), the old weigh house on Nieuwmarkt, or lunch with shopping at **La Place** (➤ 76), the cafeteria of the Vroom en Dreesmann department store.

🕘 3:00pm

Most roads in Medieval Amsterdam lead to ⑬ **De Dam** (➤ 67), where you could wander around the **Royal Palace** (Koninklijk Paleis, right), or explore some of the more innovative shops away from the main retail streets.

🕘 4:00pm

An easy stroll through the university district, past the home of the former East India Company, takes you to **Waterlooplein**. Around here you can search for some end-of-day bargains at the flea market; check out the worrying water levels (➤ 14) in the town hall; visit ⑭ **Rembrandthuis** (➤ 70), the artist's home and enjoy an afternoon coffee at the leaning café, **De Sluyswacht** (➤ 76).

⏱ 5:30pm

Back towards Centraal Station you will find some of the oldest parts of the city, such as the Oudezijds Voorburgwal and at this time of day you'll also experience how the day's commerce gives way to the night's activities in the ☆ **De Wallen**, the red-light district (➤ 56).

⏱ 7:00pm

Acquire a taste for *jenever* (Dutch gin) at a traditional tasting house such as **De Drie Fleschjes** (➤ 75) or **Wynand Fockink** (➤ 76).

⏱ 8:00pm

Dine out on excellent Thai or Chinese on **Zeedijk** (➤ 57), or remind yourself that you are in one of the great fishing nations with the superb seafood at **Lucius** (➤ 77).

⏱ 10:00pm

It is best to end your day where it started, at the Begijnhof. Just opposite is the legendary **Café Hoppe** (➤ 74) where you can help to maintain its reputation for pumping more beer for its size than any other brown café in the Netherlands.

18 Centraal Station

Beurs van Berlage 17

15 Ons' Lieve Heer op Solder

NEMO 20

19 Scheepvaarthuis

13 De Dam

Madame 16 Tussauds

12 Amsterdam Museum

11 Begijnhof

14 Rembrandthuis

⑥ De Wallen

Amsterdam's red-light district, known as De Wallen, is outrageous. Prostitutes pout in the glare of pink lighting. A sign on the window of a coffeeshop reads "Dear Customers, Please roll your joints inside the shop, thank you." Every big city has its red-light district, where the normal rules of society are suspended, but nowhere is it quite like Amsterdam.

Some visitors are intrigued by this area; one of Amsterdam's main attractions, it offers a vivid slice of a lifestyle that, in other cities, is largely concealed. Others feel very uncomfortable about venturing into the compact, ragged triangle enclosed by Warmoesstraat, Zeedijk and Damstraat. Yet to avoid the area completely would be to miss an important

The legendary red-light district may not be to everyone's taste

dimension of the city. It is interesting to note that prostitutes in Amsterdam pay the highest rate of taxes based on income and are given regular health checks by law and even have their own union.

As well as being a fascinating social phenomenon that is generally safe to visit, the slumping houses and upright churches make it clear that there is plenty of history here, too, and any visitor should explore the maze of streets that marks the historic core of Amsterdam, preferably by day.

Warmoesstraat and its continuation, **Nes,** comprise the oldest street in the city, which grew up as the eastern bank of the Amstel. At the same time, the **Zeedijk** (sea dyke) was built as a barrier to high tides and storms on the Zuiderzee. Between the two, the present warren of alleyways began to develop. From Amsterdam's earliest days as a port, the area catered for sailors who came ashore in need of alcohol and female company. Now, as then, between the brothels and bars, there are some notable ecclesiastical attractions There are also some more peaceful areas in the red-light

district. The corner of Grimburgwal/Oudezijds Achterburgwal, with the Huis aan de drie Grachten (House on the Three Canals) built in 1610 – one of the loveliest step gable buildings in the city – is especially attractive. And, you will not notice any red-light activity at the tranquil southern end of Oudezijds Achterburgwal, which was dug in 1367 and lined with a total of 19 monasteries until the "Alteration". You can go through the small gate with a pair of spectacles hanging above it. This is the former seniors' residence with a beautiful inner courtyard that now belongs to the university. Book lovers will find it hard to resist a visit to the antiquarian bookshop in the adjacent passage.

Insider Tip

Oude Kerk

As early as 1300, a small chapel stood on the present site of the **Oude Kerk** (Old Church), dedicated to St Nicholas, who protected

Continued on page 60

The Oldest Church in Amsterdam

Dating back to beginning of the 14th century, the church building was expanded in 1370 with the addition of two choir chapels and the ambulatory. The Oude Kerk remained unscathed by the two fires that devastated medieval Amsterdam. Some of the other chapels were donated by fraternities and guilds. When the choir was modified in the 16th century, work was financed – as was customary at the time – by a lottery.

❶ Bell tower: Reconstruction of the tower followed in the 16th century. The short Gothic tower was replaced by the high west tower we see today and has housed a carillon (by the famous bell caster Hemony), considered to be one of the finest in the Netherlands, since 1658. If you want to climb the tower of the Oude Kerk you need to do so by guided tour (reservation in advance) but you will be rewarded with a spectacular view over the old city from the top.

❷ South portal: Also dating from the 16th century is a portal on the south side with the coats of arms of Emperor Maximilian I and King Philip the Fair. It provides access to the Iron Chapel where the town privileges, including the customs regulations from 1275, were kept until they were moved to the community archives in 1872.

❸ Interior: Today, the Oude Kerk continues to fulfil its original purpose as a sacral building but following extensive restoration work in the 1990s, the church is now also used for art exhibitions, lectures and concerts. Much of the precious original decoration was lost during the turmoil of the 16th century.

❹ Renaissance stained-glass windows: The stained-glass windows in the Lady Chapel are especially notable. They were initially set in place in 1555 and renewed, maintaining much of their original form, in the 18th century.

❺ Choir: The elaborate carving of the choir pews dates from the first half of the 16th century.

❻ Grand organ: The Baroque grand organ (1724–26), with its rich gold and wood decoration, is really magnificent.

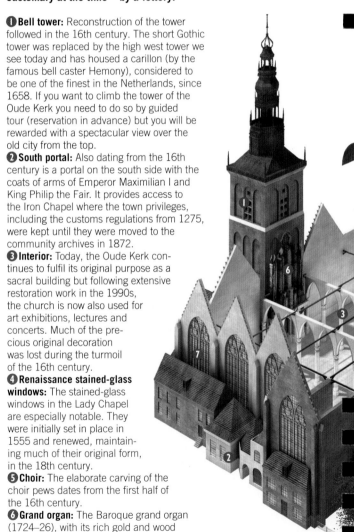

❼Tombstones: As in the Nieuwe Kerk, many of Amsterdam's famous citizens have their final resting place here in the Oude Kerk. Rembrandt's wife Saskia, who died in 1642, is buried here along with several admirals including Jacob van Heemskerk and Willem van der Zaan.

The nave and aisles have a barrel vault ceilings

Medieval Amsterdam

people against the dangers of water. In the 15th century, the basic stone structure was established, making it the oldest building in Amsterdam.

It has weathered the turbulence of the city remarkably well – though some dignity has been lost with new accoutrements such as the open-air urinals in the square outside. Inside, you are likely to find much of the space used for a temporary exhibition, but the fine stained-glass windows are undiminished and memorials to the illustrious dead are visible everywhere. Rembrandt's wife, Saskia, is buried beneath one of the 2,500 gravestones.

A church has stood on the site of Oude Kerk since the 14th century

➕ 203 F1

Oude Kerk
➕ 203 F1 ✉ Oudekerksplein 23 ☎ 020 6 25 82 84; www.oudekerk.nl
🕐 Mon–Sat 10–6, Sun 1–5. Closed 1 Jan, 26 April, 25 Dec 🚌 4, 9, 16, 24, 25 to Damrak 💶 €7.50; Museumkaart and I amsterdam City Card holders free

⑪ Begijnhof

A stake in the lawn at the Begijnhof, Amsterdam's oldest courtyard, bears the motto: "May peace prevail on earth." And, as long as the tourists keep their voices down, it does prevail here, in a broad, green and pleasant square, moments away from the centre of one of Europe's most energetic cities.

Lambert le Bègue founded the order of the Begijns in 1170, for women from wealthy Catholic backgrounds who had lost (or never acquired) a husband. The Begijnhof was a more liberal alternative to entering a convent: Begijns lived in comfortable housing while ministering to the poor and elderly, but were not required to take strict religious vows.

HOW TO BEHAVE

The residents of the Begijnhof tolerate tourism, but request visitors to follow some common-sense rules to avoid invading their privacy. Photography is permitted, but you should not photograph the interiors of individual houses. Voices should be kept down.

The Begijnhof was founded in the mid-14th century, but the original wooden houses have been lost. At No 34 is the **Houten Huys** (wooden house), built around 1530, and the oldest surviving home in the city. Most of the rest were constructed in the 16th, 17th or 18th century, though some are less than 100 years old. Around the corner from the café/information centre at No 35 is a wall in which eight biblical tablets are embedded, preserved when some of the houses were demolished. The last Begijn died in

The Begijnhof is a popular place for visitors

Medieval Amsterdam

1971, but the houses are still occupied by unmarried women. Their prim houses, beneath elaborate gables, are arranged around well-tended lawns.

Covering most of the southern half of the Begijnhof is the **Engelse Kerk**, built towards the end of the 15th century and for 100 years the sisters' place of worship. It was closed after the "Alteration" to Protestantism (➤ 64), and lay idle until 1607 when it was lent to English-speaking Presbyterians. Some of the congregation later became the Pilgrim Fathers. The church is now part of the Church of Scotland. The pulpit has panels decorated by a young Piet Mondriaan (1872–1944). Besides Sunday services (at 10:30am), the church is now used for concerts.

A stained-glass window in Begijnhofkapel dedicated to Joost van den Vondel and Thomas a Kempis, two Dutch Catholic writers

The Begijnhofkapel

The **Begijnhofkapel,** the Catholic church built in 1671, is just five paces away from the Engelse Kerk, but not at all obvious. After the "Alteration", Amsterdam's Catholics were obliged to worship clandestinely: the authorities turned a blind eye, as long as there was no evidence from the street of a church. Anonymous doors conceal an opulent interior: look for the stained-glass window dedicated to the Dutch national poet, Joost van den Vondel, to the right of the altar.

✚ 204 C4 ⊠ Begijnhof
☎ www.begijnhofamsterdam.nl
🕓 Daily 9–5; no groups. Begijnhofkapel: Sat, Sun 9–6, Mon 1–6:30, Tue–Fri 9–6:30 🚋 1, 2, 5 💲 Free

---

INSIDER INFO

- Both entrances are hard to find. The main way in is from **Gedempte Begijnensloot,** reached from Kalverstraat along a lane called Begijnensteeg. A second entrance is from the square known as Spui, underneath an arch that looks like an ordinary doorway.
- During the middle of the day, the Begijnhof can become jammed with visitors; plan to be there in **the first or last hour.**
- For more information about the Begijnhof and its chapels you can go just around the corner to the interesting Begijnhof **bookstore and gift shop** which is next to the presbytery at Nieuwezijds Voorburgwal 371; it is open Tuesday to Saturday 10–4.

Insider Tip

⑫ Amsterdam Museum

Amsterdam is an extraordinary city, and its strange, exciting history is explained in masterful manner at this city museum. The human and economic intrigues that have helped create Amsterdam are laid bare in a venue that is as jumbled as the city itself, and a visit early in your stay will help you to understand and enjoy Amsterdam all the more. The covered alley next to the museum is the Schuttersgalerij with portraits of guardsmen.

The Amsterdam Museum documents the history of the city

The museum occupies a large complex of historic building and has two main entrances. The most accessible is the doorway at Nieuwezijds Voorburgwal 357, which also puts you in the right place to begin your tour around the chronologically laid out galleries.

The museum's distinct location and shape are due to its origins and use. It was established in 1414 as a convent, but after the "Alteration" to Protestantism (►64), it became the city's orphanage. The girls' and boys' halves were separated by a deep (and unsavoury) trench, which traced the line of the walkway that now slices through the museum.

Young City

The rooms give a strictly chronological account of the growth of the city, from the first settlements formed on small, raised mounds of solid clay. These artificial mounds protected the settlers from the tides in the low-lying marshes. Gradually the mounds grew together, and Amsterdam acquired the critical mass necessary for its inhabitants to transcend subsistence lifestyles.

Medieval Amsterdam

The first dam was built on the Amstel in 1270, something of a turning point for the infant city. Its immediate effect was to impede trade – the barrier meant that cargo vessels were obliged to unload – and the goods moved onwards, creating employment in Amsterdam.

Pragmatism and innovation marked the next few centuries. The earliest known "map" of the city, Cornelis Anthonisz's 1538 *Bird's-Eye View of Amsterdam*, is displayed next to a digital version highlighting the city's growth. Other paintings in the museum include a 1593 work, showing a lottery being conducted in aid of a lunatic asylum.

Mighty City

Amsterdam was central to rapid economic growth in the 14th and 15th centuries, as enhanced maritime technology brought more trade. **Room 5** shows how trading with Asia began in earnest in 1595, by several competing companies, which merged in 1602 and became a more potent force – the Vereenigde Oostindische Compagnie (VOC, ➤ 18), the most powerful trading association in the world. Over the next two centuries, nearly a million people sailed from Holland, and some estimates suggest only one in three returned. The eastbound adventures were much more effective than those to the west. On the North American mainland, Nieuw Amsterdam was founded in 1613. The Dutch made what has been called the worst land-swap deal in history. They took Suriname in exchange for Nieuw Amsterdam – or New York, as the British called it. Suriname was ceded by the British to the Dutch in exchange for Nieuw Amsterdam in exchange for Nieuw Amsterdam New York, given to the English for Suriname, a small marshy

Amsterdam managed to turn the religious turmoil that swept across Europe in the 16th century to its advantage. Skilled Jewish people and Protestants, expelled from other European countries, were given a (guarded) welcome. The city was not immune to the strife, and its version of the Reformation – known as the "Alteration" – took place after considerable bloodshed in the second half of the 16th century. **Room 10** gives an insight into the religious struggles, and also features a replica of the carillon from the Munt Tower, which you are at liberty to try out.

Modern City

Amsterdam's mercantile and artistic glory dwindled in the 19th century, but the city continued to find innovative solutions to the special problems it faced. One is described in **Room 16:** J C Sinck's hoist was used to rescue horses that fell into the canal. It comprised a wagon with a crane attachment and harness, looped around the unfortunate animal. A rescue operation cost 40 guilders – a small price to pay to prevent the loss of such a valuable asset.

The Regent's Chamber

The 20th-century section is particularly interesting, focusing on immigration, social welfare and, of course, World War II. During the "Hunger Winter" of 1944–45, more than 2,000 Amsterdammers died under Nazi occupation.

As the docks wound down during the 1970s and early 1980s, the city went into decline, with 40,000 people leaving each year. Social upheavals since the 1960s are described with a dose of humour: amid the sober graphs of population growth is a diagram of the rise of coffee-shops between 1980 and 1999, using the marijuana plant as the symbol of magnitude.

Medieval Amsterdam

The museum brings you up to date with the contemporary community. Fewer than one in three Amsterdammers have always lived in the city, and the rate of "residential turnover" is high, making it an exciting cosmopolitan place to live. Although this is Amsterdam's historical museum, it reflects the changing face of the city, with engaging, hands-on multi-media exhibits that are very much of the 21st century.

The courtyard area of the museum's café

TAKING A BREAK

The **Museum Café Mokum** is housed in an old, large cowshed belonging to the former convent that is now the museum. Outside is an airy courtyard with additional tables and chairs to enjoy a light lunch after visiting the museum or if you've been shopping in the nearby streets.

✚ 205 D4
✉ Nieuwezijds Voorburgwal 357, Kalverstraat 92
☎ 020 5 23 18 22; www.amsterdammuseum.nl
🕐 Daily 10–5. Closed 1 Jan, 26 April, 25 Dec
🍴 Museum Café Mokum, ground floor (€€); daily 10–5
🚌 1, 2, 4, 5, 9, 11, 14, 16, 24, 25
💰 €10; free to Museumkaart and I amsterdam City Card holders

INSIDER INFO

- Rent an audio tour or pick up the **free plan at the entrance**; despite some reasonable signposting, you could get hopelessly lost without a map.
- The shop has a great range of **appealing small gifts** – a good place to do your souvenir shopping.

⑬ De Dam

Almost all visitors to Amsterdam find themselves passing through De Dam, as the square at the centre of the city is concisely known. This was where the Amstel River was first dammed in the 13th century (today the river flows via underground pipes into the IJ). The square is central to the city and the country, containing both the Royal Palace and the National Monument. Initially, the unruly architecture may disappoint, as well as the fact that the whole place is decked in overhead power cables for trams. Although De Dam can largely appear as a tourist thoroughfare, it remains at the historical heart of the city.

Koninklijk Paleis

The Dutch monarchy is distinct from most royal families – it was established, by common consent, less than two centuries ago. The Royal Palace is also rather different from the norm. From its imposing bulk and location on Amsterdam's main square, you could be forgiven for taking it for a city hall; that was, indeed, its intended purpose. Trams pass within 2m (6ft) of the south wall, and from the front door, His Majesty has an excellent view of many of the quaint excesses of life in Amsterdam, such as people idling around the Nationaal Monument while smoking marijuana.

Once the city hall now the Royal Palace

The palace was built in the mid-17th century, when Amsterdam was the greatest trading city in the world. At the time, the poet Constantijn Huygens (1596–1687) called it "the eighth wonder of the world". When Louis Napoleon took control of the Netherlands, he first resided in Utrecht but soon moved to Amsterdam. The only building grand enough to house him, he said, was the city hall. On the **pediment** is an allegory of Amsterdam's maritime prominence with the oceans paying homage to her. Above, on the dome, is a Dutch sailing ship acting as a weather vane.

It's worth walking around the outside of the palace to gauge the sheer scale of the place, and to see the **sculpture of Atlas** supporting a giant copper globe on the rear roof facade – but beware of the trams that encircle it. Even the row of four lamp posts at the front of the palace is decorative, each protected by lions and topped by a crown.

Medieval Amsterdam

Nationaal Monument

The Nationaal Monument marks the suffering during the Nazi occupation in World War II, a traumatic time for the city and the country. The white column was designed by John Rädecker and unveiled to public on 4 May 1956, 16 years after the German invasion. Critics say the design is nothing more than a giant version of the traffic bollards, and you can see their point. Look closely at the overgrown salt cellar, and representations of motherhood and repression are evident, while a flock of doves flutters down the back of the monument. Urns arrayed around it contain soil from the states of the Netherlands, and the greatest former Dutch possession, Indonesia.

Nationaal Monument, Dam Square

Nieuwe Kerk

The Nieuwe Kerk is the church used for the investiture of Dutch monarchs and, in 2002, the wedding of the current royal couple. Despite its name, the church is centuries old. It's at its loveliest on a sunny morning, when the gold figures on the sundial above the deep window on the south side glitter like a necklace. Until the coming of "railway time" at the end of the 19th century, all the city's clocks were synchronized to this sundial. The original "New Church" was founded in 1408, but fire destroyed the first two versions. Its present shape dates from the early 16th century. In 1578, the Dutch Reformed Church took it over, and cleared it of statues, altars and murals. A fire was started in 1645 by plumbers melting lead to repair the roof, which destroyed everything except the walls and pillars. This allowed the interior to be reconstructed with the best that the Golden Age could provide.

On the right of the entrance as you go in is a monument to **Joost van den Vondel** (1587–1679), national poet and contemporary of Rembrandt, whose remains are in an urn in the church. Many naval heroes – commonly regarded in the 18th and 19th centuries as the closest thing to royalty – are buried here, notably **Michiel de Ruyter** (1606–1676), an admiral in the Dutch fleet who fought in the Second and Third Anglo-Dutch Wars. In the course of the former, he sailed up the Thames Estuary almost as far as London; he died in the latter, and the battle in which he lost his life is depicted on his tomb. The church is also one of the country's most-visited exhibition venues, with regular displays of art and "world

INSIDER INFO

- The **free audio tour** is worthwhile
- If you find yourself visiting the Royal Palace in October, the yearly **exhibition of the Royal Awards for Painting** is interesting too.

religion" treasures. There is also a shop (daily 10–5, no entrance fee), offering mostly exhibition-related items and books.

TAKING A BREAK

Looking north along Nieuwendijk from De Dam, a succession of fast-food outlets stretches into the distance. On the square itself is the **'t Nieuwe Kafé** (daily 8:30–6, tel: 020 627 2830, www.nieuwe-kafe.nl), which sprouts from the Nieuwe Kerk and is an excellent venue for relaxing and people-watching. For something different, try a selection of authentic *jenevers* in the **Wynand Fockink** tasting house (►76) at Pijlsteeg 31, tucked away in a lane behind the Grand Hotel Krasnapolsky. **Insider Tip**

Koninklijk Paleis
🔢 205 D5
☎ 020 6 20 40 60; www.paleisamsterdam.nl
🕐 Generally: daily 11–5; except for official royal family receptions. Current calendar on the website
🚊 All trams to and from Centraal Station
🎫 €10; children under 5 free

Nieuwe Kerk
🔢 205 D5
☎ 020 6 38 69 09; www.nieuwekerk.nl
🕐 Daily 10–5. Closed 1 Jan, 25 Dec
🚊 All trams to and from Centraal Station
🎫 €15; I amsterdam City Card holders free

Relax at t' Nieuwe Kafé on Dam Square

At Your Leisure

⓮ Rembrandthuis

Rembrandt's delightful house was the artist's residence between 1639 and 1658. You enter through the building next door, and descend to the kitchen, where you can see the first of several "box-beds" – the maid slept in what was effectively a cupboard with a mattress inside.

The ground level is the grandest, with the entrance hall especially opulent. As a dealer in art, as well as a painter, Rembrandt knew the value of making a good impression. The anteroom has an impressive marble-effect entrance and fireplace that are actually painted wood. There are plenty of paintings by his contemporaries on show and there are reproductions of some of these works of art on sale in the shop.

Picasso took many ideas from Rembrandt's etchings, saying: "Bad artists copy, good artists steal". The salon (drawing room) doubled as Rembrandt's bedroom.

A narrow spiral staircase leads to a mezzanine floor, where you find an extraordinary collection of *objets d'art*. The artefacts include a hammock from South America, porcelain from China and, among

Rembrandt, his family and his pupils dined in this kitchen

the exhibits from the natural world, are a dazzling blue butterfly and three turtle shells.

The biggest room in the house is the large studio on the second floor, the north-facing room where Rembrandt and his pupils worked.

On the third floor, pause to look down on the rear of the house – and the modern apartment block that backs on to it – before beginning your descent. As you leave the building, look out for the fine gateway to the left (west), which shows two sulky figures in relief beneath the triple-cross symbol of Amsterdam.

There are changing exhibits and the artist's etchings on display, as well as several exhibitions devoted to works by Rembrandt, and those that have been inspired by him. The audio tour (free) is interesting and well presented.

✚ 206 B3 ✉ Jodenbreestraat 4
☎ 020 5 20 04 00; www.rembrandthuis.nl
🕐 Daily 10–6. Closed 1 Jan, 26 April
🚇 Waterlooplein 🚌 9, 14
💶 €12.50; Museumkaart and I amsterdam City Card holders free

15 Ons' Lieve Heer op Solder

Ons' Lieve Heer op Solder ("Our Lord in the Attic"), is a marvellous museum. The first three floors give an insight into 17th-century life in Amsterdam, with rooms preserved in the style created by the owner, Jan Hartman. On the three upper floors, a dazzling Catholic church, dripping in statuary and silver, has been forced into the narrow confines of the house. After the "Alteration" to Protestantism, Catholics were obliged to worship clandestinely and several wealthy families transformed parts of their homes into chapels, but this is the only one that has been preserved.

🔒 206 A4

✉ Oudezijds Voorburgwal 40

☎ 020 6 24 66 04; www.opsolder.nl

🕐 Mon–Sat 10–5, Sun and public holidays 1–5. Closed 1 Jan, 26 April and for special events

🚊 4, 9, 16, 24, 25 Damrak

🎫 €8; Museumkaart and I amsterdam City Card holders free

16 Madame Tussauds

All the usual waxwork suspects are here, including Barack Obama and his winning smile. Uniquely Dutch figures, such as Princess Beatrix and Anne Frank working on her diary are here too. 👥 Visitors are allowed to touch the models of celebrities, take photographs (expect to queue at some of the more popular choices) and even work on their stomach muscles next to David Beckham.

🔒 205 D5

✉ De Dam 20

☎ 020 5 22 10 10; www.madametussauds.com

🕐 Daily 10–6:30 (to 8:30pm in school holidays). Closed 26 April

🚉 Centraal Station 🚊 Magna Plaza/Dam, Bijenkorf/Dam 🎫 €22

17 Beurs van Berlage

One building stands out on Damrak: the superb, red-brick former stock exchange. Hendrik Petrus Berlage, who designed the Beurs a century ago, believed in the "higher life of the organization". He had trades unions in mind, but was, nevertheless, sufficiently commercially aware to accept the contract to design Amsterdam's hive of capitalism.

Berlage was not the judges' first choice: the original winner of the competition to build a new home for the Amsterdam Stock Exchange was discovered to have pinched the plan of the facade from the town hall at Nantes in France. Berlage set to work in 1898 with rather more enthusiasm than fortune, planting a monument in red brick on unsuitable foundations. Nine million bricks were supported by nearly 5,000 piles, but cracks began to appear within a year or two of its completion in 1903. Repairs succeeded in holding it together, and the

place survived a demolition threat in the 1950s.

Sadly, the tower, which at 40m (130ft) high offers a wonderful view of the city, is no longer open to the public, but the former trading floor and other halls in the building are used as venues for important exhibitions, shows, concerts – and even a royal wedding. What was once the main entrance foyer now houses a café, home to a magnificent tile tableau by Dutch Symbolist artist Jan Toorop. It offers good views over Beursplein.

✚ 203 F2
✉ Beursplein
☎ 020 531 3355; www.beursvanberlage.nl
🕐 For exhibitions only – times vary.
Café: Mon–Sat 10–6, Sun 11–6
🚊 Dam 🚌 4, 9, 16, 24, 25 🚉 Centraal Station
🎫 Varies

🔢 Centraal Station

A strange thing about this remarkable building is how few visitors appreciate it. The magnificent facade stretches 400m along an artificial island that cuts off the IJ River from the city and even the building works for Amsterdam's new underground line, do not diminish its majesty.

The style is Northern Renaissance, and the architect was PJH Cuypers – who also designed the Rijksmuseum (➤ 120), which has a very similar character. The best place and time to appreciate the overall view of the station is about 100m back from the station entrance, on an afternoon when the sun picks out the decoration. The eastern tower supports the rail traveller's essential – an elegant clock – while the corresponding face of the western tower carries a device showing the wind direction.

A series of images celebrate the commercial life of the city: manufacture, trade and export. Inside, the unlovely 1970s refurbishment has been improved by renovations, but the highlight remains on platform 2B, where you will find the elegant old **Wachtkamer Eerste Klasse**, the first-class waiting room, now divided into two café/restaurants (➤ 75). Lions flank the original entrance, along with a portrait of a wistful Dutch girl who is adorned with roses.

✚ 206 A5
✉ Stationsplein
🕐 Open 24 hours; access between midnight and 5am restricted to passengers with tickets
🍴 Many refreshment facilities in the shopping area beneath the platforms, and on platform 2
🚌 1, 2, 4, 5, 9, 13, 16, 17, 24, 25, 26 🚉 All

🔢 Scheepvaarthuis

The name of this unusual edifice translates simply as "shipping house", but it is also popularly known as the "house with 1,000 windows". Originally designed to house maritime companies, the whole facade is awash with images celebrating navigation, and bold announcements of the great seas from the Middellandse Zee (Mediterranean) to the

The Scheepvaarthuis with its umpteen windows

Interactive science and technology centre NEMO

wonderful decoration and stained glass on the stairwell.

➕ 206 B4
✉ Prins Hendrikkade 108
☺ Much of the interior is open only to hotel guests 🚇 Centraal Station 🚌 Any serving Centraal Station 🚊 Centraal Station

De Ruijterkade

18 Centraal Station

Stations-plein

Prins

Hendrikkade

Geldersekade

19 Scheepvaarthuis

Oosterdok

NEMO 20

20 NEMO

This local landmark is a dramatic addition to the skyline, appearing like a sinking ship out of the Oosterdok. The walk up the rim of the building is fun and ends with a superb view from the roof terrace. This imaginative and state-of-the-art interactive hands-on science and technology centre contains a variety of exhibits over five floors. 🔍 The deliberately playful approach to science (where it is forbidden *not* to touch) is designed to appeal to children between the ages of 6 and 14. New attractions are added all the time.

➕ 207 D4 ✉ Oosterdok 2
☎ 020 5 31 32 33; www.e-nemo.nl
☺ Tue–Sun 10–5 (also Mon during Dutch school holidays and June–Aug). Closed 1 Jan, 26 April, 25 Dec 🍴 Café (€€)
🚇 Centraal Station 🎫 €13.50; reduction for Museumkaart and I amsterdam City Card holders

Indische Oceaan (Indian Ocean). It was designed by J M van der Mey and is the first example of Amsterdam School design. Some visitors see geometrical elements borrowed from the Scottish designer Charles Rennie Mackintosh, or even imagery from the Mayan civilization of Central America.

The building is now the Grand Hotel Amrâth (➤ 44). Nobody will mind if you pop inside to see the

Where to...
Eat and Drink

Prices

Expect to pay per person for a three-course meal, excluding drinks and service:

€ under €20   €€ €20–€40   €€€ over €40

CAFÉS AND BARS

De Bakkerswinkel €

Be assured that the breads and pastries on display taste as fresh and delicious as they look and smell. The coffee is good and, all-in-all, this is an excellent choice for a snack or light lunch, such as soup, quiche or a sand-wich. Or, if you are in the area later in the afternoon, stop by for high tea – when scones and other tasty home-made treats are available.

🚼 203 F2
✉ Warmoesstraat 69
☎ 020 4 89 80 00; www.debakkerswinkel.nl
🕐 Mon–Fri 10–5:30, Sat, Sun 8–6

Café de Dokter €

Hidden away down a side street off Kalverstraat, the 200-year-old Café de Dokter, once a doctor's surgery, now dispenses medicines of a dif-ferent kind at what is claimed to be Amsterdam's smallest brown café (► 26). It's moody and candlelit, even on a bright sunny afternoon, and looks more like a junk shop than a bar. Lamps and old bottles gather dust, musical instruments hanging on the walls rust away, and the telephone is old enough to have bells on it (but, surprisingly, it does work).

🚼 205 D4   ✉ Rozenboomsteeg 4
☎ 020 6 26 44 27; www.cafe-de-dokter.nl
🕐 Tue–Sat 4pm–1am

Café Hoppe €

This convivial brown café is said to date from 1670. If you want to soak up the atmosphere, go into its dimly lit, standing-only older half (it has sawdust on the floor and barrels set into part- panelled walls). For comfort, try its relatively modern half: it has a terrace over-looking Spui Square, and waiter service. This is a place to come and drink, though there are a few snacks, such as soup and sandwiches, on offer.

🚼 205 D4
✉ Spui 18–20
☎ 020 4 20 44 20; www.cafehoppe.com
🕐 Sun–Thu 8am–1am, Fri–Sat 8am–2am

Café de Jaren €/€€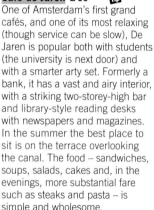

One of Amsterdam's first grand cafés, and one of its most relaxing (though service can be slow), De Jaren is popular both with students (the university is next door) and with a smarter arty set. Formerly a bank, it has a vast and airy interior, with a striking two-storey-high bar and library-style reading desks with newspapers and magazines. In the summer the best place to sit is on the terrace overlooking the canal. The food – sandwiches, soups, salads, cakes and, in the evenings, more substantial fare such as steaks and pasta – is simple and wholesome.

🚼 205 E4
✉ Nieuwe Doelenstraat 20–22
☎ 020 6 25 57 71; www.cafe-de-jaren.nl
🕐 Sun–Thu 9:30am–1am, Fri-Sat 9:30–2am

Café Luxembourg €/€€

This quintessential grand café, popular with Amsterdam's media set, has the languorous air of a smart Parisian café, and looks as if it's been around for a 100 years (which it hasn't). Choose between the covered terrace overlooking Spui square, the leather banquettes inside, a pew at the long marble-topped bar or the reading tables stocked with international magazines and newspapers. The food – anything from soups and salads to steaks and indulgent pastries – is excellent. The club sandwiches are renowned.

➕ 205 D4 ✉ Spui 24 ☎ 020 6 20 62 64
🕐 Mon–Fri 8am–1am, Sat, Sun 9am–1am

De Drie Fleschjes €

The smart "Three Little Bottles" is the city's best known *proeflokaal* (tasting house, ➤ 31). It dates from 1650, and has rows of ancient wooden casks running its length. All the various liqueurs and *jenevers* (➤ 44) are detailed on boards that hang from hooks over the bar, and on the counter-top are decanters of flavourings to add to the *jenevers*. The *proeflokaal* is tiny with virtually no seating inside, but in summer there are tables outside on the pretty cobbled square.

➕ 203 E2
✉ Gravenstraat 18 ☎ 020 6 24 84 43
🕐 Mon–Sat 1:30–8:30, Sun 2–7

Esprit Caffe €

The Esprit fashion store backs on to this hip "*lunchcafé*". The minimalist decor, with exposed metal girders to the fore, and the giant windows overlooking Spui square, ensure maximum attention for the clientele and the fashionable café staff. The food, though an unremarkable selection (consisting mostly of sandwiches, pastas, salads, burgers, bagels and ice cream), is surprisingly decent, and outdoor seating covers a large area of the square when it's sunny.

➕ 205 D4 ✉ Spui 10
☎ 020 6 22 19 67; www.caffeesprit.nl
🕐 Mon–Fri 10–6, Thu 10–8

't Gasthuys €

Atmosphere oozes from every pore of this down-to-earth café, which is especially popular with students. Downstairs is a long narrow bar. Steep stairs climb to another two tiny rooms up among the rafters, and there is a canalside terrace. 't Gasthuys bills itself as an *eetcafé* (➤ 32), and, miraculously, produces good, inexpensive, no-nonsense food, which comes in the form of sandwiches, as well as substantial main courses consisting of a variety of meat dishes served with salad and chips.

➕ 205 D4 ✉ Grimburgwal 7
☎ 020 6 24 82 30; www.gasthuys.nl
🕐 Daily noon–4:30, 5:30–10

Grand Café Restaurant 1e Klas €/€€

This over-the-top neo-Gothic room, with its lofty ceiling, pillars painted onto walls and monumental carved bar, used to be the Centraal Station's first-class waiting room. Softly lit and dotted with ornaments, it's quite a sight, and worth a visit even if you're not waiting for a train. You can enjoy the surroundings for the price of a drink, a sandwich or a bowl of lobster bisque, or have a full meal (choose from an international menu).

➕ 206 A5 ✉ Centraal Station, platform 2B
☎ 020 6 25 01 31; www.restaurant1eklas.nl
🕐 Daily 8:30am–11pm

In de Waag €/€€

This café/restaurant is in the Waag, the turreted, Disneyesque medieval gatehouse turned weigh house (Waag), originally built in 1488, that dominates the Nieuwmarkt. Inside it is grand yet intimate, with bare walls, wooden tables and vaulted ceilings lit by 300 candles. The sandwiches at lunchtime are recommended, but dishes from the more elaborate and eclectic dinner menu have received mixed reviews.

➕ 205 E5 ✉ Nieuwmarkt 4 ☎ 020 4 22 77 72;
www.indewaag.nl 🕐 Daily 9am–1am

Medieval Amsterdam

In de Wildeman €

The immaculately kept "Savage", founded as a liqueur distillery in 1690, now accurately bills itself as a *bierproeflokaal* – a beer-tasting house. There are more than 200 bottled beers on offer, and 17 beers on tap. With its beautiful old bar and ancient liqueur barrels, it's atmospheric enough to entrance even teetotallers.

➕ 203 F3 ✉ Kolksteeg 3
☎ 020 6 38 23 48; www.indewildeman.nl
🕐 Mon–Thu noon–1am, Fri–Sat noon–2am

't Loosje €

With its historic wall tiles, this student café in the Nieuwmarkt area starts filling up in the morning at breakfast time and by the evening it is bursting at the seams. You can either sit outside on the street terrace or stand at the crowded bar counter, where you can chose from eight draft and 20 bottled beers.

➕ 205 E5 ✉ Nieuwmarkt 32
☎ 020 6 27 26 35; www.loosje.nl
🕐 Sun–Thu 8:30am–1am, Fri–Sat 8:30am–3am

De Ooievaar €

Insider Tip

"The Stork" is the Netherlands' smallest tasting house: no bigger than a small living room, it feels crowded with just 10 customers. Though it occupies the corner of an ancient, tipsy house, and has old tiled and panelled walls and liqueur-lined shelves inside, the bar has in fact been here only since the mid-1990s. Despite its dubious location at the entrance to the Zeedijk (➤ 57), it's a thoroughly civilized bolthole

➕ 206 A5 ✉ Sint Olofspoort 1
☎ 020 4 20 80 04 🕐 Daily noon–1am

La Place €

The bustling self-service caféteria of the Vroom & Dreesmann (V&D) department store (➤ 79) is ideal for a quick, inexpensive but tasty lunch. It offers a vast range of hot and cold food, from pastries and a salad bar to Thai dishes and steak and chips, as well as a choice of freshly squeezed juices. On the Kalverstraat side is a very tempting bakery/takeaway deli department perfect for picking up breakfast or creating a picnic. Choose from a variety of breads, tasty sandwiches, pastries, quiches, cakes and pies.

➕ 205 D4 ✉ Kalverstraat 203
☎ 020 2 35 83 63; www.laplace.nl
🕐 Sun, Mon 11–8, Tue, Wed, Fri, Sat 9–8, Thu 9–9

De Sluyswacht €

An alarmingly sloping 17th-century former lock-keeper's house has been turned into a brown café, right across the road from the Rembrandthuis. Wonderfully unassuming, it's cosy and friendly inside. You can also sit out on the large terrace, and admire the views down the Oudeschans.

➕ 206 A3 ✉ Jodenbreestraat 1
☎ 020 6 25 76 11; www.sluyswacht.nl
🕐 Mon–Thu 12:30am–1am, Fri–Sat 11:30am–3am, Sun 11:30–7

Villa Zeezicht €

Insider Tip

This cosy café occupies a prime canalfront spot: its picture windows overlook, and its wicker chairs partly cover, the Torensluis bridge, one of the widest in the city. Inside, the hotchpotch of battered old furniture, the jazz music playing in the background, and the informal young staff all help make this a thoroughly laid-back place. On offer are quiches, sandwiches, croissants and famously good apple pies.

➕ 205 E3 ✉ Torensteeg 7
☎ 020 626 7433 🕐 Daily 9–9

Wynand Fockink €

This enchanting little time capsule of a tasting house is hidden down an alley behind the Grand Hotel Krasnapolsky and dates from 1679. Bottles of its own liqueurs (made in the distillery next door) line the sagging shelves behind the bar, including obscure concoctions with unlikely names such as Parrot Soup. As well as countless plain *jenevers* (Dutch gin), a dozen flavoured varieties are offered. For food, though, you'll have to rely on peanuts.

➕ 205 D5 ✉ Pijlsteeg 31
☎ 020 6 39 26 95; www.wynand-fockink.nl
🕐 Bar: Daily 3pm–9pm

RESTAURANTS

Bird €

Good-value Thai food is served in this cramped, hectic, no-frills snackbar. You can either take it away or eat in at one of the few tables and window seats (the latter is ideal for watching the fascinating comings and goings along Amsterdam's most notorious street). The sensational chicken and coconut soup is a meal in itself. The Bird restaurant (daily 5–11) across the street serves similar fare in more comfortable but less atmospheric surroundings.

➕ 206 A5 ✉ Zeedijk 77
☎ 020 4 20 62 89; www.thai-bird.nl
🕐 Daily 2pm–10pm

Brasserie Harkema €€

Named after the building's previous occupant, a tobacco company, this stylish, Parisian-style brasserie offers light fare during the day, then in the evening, the menu focuses on classic dishes with a modern twist. Dishes include green spaghettini with goat's cheese or guinea fowl stuffed with pastrami. There is a strong wine list. The dining area is airy and open with a modern decor, overlooked by a glass mezzanine *(entresol)* level. Service can be a bit hit or miss at times.

➕ 205 D4 ✉ Nes 67
☎ 020 4 28 22 22; www.brasserieharkema.nl
🕐 11am–1am (lunch noon–4, dinner 5:30–11)

De Goudvisclub €

The "Goldfish Club" offers Asian cuisine served in small portions,

each €7, that are designed to be shared. The communal tables are full of lively groups of young people snacking on a wide selection of small dishes. When the kitchen closes, the restaurant transforms into a cocktail bar.

➕ 203 E2 ✉ Spuistraat 4
☎ 020 7 37 21 21; www.degoudvisclub.nl
🕐 Tue–Thu, Sun 4–1, Fri, Sat until 3am

Kamasutra €€

It was only a matter of time before someone in the red-light district had the idea to theme their restaurant around the ancient Indian text. The murals may take inspiration from the Kama Sutra, but the main draw is the food. The menu offers few surprises, but the dishes, such as chicken *tikka* and *saag paneer*, are well made and reasonably priced.

➕ 203 F2 ✉ Lange Niezel 9
☎ 020 6 26 00 03; www.restaurantkamasutra.nl
🕐 Daily 2pm–midnight

Kantjil & de Tijger €/€€

Unlike most of the city's Indonesian establishments, the "Mouse-deer and the Tiger" is a large, austere and modern-looking restaurant, with a busy buzz to it. It serves some of the best Indonesian food in Amsterdam, and there are extensive explanations on English menus of all the various options. As well as three types of full-blown *rijsttafel* (rice table, ► 46), you can order an inexpensive mini-*rijsttafel*, where all the dishes come on a single plate. If you want takeaway, visit the outlet on Kinkerstraat 83.

➕ 204 C4 ✉ Spuistraat 291–293
☎ 020 6 20 09 94; www.kantjil.nl
🕐 Daily noon–11

Het Karbeel €/€€

By day, this 16th-century building, in the heart of the red-light district, is a busy sandwich shop. In the evening, it transforms into an intimate bistro specializing in mouth-watering fondues, such as blue cheese, traditional and mushroom, as well as a *fondue du jour*. Soups, salads and a few decadent desserts are also on offer and there are several good wines sold by the glass. The service is friendly as well as efficient.

✚ 203 F2 ✉ Warmoesstraat 16
☎ 020 6 27 49 95; www.hetkarbeel.nl
🕐 Daily 9:30am–11pm

Lucius €€/€€€

Huge ceiling fans keep this long, narrow and busy Dutch/French seafood bistro from overheating. While waiters bustle amid tiled walls, marble-topped tables and an aquarium, peruse boards detailing platters of *fruits de mer*, mussels and french fries as well as local oysters. Other specialities include blue shark, smoked eel and herring served with old *jenever*. To keep the cost down, there's a small selection of set meals. The wine list is long, service isn't as polished as the tables, but the food is pre-pared to perfection.

✚ 204 C4 ✉ Spuistraat 247
☎ 020 6 24 18 31; www.lucius.nl
🕐 Daily 5pm–midnight

Hemelse Modder €€

Pleasant restaurant, in a quiet corner of the old town, that serves French-Dutch specialties made from organic and local ingredients. Try to get a table by the window so that you can enjoy the lovely view of the canal.

✚ 206 B4 ✉ Oude Waal 11
☎ 020 6 24 32 03; www.hemelsemodder.nl/en
🕐 Daily from 6pm

&Samhoud Places €€€

This oddly named restaurant boasts two Michelin stars. The upstairs section of the new building serves the highly-acclaimed inventive creations of the culinary world's newest shooting star, chef Moshik Roth. For those on tighter budgets, there is the more casual down-stairs lounge.

✚ 206 C4 ✉ Oosterdokskade 5
☎ 020 2 60 20 94; www.samhoudplaces.com
🕐 Tue–Fri noon–1am, Sat 3–1

Nam Kee €

Be warned: if decor and ambience are more important than excellent-value, no-frills food, Nam Kee (which has two other branches, one on Nieuwmarkt, the other on Heinekenplein) may not suit you. There are two plain white-tiled and cramped dining rooms and you may have to share a table as the restaurant is invariably packed. The menu offers giant portions of delicious fried noodles, along with lots of sweet and sour and Cantonese dishes.

✚ 206 A4 ✉ Zeedijk 111–113
☎ 020 6 24 34 70; www.namkee.net
🕐 Daily noon–midnight

New Dorrius €€

As part of the Crowne Plaza Hotel, the sleek upscale interior of the restaurant is a welcome respite from the hazy cafés and informal eateries otherwise found around here. Behind the long bar, some good-quality cocktails are created with authentic Dutch spirits. For dessert try the home-made buttermilk ice cream or the pina colada panna cotta. Staff provide first-rate service.

✚ 203 F2 ✉ Nieuwendijk 60
☎ 020 4 20 22 24; www.newdorrius.nl
🕐 Mon–Sat 6–11

Supper Club €€€

In this windowless, stark white warehouse of a room, you eat off your lap reclining on long rows of mattresses arranged along walls like giant bunk beds. You're enter-tained by mellow music, cinematic images such as rocket launches and naked swimmers projected onto one wall, and maybe live music and DJs. Go for the whole sensual experience, not for the mediocre food. Everyone eats the same dishes, served by nubile young waiters and waitresses at the same time: set aside four hours for dinner. The same company operates a supper-club cruise.

➕ 205 D5 ✉ Jonge Roelensteeg 21
☎ 020 3 44 64 00; www.supperclub.com
🕐 Daily 7:30pm–1am

Vermeer €€€

With its beamed ceilings, brass chandeliers and marble floors, the Vermeer occupies one of the 17th-century houses incorporated into the otherwise modern NH Barbizon Palace Hotel. It's as formal a place to dine as anywhere in Amsterdam (one Michelin star). Start with an aperitif by the fire in the lounge, then enjoy chef Chris Naylor's palate-teasing combinations such as duck with grapefruit, capers and artichoke, followed by a millefeuille with cloves, honey, figs and pears. Also recommended is the "Van het Land" set menu that consists of locally sourced, seasonal ingredients, which can include white truffles, artisan cheeses and northwest Atlantic monkfish.

➕ 206 A5 ✉ Prins Hendrikkade 59–72
☎ 020 5 56 48 85; www.restaurantvermeer.nl
🕐 Mon–Sat 6:30pm–8pm

d'Vijff Vlieghen €€/€€€

With nine dining rooms spread through five 17th-century canal houses, the "Five Flies" is a romantic, Golden Age time warp. You may be lucky enough to end up sitting next to an original Rembrandt etching, or in a chair once occupied by Elvis Presley or John Wayne (every seat has a little plaque naming a famous visitor). The modern Dutch cooking is imaginative and beautifully presented, and the set seasonal menu is good value. Service is formal, and the clientele mostly well-heeled foreigners.

➕ 204 C4 ✉ Spuistraat 294–302
☎ 020 5 30 40 60; www.thefiveflies.com
🕐 Daily 6–10

Where to...
Shop

For the most part, the shops in the city centre tend to be international chains. Kalverstraat and Nieuwendijk, the main pedestrianized shopping thoroughfares, are bustling and have the best range of everyday high street shops. Beyond these streets lie a few pleasant surprises, such as the grandiose Magna Plaza Shopping Center, and, in among the graphic sex emporia of the red-light district, some fun and some very old shops.

KALVERSTRAAT AND ROKIN

Kalverstraat is named after a calf market that was held in this area during the 15th century. The southern (Muntplein) end has more style. Worth a browse are the department stores of **Maison de Bonneterie** (Rokin 140–142, tel: 020 5 31 34 00, www.debonneterie. nl), royal-appointed, stylish, with chandeliers under its dome and a smart café, and **Vroom & Dreesmann** (Kalverstraat 203; www. vd.nl), part of a chain, pitched more mid-range, with the good La Place café (▶ 76).

Across the street is the **Kalvertoren shopping mall** (Kalverstraat 212–220, www. kalvertoren.nl) – its most interesting feature is its glass-towered café on the top floor, which enjoys wide views over the canals. **Rokin**, parallel to Kalverstraat, is a busy tram thoroughfare, so not particularly pleasant for a stroll. However, it has a few old-fashioned antiques shops such as **Premsela & Hamburger** (No 98, tel: 020 6 24 96 88, www.premsela.com), which has

Medieval Amsterdam

dealt in silverware since 1823. Rokin's one unmissable shop, however is the tobacconist **PGC Hajenius** (Nos 92–96, tel: 020 623 7494, www.hajenius. com). The art deco, marble-walled interior looks much as it did when it was designed in 1915, and there are displays of handmade clay pipes, a wall of humidor lockers rented by clients, a bar, a library of books on smoking, and often cigar tastings.

AROUND DE DAM

De Bijenkorf (Dam 1, www.de bijenkorf.nl; Sun, Mon 11–8, Tue, Wed, Sat, 10–8, Thu, Fri until 9), which translates as "The Beehive", is the most famous department store in the country. It has the requisite cosmetics counters and luxury brand stores such as Louis Vuitton and Gucci, along with a good café with picture windows on to the Damrak. Clubbers should check out the Chill Out collection on the fifth floor for glow-in-the-dark accessories.

Across the square is the **Amsterdam Diamond Centre** (Rokin 1–5, tel: 020 624 57 87, www.amsterdamdiamondcenter.nl), where you can watch cutters at work and buy watches as well as diamonds. The shops just around the corner on Damstraat peddle classic Dutch souvenirs, such as cheeses, clogs and canal-house fridge magnets.

Behind the palace, on Nieuwezijds Voorburgwal, is the **Magna Plaza Shopping Center** (Magna Plaza, Nieuwezijds Voorburgwal 182, www.magna plaza.nl), in a splendid neo-Gothic building that used to be the main post office. It's devoted mainly to clothes boutiques and shoe shops. Beer-drinkers should not miss **De Bierkoning** (▶ 27), round the corner at Paleisstraat 125.

NIEUWENDIJK

Few of the shops on this scruffy pedestrian street are likely to detain you on your way between Dam Square and the train station. One exception, however, may be **Oud Amsterdam** (No 78, tel: 020 624 45 81, www.oudamster dam.nl), established almost three centuries ago in 1710, a specialist liqueur shop.

SPUIKWARTIER

Better known for its cafés and restaurants, this area also has a concentration of new and second-hand bookshops and a book market (▶ 77). For less literary pleasures, such as home-made ice cream and apple turnovers, pop in to **Lanskroon** (Singel 385, just off Spui, tel: 020 623 77 43, www.lanskroon.nl). The pâtisserie has a tiny sit-down area.

AROUND THE RED-LIGHT DISTRICT AND NIEUWMARKT

Among the grungy coffee shops and "smart" shops on Warmoesstraat are some interesting outlets. The **Metropolitan Deli** (No 135, tel: 020 330 19 55; www.metropolitandeli.nl) is stocked with treats such as home-made ice cream and organic chocolates. **Condomerie** (No 141, tel: 020 627 41 74, www.condomerie.com), the world's first specialized condom shop, puts a little fun and glamour into the concept of contraception: here, you can buy condoms in fun packs, condoms disguised as lollipops or a flip-top aluminium case in which to keep them – there's plenty of choice.

Just south of Nieuwmarkt, at Kloveniersburgwal 12, is **Jacob Hooy** (tel: 020 5 05 27 44, www. jacob-hooy.nl). Founded in 1743, this delightful pharmacy, lined with 19th-century drawers, specializes in aromatherapy remedies and health foods.

Further down Kloveniersburgwal, at No 39, is the **Head Shop** (tel: 020 6 24 90 61, www.headshop.nl), which opened back in 1968, and offers all sorts of dope-smoking paraphernalia.

Little **Nieuwe Hoogstraat** is un-expectedly lined with fun, gift-ori-ented boutiques.

De Hoed Van Tijn (No 15, tel: 020 6 23 27 59, www.dehoedvan tijn.nl) is an elegant hat shop, and **Joe's Vliegerwinkel** (No 19, tel: 020 6 25 01 39, www.joes vliegerwinkel.nl) specializes in kites (custom-made on request) and other flying toys, such as Frisbees.

At the end of the street stands 🏠**Knuffels** (tel: 020 4 27 38 62), a children's toy shop (and clog factory) with a delightful collection of toys, mobiles and wooden shoes. Just down the street is the **Rembrandthuis** (▶ 70), whose shop sells good-quality reproductions of Rembrandt's etchings.

MARKETS

Nieuwmarkt (May–Sep Sun 9–5): an antiques market.

Oudemanhuispoort (Mon–Sat 10–4): this moody passageway through the university has a few permanent second-hand book stalls under its arches.

Spui (Fri 10–6): second-hand and antiquarian books and prints; (March–Dec Sun 10–6): a few stalls selling decent modern art.

Waterlooplein (Mon–Sat 9–5): the city's best and liveliest flea-market. It's good for things such as leather jackets, second-hand records, film posters and bicycle chains. Many visitors just come to rummage through the piles of unwanted clothes, or nose around the stalls with an obligatory plastic tray of fries and mayonnaise in hand.

Where to...
Go Out

A night out in the city centre can be as seamy or as sophisticated as you wish. You could take in the repulsive yet compulsive spectacle of the red-light district, spend an evening at the opera or catch a modern jazz jam session.

THE RED-LIGHT DISTRICT AND AROUND

At night, purple and red neon, pervades the streets bounded by Zeedijk, Warmoesstraat and Damstraat. It lights up the prosti-tutes posing in the windows, flash-ing come-hither smiles one second, looking thoroughly bored the next. Though there are plenty of men prowling around checking out their options, many passers-by are simply curious tourists. Few people of either sex are hassled, and, thanks to the large numbers who come in the evenings to gawp, and to a con-spicuous police presence, the main thoroughfares feel safe. However, the back alleys, particularly those off the southern end of Zeedijk, are best avoided. If you want to visit a sex show, try **Theatre Casa Rosso** (Oudezijds Achterburgwal 106–108, tel: 020 6 27 89 54, www.casarosso.nl – note that there are other pretenders with similar names).

Zeedijk, once a virtual no-go area, has now been cleaned up over the last decade or so. Its more respectable northern end is lined with restaurants and characterful cafés, such as **De Ooievaar** (▶ 76) and, facing it at No 1 Zeedijk, **In 't Aepjen.** Translating as "In the Little Monkey", this ancient timber-framed building used to be a doss-house where sailors could barter a

Medieval Amsterdam

bed for the night, even exchanging their pet monkeys. This café claims to be the oldest in town, dating back to 1560. It's certainly one of only two original wooden structures in the city, the Houten Huys (➤61) being the other and oldest one.

Nieuwmarkt, ringed with more cafés, is also far more salubrious than it once was. **In de Waag** (➤75) is its most interesting haunt. If you're looking for a brown café, **'t Loosje** (➤76) should fit the bill. **Bekeerde Suster** (one of the Beiaard group), just south at Kloveniersburgwal 6–8, has a small, excellent on-site brewery.

Seedy Warmoesstraat must have more coffeeshops than any other street in Amsterdam. Intermingled with them are gay venues, such as **Getto** (No 51, tel: 020 4 21 51 51, www.getto.nl), a kitsch cocktail bar with DJs. Loud, live rock music is the attraction most nights at **Winston** (No 129, tel: 020 6 23 13 80, www.winston.nl, club open daily 9pm–3am, Fri–Sat to 4am), a club, hotel and restaurant.

SPUIKWARTIER

The area around Spuistraat south of Raadhuisstraat has a concentration of restaurants, cafés and bars, including some of the city's best brown and grand cafés. Most can be found at the southern end of Spuistraat and on Spui. As well as those recommended on pages 74–78, **Dante** (Spuistraat 320, tel: 020 7 74 74 73, www.amsterdam-dante.nl) attracts the "beautiful" people who compete with the slick modern decor. More hip late-night bars are clustered on Nieuwezijds Voorburgwal, just south of Dam Square.

MUSIC AND THEATRE VENUES

Amsterdam's opera house, the **Muziektheater** (Waterlooplein 22, tel: 020 5 51 81 17, www.het-muziektheater.nl), forms a single complex with the Stadhuis or city hall. The imposing marble, brick and glass structure is home to the Netherlands Opera and National Ballet and boasts a full programme of opera, ballet and modern dance eleven months of the year (no performances in August). From October to May, free half-hour concerts take place on Tuesdays at 12:30pm in the minor hall, **Boekmanzaal**, and throughout the year you can take a backstage tour on Saturdays at noon.

Beurs van Berlage (Beursplein, Damrak 243, tel: 020 5 31 33 55, www.beursvanberlage.nl, ➤67–68), the old Beurs (stock exchange) designed by Hendrik Berlage and completed in 1903, is a prime example of the Amsterdam School of architecture. Exhibitions often occupy the impressive main hall, while the Netherlands Philharmonic and Chamber orchestras perform in two further halls – one of which has, as its stage, a giant, free-standing glass box.

It goes without saying that there is always a band or a DJ on playing somewhere. There are pop and rock concerts and DJ nights at **Bitterzoet** (Spuistraat 2, tel: 020 4 21 23 18).

And there is live jazz at the **Cotton Club** (Nieuwmarkt 5, tel: 020 6 26 61 92, www.cotton clubmusic.nl) and at **Bethany's Jazz Club** in Bethanienklooster (Barndesteeg 6a, tel: 020 6 25 00 78, www.bethanienklooster.nl) on Tuesdays, Thursdays and Sundays.

The stylish **Paleis van de Weemoed** is a theatre restaurant full of nostalgic red-light charm, on Fridays and Saturdays they have dinner shows with burlesque and music performances (Oudezijds Voorburgwal 15–17, tel: 020 25 69 6 64 www.paleis-van-de-weemoed.nl).

Insider
Tip

Canal Ring – West

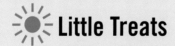 **Little Treats**

An evening gliding through the canals

For a memorable experience **cruise** the canals (► 88) while enjoying wine and appetizers by candlelight.

Authentic Dutch *pannekoeken*

Tuck into one of the many varieties on offer at the **Pancake Bakery** (► 110), the bacon and apple pancakes are simply delectable.

Spend the night in the Hotel de Windketel

Across from Café Amsterdam (► 109) is a little **octagonal tower** that is the smallest hotel in Amsterdam.

Getting Your Bearings

The most romantic photographs of Amsterdam are taken in the western part of the city – which is also where the real soul of Amsterdam resides. Beautiful waterways and quiet courtyards, the trendiest and most liberal locals and authentic *bruin cafés* can all be found here. Almost any street you walk along is likely to reveal at least one of the following: a lovely old house embellished with a beautiful tablet or gable; an intriguing shop or café; or a charming canal view.

The best way to get an overview of the area is to take a boat trip, then to walk around the fascinating streets here.

View from the Westerkerk

The hub of bohemian lifestyles is the Jordaan, the working-class fringe of Amsterdam that has become the most sought-after neighbourhood in the city. The elegant old *hofjes* (almshouses) that dot the district are now desirable homes, most of which tolerate visitors. Between the Jordaan and the city centre, the Nine Streets area (➤ 111) squeezed into a neat three-by-three grid is another fashionable patch with boutiques, good cafés and restaurants. Going further west, the gentrification now extends to a disused gasworks. Most visitors stick to a fairly narrow strip from the Anne Frank House via the Westerkerk to the entertainment zone around Leidseplein, but it's well worth straying away from the beaten tourist trail to discover the Amsterdam that entrances the locals.

The interior of the Westerkerk

Getting Your Bearings

TOP 10
★ Grachten ➤ 88
★ Jordaan ➤ 92
★ Anne Frank Huis ➤ 96
★ Westerkerk ➤ 101

At Your Leisure

Westergasfabriek 25

Westerpark 25

Haarlemmerweg

Nassau-plein

Haarlemmer Houttuinen

Van Hallstr

Kattensloot

2e Goudsb. dwstr.

Brouwersgracht

Grachten ★

Jordaan ★

Singelgracht

Frederik Hendrik-plantsoen

Nassaukade

Amsterdam Tulip Museum 24

★ Nieuwezijds Voorburgwal

Anne Frank Huis ★

Westerkerk 10 23 **Homomonument**

Raadhuisstraat

0 — 250 m
0 — 250 yd

Rozengracht

Prinsengracht

Keizersgracht

Herengracht

Singel

Elandsgracht

Nassaukade

★

Koningspl.

Munt-plein

American Hotel 22 21 **Leidseplein**

Overtoom

Stadhouderskade

Weteringschans

Vijzelstraat

85

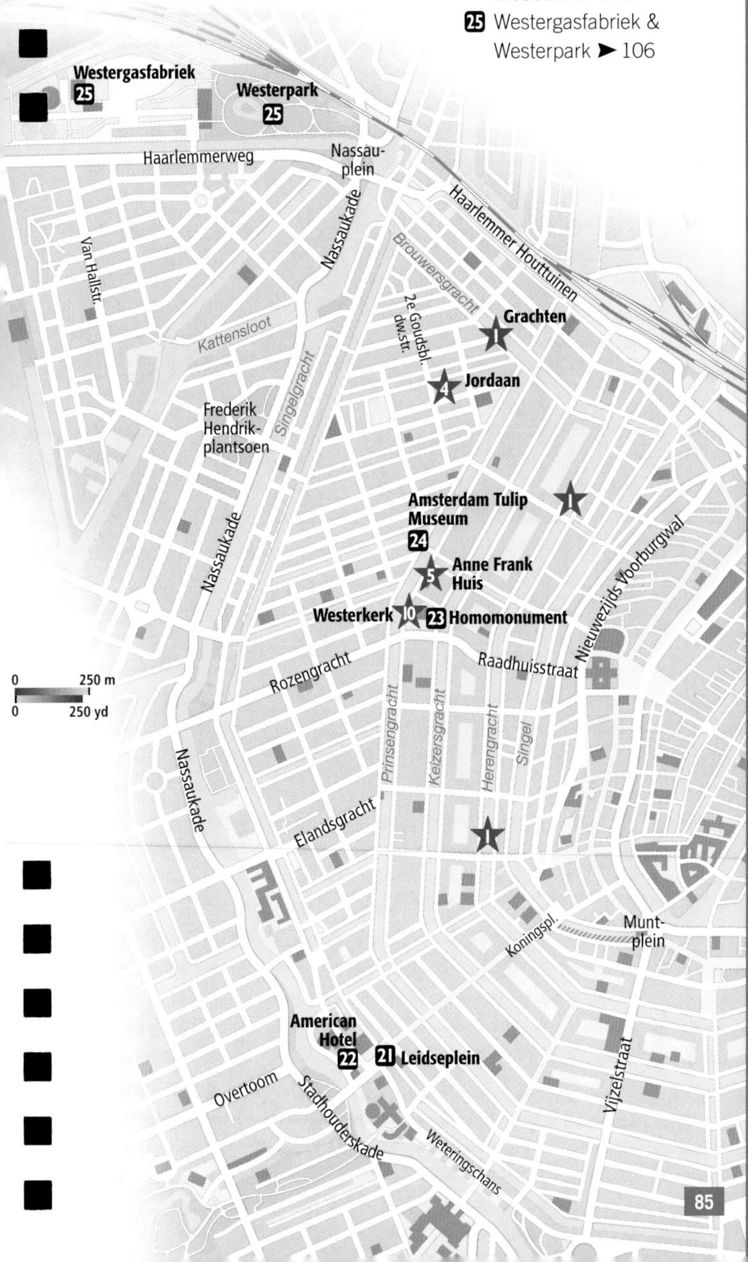

The Perfect Day

If you're not quite sure where to begin your travels, this itinerary recommends a practical and enjoyable day exploring the western canal ring. It takes in some of the best places to see and suggests you to start your adventure with a leisurely boat ride. For more information see the main entries (►88–106).

🕘 9:00am

Beat the crowds by taking the first boat of the day around the ⭐**canals** (above, ►88). You will circumnavigate the whole city, but the prettiest and most interesting parts are around the western canal ring.

🕙 10:00am

Wander over to **21 Leidseplein** (►103) before it gets too overrun with beer-drinking, dope-smoking tourists. Enjoy a coffee at an outdoor terrace – or, on a cool or damp day, warm up instead in the opulent setting of the Café Américain at the **22 American Hotel** (►103).

🕚 11:00am

Walk north and work up an appetite for lunch with a long stroll around ⭐**Jordaan** (►92), admiring some superb views and calling in at one or two of the *hofjes* (courtyards) that offer sanctuary from the city.

🕐 1:00pm

From anywhere in the Jordaan, you are not far from lunch at a café in the chic and cheerful **9 Straatjes,** or "Nine Streets" (►111). Perhaps go window shopping; this is the area where you will find some of Amsterdam's most imaginative stores. Alternatively, have lunch on the roof-terrace at **Werck** (►111), a contemporary café-restaurant that was once the coach house of Westerkerk, at the northwest corner of Nine Streets.

🕓 2:30pm

Visit the 🌠 **Westerkerk** (➤ 92–93), the location for the (now lost) tomb of Rembrandt. In summer (April to October), you can climb the stairs to the top of the tower.

🕓 4:00pm

Have another break for coffee, perhaps at the cosy **Café Chris** (➤ 107) close by on Bloemstraat or, on a fine day, at one of the canalside cafés, such as Café 't Smalle (➤ 108).

🕓 5:30pm

Take advantage of late opening hours to visit the 🌠 **Anne Frank Huis** (➤ 96) when it's quieter than usual, and allow time to wind down afterwards.

🕓 7:30pm

There are plenty of brown cafés (➤ 31) to choose for an aperitif. Alternatively, go to Leidseplein (below) for some beer and people-watching.

Westergasfabriek ● 25   25 **Westerpark**

Grachten

Jordaan ☆

Amsterdam Tulip Museum 24
☆ **Anne Frank Huis**
Westerkerk 23 **Homomonument**

American Hotel
22 21 **Leidseplein**

🕓 8:00pm

Have a laid-back dinner in a classic *eetcafé* such as **Café de Reiger** (➤ 109). If you want a swankier venue, the **Bordewijk** (➤ 103) is a reliable bet for great food.

🕓 10:00pm

Blow the rest of your cash, or make a fortune, at the **Holland Casino** (➤ 113). Or check out the music on offer at the **Melkweg** or **Paradiso** (➤ 113), two of Amsterdam's finest venues.

★Canal Tour

The city was made to be enjoyed from the water. Several million tourists take a tour each year around Amsterdam's canals aboard a combined fleet of around 120 sightseeing boats. At a gentle pace you can appreciate the grace of the canal houses, the profusion of greenery and the appeal of canalside living.

Choosing Your Tour

Each operator has a different starting point and itinerary. Competition between the rival companies keeps prices low and standards high. Most companies now use a pre-recorded commentary; it's the only way they can cater for the many different nationalities on their tours. Amsterdam Canal Cruises, just opposite the Heineken Experience (➤ 148), offers an appealing route through some of the best waterscapes.

MANAGING THE WATER

The level of Amsterdam's water is kept constant thanks to a system of locks. Local people say the 3m (10ft) depth is actually made up of equal parts of water, bicycles and mud. The bicycles are periodically removed, along with old refrigerators, bedframes and anything else that can reliably sink without trace.

Circuit of the City

This itinerary is based on the Amsterdam Canal Cruises tour (➤ 91). Like most routes, it goes clockwise around Amsterdam and takes in the Amstel River, the natural waterway that led to the city's foundation. (Some tours go in the opposite direction and avoid the Amstel altogether.)

Notable sights on the Amstel are the **sluice gates,** the grand **Theater Carré** and the **Magere Brug** (➤ 156). Dominating the east bank between Keizersgracht and Herengracht is the handsome **Amstelhof,** one of the city's very first refuges.

The favourite canal on the ring is the **Herengracht,** and the Amsterdam Canal Cruises tour plies much of its length. Where it joins **Reguliersgracht,** the "Seven Bridges Canal", the boat slows to give everyone a view of the identical humped bridges stretching off along the canal.

The standard route enters **Brouwersgracht,** one of the loveliest stretches in Amsterdam, before turning north (an awkward manoeuvre) into Singel and onwards through a succession of bridges into the IJ River. The sense of breaking free from the city can be liberating, though if a big cruise ship is bearing down it can also feel intimidating.

The stretch of open water lasts for 1km (0.6 miles), taking you past the futuristic **EYE Film Instituut** building and the Overhoeks Tower high-rise, which was

A boat tour allows you to see and experience Amsterdam at a different pace

previously used by the oil giant Shell, and is now being redeveloped into a hotel. The new **IJdock** complex with the Palace of Justice and the Muziekgebouw aan't IJ are also visible across the water. The vessel turns south under two swing bridges – one carrying eight railway tracks into the main station – and into **Oosterdok.** This used to be the main harbour until the railway closed it off from the IJ. Your field of vision is filled by the vast copper "hull" of science center **NEMO** (► 73). Here you will also see many freight ships sharing the waters with large floating hotel vessels. Sailing Home, a luxury floating hotel and restaurant, is usually moored near NEMO. It was originally built as a freighter in 1927 but now functions as an alternative to a land-based hotel (tel: 65 1 57 10 70).

HOUSEBOATS

The dwellings of all shapes and sizes that are moored to the banks of Amsterdam's canals are a relatively new addition to the city's waterscape. The practice of living aboard houseboats began at the end of World War II, when accommodation in the city was scarce. Now, there are around 2,500 – all of them are legitimate, with access to electricity and drinking water. Many of them are made from the blackened hulks of old steel freight barges; every few years, these have to be towed to a shipyard for the soundness of their hulls to be checked. Increasingly, though, the design is a concrete box. This requires no maintenance and provides more living area – it is possible to have a floor below the surface of the canal (look for narrow windows just above the waterline for evidence of this). On top of the concrete base, some people have built proper brick houses, sometimes with a garden or patio area. Houseboat sewage is no longer drained into the canals but piped into the city's sewerage system. They do lack central heating; most houseboats are heated by use of small furnaces. To see what life is like aboard, you could visit the **Houseboat Museum** (► below; Prinsengracht, tel: 020 4 27 07 50, www.houseboatmuseum.nl, March–Oct Tue–Sun 11–5, Feb, Nov–Dec Fri–Sun 11–5, closed most of Jan and some holidays, €3.75), which is moored on the west bank of Prinsengracht, just south of its junction with Berenstraat.

Sightseeing boat opposite Centraal Station

Most boats turn around here to go back past NEMO and back to their moorings; the Amsterdam Canal Cruises trip carries on back into the Amstel to return to Singelgracht.

Canal Tours
✉ Most cruise companies have a stop/jetty in and around the Damrak basin opposite Centraal Station

Amsterdam Canal Cruises
✉ North bank of Singelgracht directly opposite the Heineken Brewery
☎ 020 6 26 56 36; www.amsterdamcanalcruises.nl
🕐 Tours: April–Sep 10–6, every 30 min; Oct–March 10–5, every hour.
The journeys are non-stop and take around 75 min 💶 €15

INSIDER INFO

- Such is the extent of competition that **buying a ticket in advance** can undercut the "turn-up-and-go" price – budget hotels and backpacker hostels sometimes advertise discounts of one third or more.
- Most operators offer discounted online tickets.
- Don't board with a thirst or an empty stomach: **few of the vessels have refreshment facilities,** except for the evening dinner cruises.
- In summer, 80 or more canal boats can be on the water during the day, along with numerous smaller craft and dozens of erratically steered Canal Bikes. Congestion can be severe, adding a lot of time to the average trip; and some departures may be fully booked with tour groups. **Try to be aboard one of the first departures of the day**, at around 9am; from 10am, the "rush-hour" begins and lasts until 5 or 6pm.
- Canal Bike (tel: 020 6 23 98 86, www.canal.nl, daily 10–6 and 10–10 in summer) offers a "rent it here, leave it there" service of four-seater 🚲 **pedal-boats** for do-it-yourself tours between any of four locations at key tourist sites. You can pick up and/or drop off a Canal Bike at three points in the western canal ring – the north side of Leidseplein, Keizersgracht where Leidsestraat crosses it, and outside the Anne Frank Huis. The fourth option is the company's main base, on Weteringschans, close to the Rijksmuseum entrance.

Insider Tip

⭐Jordaan

Nowhere in Amsterdam is better preserved than this former working-class area, and anywhere you wander within the tight web of streets and canals is likely to reward you with a rich mix of impressive architecture, intriguing shops, dreamy views and a village ambience. These pages provide a walk that can be used as a basis for exploring the area, from which you can (and should) deviate at will, maybe with a glimpse into one or more of the hidden courtyards that make the Jordaan so special.

The Golden Age of the 17th century was accompanied by a population explosion, as Amsterdam enticed craftspeople and drew fortune-seekers from all over Europe. As the wealthy staked their claims around the new canal ring, an area of high-density housing was created beyond it in what had been green fields.

The name "Jordaan" derives from the French word *jardin,* though with tens of thousands of people packed into the area there was little resemblance to a garden. The area forms a finger of land curling around the west of the canal ring, flanked by Prinsengracht to the east and Lijnbaansgracht to the west. The northern boundary is Brouwersgracht, with Looiersgracht marking the southern edge – and the start of this stroll.

Egelantiersgracht, one of the most photogenic canals in Amsterdam

West of Prinsengracht

As soon as you are west of Prinsengracht, the character of the city changes; the pace of life dwindles along with the size and ambition of the buildings. The bridge along Looiersgracht is an excellent viewpoint. Head northwest along Eerste Looiersdwarsstraat, past some interesting shops whose contents fall somewhere between antiques and junk.

The street name turns into **Hazenstraat**: this strip contains a range of fancy stores, where you should be able to find just the grade of olive oil you need at Olivaria (► 106). Your reverie may be rudely interrupted by the only big street in the Jordaan: **Rozengracht**. With four tram routes and a huge amount of other traffic cutting through a rather down-at-heel string of shops, it seems to be disconnected from the rest of the neighbourhood.

Once safely across, you hit **Bloemstraat** – but don't expect to see too many blooms along this street, nor along many others in the Jordaan. Walk towards the unmistakable tower of the **Westerkerk** (► 101), which serves as an instant beacon for the befuddled tourist (or local). Before you reach Westerkerk, turn left along **Eerste Bloemdwarsstraat**; this will take you to the area where several *hofjes* (► 94) are concentrated. Zigzag towards **Westerstraat**, making sure you take the **Eerste Leliedwarsstraat** bridge over **Egelantiersgracht** to enjoy what is, perhaps, the finest canal perspective in Amsterdam.

Canal Ring – West

Westerstraat is effectively Jordaan's high street but its appeal is muted by all the parked cars. Take the street heading north from the centre of **Lindengracht,** and within five minutes you will emerge at the northernmost point of the Jordaan.

From here, you can embark on Walk 1 (► 180–183), or Walk 3 (► 187–189), venture westwards to **Westergasfabriek** and **Westerpark** (► 106), or just wander back a different way, to see more facets of this multi-dimensional district.

The Hofjes of Jordaan

The Jordaan hides its secrets well. Behind a succession of innocuous doorways are hidden courtyards, most built by the high and mighty for the benefit of the poor and lowly. They tended to shelter the elderly of a particular religious denomination, and some of them still adhere to the original faith. These *hofjes* range in style from collections of houses spilling on to a workaday yard, to prim cottages precisely arranged around well-kept gardens. These can be found in other parts of Amsterdam, too, but the highest concentration is in the Jordaan. They are usually open to the public on weekdays between 9am and 5pm.

If you have time to visit only one Jordaan *hofje,* make it **Karthuizerhof** (Karthuizerstraat 89–171): grander and lovelier than all the others, the Huiszittenweduwenhof (the names of the founders) consists of a large courtyard whose central point of interest is a pair of ornate water pumps. All the dwellings are arranged strictly symmetrically, as was the style in the mid-17th century, when it was built. Note how, on the upper level, a space has been left where a window should be, helping to reveal the extent of the *hofje.*

Claes Claesz Hofje (Egelantiersstraat 34–54) is one of the most accessible *hofjes.* It is buried in a tightly packed area of the Jordaan, and merges with the houses on Egelantiersstraat, the parallel Tuinstraat and Eerste Egelantiersdwarsstraat, where the main entrance is located. Claes Claesz Anslo was a Mennonite textile merchant who

Statues dot the Jordaan area, such as this one honouring the life of Theo Thijssen

A well-kept, fenced garden is the centrepiece of this courtyard on Egelantiersstraat

founded the *hofje* in 1626. It comprises three linked courtyards, in which the greenery runs wild, and is nowadays a hall of residence for music students.

There is a second entrance around the corner, just next to the Taverne restaurant that intrudes into one of the courtyards; if you exit through this doorway, and look above the entrance to the restaurant, you can see a particularly splendid tablet showing the coat of arms of the founding family.

St Andrieshofje (Egelantiersgracht 107–145) is a complete contrast to the Claes Claesz Hofje – a model of calm and order, with well-tended gardens and demure, lopsided cottages, once home to 66 Catholic widows.

You will be fortunate to find **Zevenkeurvorstenhof** (Tuinstraat 199–225) open even during the day; if you do, the reward is a concise courtyard that manages to shut out the city entirely.

The most attractive feature of **Bosschehofje** (Palmgracht 20–26) is the main entrance, viewed from the street. High above the gate is a big, extravagant tablet; beneath that, a porthole; and a keystone above a stout brick archway. Take a look inside, which is like any ordinary communal living space, with children scuttling about and washing drying, though there are good views over the back wall to the rears of some handsome houses.

✉ 202 C2

INSIDER INFO

- The alignment of the streets and canals in Jordaan mean that the best **light for photography** is usually in the late afternoon.
- If you find yourself in Amsterdam for **King's Day on 26 April**, the Jordaan is a good place to celebrate.
- To experience life on an Amsterdam houseboat, **check out the Houseboat Museum (▶** 90) moored on Prinsengracht at Johnny Jordaan Plein.

⭐ Anne Frank Huis

A prettier location is hard to imagine: in the benevolent shadow of the Westerkerk, on one of Amsterdam's loveliest canals, stands a well-proportioned merchant's house, built in 1635. Yet behind its handsome exterior lay a sanctuary, a prison and, ultimately, a place of betrayal. Prinsengracht 263 is now a shrine to the victims of World War II and, in particular, to a teenager whose eloquence has endured into the 21st century.

For 25 months, the Frank family and the van Pels family lived in fear in the annexe at Prinsengracht 263. As the war drew to a close, they were discovered and deported. Only Otto Frank, Anne and Margot's father, survived; the others died in Nazi death camps. When Otto went back to the house, one of the people who had helped them hide returned Anne's diaries, which were subsequently published to wide acclaim.

It is usually very crowded outside the Anne Frank House

The house where they had hidden remained empty for years. In the late 1950s a plan was put forward to demolish it, which led several prominent citizens to establish the Anne Frank House. Its primary goal is the preservation of the annexe, but increasingly the organization is concerned with education about the dangers of racism.

Anne Frank's story unfolds as you pass through a series of rooms on the prescribed tour. There are no guides: you proceed at your own pace. Having entered through the modern building at Prinsengracht 267, you pass through a video room that sets the scene in No 265. You then enter the house on the ground floor, at what was the warehouse and spice-grinding room.

Otto Frank had moved his family from the German city of Frankfurt in 1933, when Adolf Hitler came to power. In Amsterdam he set up two businesses: Opekta, making pectin as a setting agent for jam, and a spice company called Pectagon. The herbs and spices had to be kept in the dark – an ideal excuse for blacking out the windows in the annexe at the back of the house.

Invasion

The Nazis invaded the Netherlands in May 1940, and gradually stripped the Jewish community of rights. Otto Frank, his wife Edith and their daughters Anne and Margot (three years older) went into hiding on 6 July 1942, after Margot was called up for a "work-force project" in Germany – a euphemism for enforced deportation to the concentration camps. In a video on the **first floor**, Miep Gies – one of the family's helpers – explains how the family hid at the back of the residence that housed Otto's business. They were joined by one of Otto's business associates, Hermann van Pels, his wife Auguste and son Peter. In November, an eighth person arrived: Fritz Pfeffer, who had fled Germany to Holland with his non-Jewish fiancée.

The hideaways were helped by four people; one was Victor Kugler, a manager for the company. After climbing the stairs and walking along a corridor, you pass through his office on the second floor. Sometimes at night, the hideaways would slip down to the office and listen to broadcasts from Britain. Otto Frank even continued his involvement in running the business, with Kugler's help.

Life in the Annexe

On the **same floor** is the office shared by three other helpers: Johannes Kleiman, Miep Gies and Bep Voskuijl. On Saturday afternoons, this acted as the bathroom for the Frank sisters. "We scrub ourselves in the dark," wrote Anne, "While the one who isn't in the bath looks out the window through a chink in the curtains." In the store room, exhibits show how persecution of Jewish people gradually increased during the German occupation. You then move in to the **annexe behind a moveable bookcase**. Here, eight people were crammed into two floors, where they had to live in near silence to avoid being overheard by employees. The door was concealed by the bookcase containing a few

Continued on page 100

Life in the Annexe

In 1957, the owner of this house donated it to the Anne Frank Foundation that subsequently opened it to the public in 1960. The museum was hardly able to cope with the enormous rush of close to 600,000 visitors annually and had to be completely renovated.

❶ **Front building:** Similar to many other houses on Amsterdam's canals, the building at Prinsengracht 263 consisted of a front and rear house. Otto Frank, Anne's father, had his company with its office and storerooms in the front house from 1940. It continued to operate during World War II. Old photographs were used to reconstruct the rooms but they are no longer furnished. Quotations from Anne Frank's diary give insights as to how they must have looked and their atmosphere.

❷ **Rear building:** When the first Jews had to register for work camps in 1942, Otto Frank arranged four rooms in the rear house in a manner that made it possible for his family and friends to go into hiding. Otto Frank's former secretary, Miep Gies, and other helpers provided them with food.

❸ **Hidden entrance:** The entrance to the secret annexe at the rear building where the family was forced to live was through a hidden door disguised as a bookcase. The rooms are no longer furnished. Anne's diary was found on the floor after the family had been arrested.

❹ **Anne's bedroom**

The hideaways were brought food by helpers

Anne Frank (1929–45)

⑤ The parent's bedroom
⑥ The Van Pels family's rooms: The furnishings were confiscated by the Nazis and a decision had to be made on reconstruction in 1962. Otto Frank however, was against the idea and only a few personal belongings and letters of the eight people who were in hiding are on display. In her diary Anne gave the Van Pels family the pseudonym Van Daan.
⑦ Attic: In the attic there are displays of photographs and other documents that show the ordeal that the occupants of the annexe suffered in various concentration camps. Videos place the individual stories within the historical context.

dusty files. Beyond this, a narrow stairway leads up to the annexe.

Each week, Victor Kugler brought Anne a copy of the magazine *Cinema and Theatre*; she cut out the pictures of idols and pinned them to the walls. She had kept her diary since her 13th birthday on 12 June 1942, a few weeks before they went into hiding: "I hope I will be able to confide everything to you," read her first entry. The last was on 1 August 1944, in which she wrote "A voice within me is sobbing."

You move from the annexe into a bare, modern **exhibition room,** where the fate of the eight is explained. On 4 August 1944, German police were tipped off about the hiding place. The eight were taken to a police station, then sent to Westerbork transit camp. Johannes Kleiman and Victor Kugler were also arrested, but eventually released. The prisoners were among the last to be sent to Auschwitz from Westerbork. Hermann van Pels was gassed soon after arrival. His wife and son were moved from camp to camp, and six months later died within a few days of each other from illness and hunger. Fritz Pfeffer perished from the same causes. Otto and Edith escaped the gas chamber, but Edith died from disease and malnutrition in January 1945. Anne and Margot ended up at Bergen-Belsen concentration camp. They died in March, just one month before the war ended in Europe, in a typhus epidemic.

After the war, Otto Frank decided to fulfil Anne's wish that her diary be published; the original is on display on the top floor. The book first appeared, in Dutch, in 1947. It has since been published in 65 languages.

TAKING A BREAK

The venue has a bright and pleasant café on the south side, looking across to the Westerkerk (daily 9–7).

✚ 203 D2

✉ Prinsengracht 263 (entrance at 267)

☎ 020 5 56 71 05; www.annefrank.org

🕐 Apr–June Sun–Fri 9–9, Sat 9am–10pm; July–Aug daily 9am–10pm; Sep–March Sun–Fri 9–7, Sat 9–9. Closed Yom Kippur

🚊 13, 14, 17 💶 €9

INSIDER INFO

- In summer, the later you visit the less likely you are to have to queue.
- If you are planning to visit at a busy time, **buy tickets in advance online** (www.annefrank.org). You'll avoid having to queue at the ticket desk. Instead, you enter through a separate door marked "online tickets".
- Most visitors **find the experience very moving;** some are visibly distressed, especially children. Build in time to come to terms with what you have seen and heard before going on to your next destination.

⭐🔟 Westerkerk

Of all the handsome churches in Amsterdam, this is the most central to the life of the city – and, indeed, to the country. The tower – a miracle of construction, given the soupy geology – dominates western Amsterdam, and Amsterdammers consider it a blessing to have been born within the sound of the Westerkerk's carillon, a mark that identifies them with the densely populated, and dearly loved, neighbourhood west of the city centre.

Westerkerk is a well-loved landmark in the area

The Westerkerk, one of the city's first Protestant churches, was built in the Renaissance style by Hendrick de Keyser (1565–1621), and opened on Whit Sunday 1631. Its spire, which can be seen for miles around and is known locally as "Langer Jan" was completed seven years later. It is over 85m (280ft) high, and contains the city's heaviest bell that weighs 7,500kg/16,500lb with a hammer that weighs 200kg (440lb).

The church is assertively plain, in deliberate contrast to the Catholic tradition. The box pews are the most elaborate furnishings: wealthy families would buy up a separate section to keep them apart from the proletariat. The large, ornate organ above the west door was added more than 50 years after the church was completed; before that, there had been heated debates about whether musical accompaniment was appropriate. It provides the one touch of extravagance in the whole church, supported on marble columns with the assistance of a cherub or two. The decoration is most lavish on the shutters, depicting Old Testament scenes.

Rembrandt's Hidden Tomb

The most notable person to be buried here is so well hidden that no one knows where he is. Rembrandt was buried in a rented grave, but after 20 years or so his remains were moved to make room for more burials. An optimistic memorial on the north side of the church claims, "Here lies buried R Harmensz Van Ryn, Born 15 July 1606, Died 4 October 1669".

Best View of the City

A climb to the top of the tower is rewarded with a fine panorama. In the 17th century, as well as glorifying God (and the city), the tower also served as an early-warning station, with a permanent watch looking out for fires or dambursts. The base is made of brick but, beyond the first gallery, the structure is wooden with a facing of sandstone or lead, reducing the tower's weight. The central circle on the floor on the first gallery, now filled in, was used to haul up materials and bells. At the fourth gallery you can see the beams that were added to absorb the vibrations from the 7-tonne hour bell; without them, the tower could shake itself apart.

The carillon bells of Westerkerk ring out over the city

TAKING A BREAK

Pause for coffee, a cocktail, or lunch at **Werck** (➤ 111). This highly contemporary café/bar/restaurant in the old coach house of the Westerkerk has a terrace with bird's-eye views of the church next door.

➕ 203 D2
✉ Prinsengracht 281
☎ 020 6 24 77 66; www.westerkerk.nl
🕐 Mon–Sat 11–3. From April–Oct there is a free organ concert at 1pm on Fridays. Tower tours: April–Oct 10–5:30 July–Sep until 7:30, every half hour
🚌 13, 14, 17
💶 Church: free. Tower: €7.50

INSIDER INFO

- The **tower climb** is not difficult for able-bodied people, though the steeper sections near the top require special care. To climb up the tower you will need to join one of the guided tours.
- Just north of the main entrance is a lintel showing **four cherubs and two skulls**.

At Your Leisure

21 Leidseplein

Leidse Square (named because it was the end of the road between Leiden and Amsterdam) began life in the 17th century, when it was used for parking horses and carts. Today, it is a hub for nightlife, awash with neon lights and revellers every evening.

A sense of timing is important when visiting the hub of the city's many tourist trails. Mornings see the square being spruced up after all the excesses of the previous night, and the eastern light illuminating the American Hotel (➤ right) to good effect.

The imposing Hirsch & Cie neoclassical property on the southern edge previously housed the fashion house but is now home to an Apple Store. Along **Marnixstraat**, marking the northeast flank of the American Hotel, there is an attractive crescent of houses – now mostly converted to hotels.

At the **AUB Ticketshop** (➤ 49), built into the Stadsschouwburg,

Night view of the Stadsschouwburg theatre, Leidseplein

you can pick up bargains for shows the same day.

✚ 204 B3

22 American Hotel

The hotel, which was built in 1900 and is a listed monument is Leidseplein's main attraction – a crazed art nouveau interpretation of a Scottish baronial castle. The exterior rewards a good, close inspection, and the interior is also well worth investigating.

Start on the northeast corner: look up and you'll see decorations of storks on one face and squirrels on the other. The gable is enlivened

The art deco interior of the Café Américain

by a stylized sunbeam. The main face of the hotel, on the southeast flank, has a fishy fountain at the front, but what may be of more interest is to the left of the café entrance (above the Café Américain; ► 107): a relief showing the hotel itself. On the southern corner, a Venus figure appears on tiles, guarded by a pair of owls, a couple of serpents and a menacing-looking bat. The words "American Hotel" are picked out in a mosaic that has the look of embroidery. Officially the Hampshire American Hotel,

The Homomonument is now an integral part of the canalscape

it is still commonly called the American Hotel.

➕ 204 B3 ✉ Leidsekade 97
☎ 035 6 77 72 17;
www.edenamsterdamamericanhotel.com
🚋 1, 2, 5

23 Homomonument

The city's tolerance is, once again, evident, in the location – next to Westerkerk – of this monument to people persecuted because of their homosexuality. The triangular slab of pink granite, beside the Keizersgracht, is based on the pink triangle symbol that gay men

and women were obliged to wear during the German occupation. It is something of a shrine, and you may see people placing flowers and tributes there.

➕ 203 D2
✉ Corner of Westermarkt and Keizersgracht
🚋 13, 14, 17

24 Amsterdam Tulip Museum

The Tulip Museum is located in an historic canal house, from the front all you see of the museum is the delightful museum shop. While the shop does take up most of the museum space, it is well worth a visit for its engaging and well designed exhibition devoted to Holland's most famous flower. It sheds light on the tulip's pre-eminence in Ottoman Empire art, and Tulipomania: in the 17th century, the most prized bulbs could fetch sums in Holland that surpassed the price of houses. Fortunately the tulips and bulbs for sale in the shop are now far more affordable.

➕ 203 D2
✉ Prinsengracht 116
☎ 020 4 21 00 95;
www.amsterdamtulipmuseum.com
🕐 Daily 10–6 🚋 13, 14, 17 💶 €15

The Tulip Museum is informative and colourful

Canal Ring – West

25 Westergasfabriek and Westerpark

The western reaches of the city, particularly north of Haarlemmerweg, have long been overlooked, which helps explain why the Western Isles (➤ 190) are so splendidly preserved. Squeezed between a canal and the main rail line, this triangle of land is occupied by a park and a former gasworks that is now home to cafés, cinemas and galleries (➤ 114) and is also a popular nightlife area. The Westergasfabriek is a clutter of buildings on the north side of the Haarlemmervaart canal, dramatically rejuvenated in 2003.

The main "avenue" takes you past several handsome structures, some of which are filled with experimental arts projects. At the eastern end, the Westergasfabriek merges with Westerpark, one of the city's

For modern art, the place to go is the Westergasfabriek

smaller parks. 🍴 In nice weather there is a wadingpool full of children splashing around in the water.

✚ 202 A5 and B5

☎ 020 5 86 07 10; www.westergasfabriek.nl

🚊 10 terminates on Van Hallstraat, from where it is a short walk north to Haarlemmerweg and across the canal to the Westergasfabriek (gates open 8am–11:30pm). Tram 3 serves Haarlemmerplein, at the east end of Westerpark

💶 Free

Where to...
Eat and Drink

Prices
Expect to pay per person for a three-course meal, excluding drinks and service:
€ under €20   €€ €20–€40   €€€ over €40

CAFÉS AND BARS

De Admiraal €/€€

This *proeflokaal* (tasting house, ►31), in an old canal ware-house, has 20 types of *jenevers* (gin) and 60 liqueurs (some with fun names such as Perfect Happiness and Lift up your Shirt), produced by its own long-established distillery. Old oak barrels, giant stone liqueur bottles and copper distillery kettles decorate the large, smart bar. Unlike most other tasting houses, it offers interesting snacks, such as herring and smoked eel, full meals and comfortable seating.

🔢 205 D3
✉ Herengracht 319
☎ 020 6 25 43 34; www.proeflokaaldeadmiraal.nl
🕐 Mon–Sat 4:30–midnight

Café Amércain €/€€€

This landmark grand café – part of the American Hotel (►103) – has an art nouveau interior so fabulous that it has been declared a listed monument. There are beautiful stained-glass motifs above stone arches and weird and wonderful chandeliers. The concise but inviting menu features burgers and finger food, including dim sum. If you prefer, you can also lap up the atmosphere for the price of a coffee or a beer. Jazz accompanies Sunday brunch.

🔢 204 B3
✉ Leidsekade 97 ☎ 020 5 56 30 00;
www.edenamsterdamamerican.com
🕐 Daily 7am–11:30pm

Café Chris €

A good choice if you're looking for a traditional brown café in the Jordaan that receives few tourists. It makes a fair claim to be Amsterdam's oldest café. It started life in 1624, when the builders of the nearby Westerkerk would receive (and presumably spend) their wages here. Quirky features include a men's toilet that is so small it is flushed by a chain from the bar area.

🔢 202 C1
✉ Bloemstraat 42
☎ 020 6 24 59 42; www.cafechris.nl
🕐 Mon–Thu 3pm–1am, Fri–Sat 3pm–2am, Sun 3pm–9pm

Café Dulac € –€€

This café, housed in a former 1920s bank, is a strong contender for the most outrageously furnished grand café in Amsterdam. Post-modern kitsch rules, in the form of trumpets and model boats hanging from the ceiling, gargoyles and naked women erupting out of the walls. It's a trendy students's haunt, with a DJ performing on some nights. Decent food comes in the form of salads, steaks, pasta and tarts.

🔢 203 E3
✉ Haarlemmerstraat 118
☎ 020 6 24 42 65; www.restaurantdulac.nl
🕐 Mon–Thu 3pm–1am, Fri 3–3, Sat noon–3am, Sun noon–1am

Café Papeneiland € Insider Tip

The diminutive "Priest's Island" is one of Amsterdam's oldest brown cafés (►31) . In the early

Canal Ring – West

17th century, its landlord sold ale as a sideline: his main source of income was making coffins. With wood panelling and old Delft tiles adorning the walls, tankards hanging from beams, a large old stove and, in traditional fashion, boiled eggs and apple pie displayed on the bar, the café oozes character from every pore.

➕ 203 E3
✉ Prinsengracht 2
☎ 020 6 24 19 89; www.papeneiland.nl
🕐 Mon–Thu 10am– 1am, Fri–Sat 10am–2am, Sun noon–1am

Café de Prins €/€€

This is a brown *eetcafé* (➤ 28) – note the typical old bar, bare wooden tables and part-panelled walls – that's always busy with diners and a young, boisterous crowd of drinkers. Its main selling points are its canalside location (with outdoor seating) close to the Anne Frank Huis, and its good, inexpensive Dutch/French food. Try the cheese fondue, the excellent quiches crammed with delicious fillings, or at lunchtime the tasty *uitsmijter* (fried eggs on bread).

➕ 203 D2
✉ Prinsengracht 124
☎ 020 6 24 93 82; www.diningcity.nl/deprins
🕐 Daily 10am–1am (kitchen open until 10pm)

Café 't Smalle €

Brown cafés (➤ 31) don't come any quainter than this tiny, split-level corner building. Candles line the bar, wood panelling covers the walls, and the stained glass dates back to the late 18th century. The café is usually packed, but retains a civilized air, with rare *jenevers* and a good range of snacks on offer, including slices of apple pie. The canalside location is simply idyllic, and there is a terrace by the water.

➕ 202 C2
✉ Egelantiersgracht 12
☎ 020 623 9617; www.t-smalle.nl
🕐 Sun–Thu 10am–1am, Fri– Sat 10am–2am

De Doffer €/€€

A roomy, brown *eetcafé*, with a second bar next door, that hits all the right notes (and that's not just the jazz music that might be playing in the background). The requisite boarded floors, panelled walls and candlelit tables are all here, with a concise menu – soup and sandwiches at lunch with dishes such as salmon with wasabi and duck confit with cassis for dinner. The café is slightly smarter than many of its counterparts, which is reflected in the clientele.

➕ 204 B4
✉ Runstraat noon–14
☎ 020 6 22 66 86; www.doffer.com
🕐 Sun–Thu noon–3am, Fri noon–4am, Sat 11am–4am

Spanjer & Van Twist €/€€

This modern, canalside *eetcafé* serves some of the best café food in Amsterdam. Most ingredients are organic. Lunches include delicious omelettes and interesting open sandwiches such as salmon, mozzarella and pesto. More substantial dinners run to fish stew, and jugged hare with turnip mash. The café is an intimate, split-level space, with an eye-catching bar backed by Mondrian-style glass. The canal-side terrace is a pretty spot in the summertime.

Insider Tip

➕ 203 D2 ✉ Leliegracht 60
☎ 020 6 39 01 09; www.spanjerenvantwist.nl
🕐 Daily 10am–1am

Tabac €

Pleasant café on one of the most beautiful street corners in Amsterdam. In summer you can sit on cushions on the roof of a small extension and watch the boats on the Prinsengracht glide by. The menu is Asian-influenced; try the delicious *Soto Ayam* (Indonesian chicken soup).

➕ 203 D3 ✉ Brouwersgracht 101
☎ 020 6 22 44 13
🕐 Sun, Mon11–1am, Tue–Thu 4–1, Fri 4–3, Sat 11–3am

De Tuin €

"The Garden" is one of the Jordaan's classic little brown cafés. Go for coffee and cake or a lunch. It has all the necessary features to make it ever so cosy: a lovely old worn bar, candles on bare wood tables, walls covered in yellowing panelling and old posters advertising beer. It's popular with the neighbourhood's young liberal set, with a wonderful mix of students, intellectuals and dedicated beer drinkers.

➕ 203 D2 ✉ 2e Tuindwarsstraat 13
☎ 020 6 24 45 59 ⏰ Mon–Thu 10am–1am, Fri–Sat 10am–2am, Sun 11am–1am

Walem Café €/€€

One of the oldest "designer bars" – hence the waitresses dressed in black, the subtly lit mirrors, and the bold plant displays – Walem is, none the less, refreshingly attitude free. The main reason for its popularity is the excellent food produced by its open-plan kitchen. For lunch you might have a simple *croque madame* (a toasted sandwich with a fried egg on top) and for dinner braised rabbit with sauerkraut cooked in Riesling. When it's fine, you can sit out by the canal, or in the garden at the rear of the building.

➕ 204 C3 ✉ Keizersgracht 449
☎ 020 6 25 35 44; www.walem.nl
⏰ Sun–Thu 10am–1am, Fri–Sat 10am–2am

RESTAURANTS

De Belhamel €€

An intimate, romantic restaurant that looks out across the lovely Brouwersgracht and right down Herengracht: try to bag a window seat when you book. Both the dining room and grotto-like bar are decked out in authentic art nouveau decor. The French food is reliably good: the menu changes often but a dinner might start with shrimp mousse, be followed by poached calf's tongue, and end with a pear

tarte Tatin.

➕ 203 E3 ✉ Brouwersgracht 60
☎ 020 622 1095; www.belhamel.nl
⏰ Daily noon–4, 6–1

Bordewijk €€/€€€

This is one of the city's most fashionable restaurants (reserve for any night). The sparse, modern dining room looks through large windows on to the lovely Noordermarkt. The exciting menu swings between Italy and France – from dishes such as Bresse pigeon with fresh morel mushrooms and polenta to Dutch shrimps with spring onions. The cheese trolley is a highlight of the meal. The daily menus are excellent value.

➕ 203 D3 ✉ Noordermarkt 7
☎ 020 6 24 38 99; www.bordewijk.nl
⏰ Tue–Sat 6:30–10:30

Café-Restaurant Amsterdam €€

It's worth making the 10-minute tram ride from Leidseplein (on tram 10 to its last stop) just to ogle at the scale of this restaurant. Occupying the gleaming hall of a former 19th-century pumping station, it could fit a dozen canal houses into the space. The largely French, brasserie-styled food – snails, steak tatare, steak and chips served Dutch-style with mayonnaise, all simply prepared and keenly priced – is worth coming for too. Book in advance or you may have to wait a while for a table. And across from the café is a little tower that houses the smallest hotel in Amsterdam (www.windketel.nl).

➕ 202 off A4 ✉ Watertorenplein 6
☎ 020 6 82 26 66; www.cradam.nl
⏰ Sun–Thu 10:30am–midnight, Fri–Sat 10:30am–1am

Café de Reiger €€

This atmospheric *eetcafé* (➤ 32) in the Jordaan is invariably packed with Amsterdammers. They come for its long candlelit bar, buzzy but laid-back vibe, and the robust, uncomplicated French/Italian/ Dutch food. The menu offers steaks and pasta. Daily specials are more interesting – try the goat's cheese soufflé, or risotto with leg of lamb. No reservations (or credit cards); arrive early to avoid a wait.

➕ 202 C2 ✉ Nieuwe Leliestraat 34
☎ 020 6 24 74 26
🕐 Tue–Fri, Sun 5–10:30, Sat noon–10:30

Chez Georges €€/€€€

You'll need to book well in advance for this small, cosy but quite formal bistro. Belgian Georges Roorda's cooking tends to be French, particularly from the Burgundy region. Don't come here for a snack; recommended is the seven-course gastronomic menu which represents excellent value – especially in comparison with the expensive wine list.

➕ 202 E2 ✉ Herenstraat 3
☎ 020 6 26 33 32; www.chez-georges.nl
🕐 Tue–Sat 6–11:30

Christophe €€€

In 2006, Christophe Royer sold his elegant, sophisticated establishment to two of his staff, Ellen Mansfield and Jean-Joel Bonsens. Though the restaurant subsequently lost its Michelin star, it is still regarded as one of the best (and most expensive) spots in Amsterdam. Ellen is the sommelier, while Frenchman Jean-Joel is head chef and the creator of such dishes as salted cod with anise and crème brûlée with lemon grass and red pepper.

➕ 203 D2 ✉ Leliegracht 46
☎ 020 6 25 08 07; www.restaurantchristophe.nl
🕐 Tue–Sat 6:30–10:30

Envy €€/€€€

Creative Italian taster-sized dishes, and great cheeses and meats, are served in this ultra-trendy, minimalist canalside restaurant. You can dine at private tables, or communally, perched on stools, at high, long tables. Before or after eating,

have a glass or two of wine in Vyne, Envy's equally fashionable sister wine bar, a few doors down along the canal.

➕ 204 B5 ✉ Prinsengracht 381
☎ 020 3 44 64 07; www.envy.nl
🕐 Sun–Thu 6pm–1am, Fri–Sat noon–3, 6–1am

Moeders €€

When "Mothers" first opened in 1990, diners bought their own cutlery and crockery and they remain all joyfully mismatched in this kitsch and cosy restaurant. The friendly waitresses will explain the menu, which features traditional Dutch as well as international food. Try the Dutch "rice table"– a spoof of the Indonesian dish, which includes no rice, but a combination of small national dishes.

➕ 204 A5 ✉ Rozengracht 251
☎ 020 6 26 79 57; www.moeders.com
🕐 Mon–Fri 5– midnight, Sat, Sun noon– midnight

🏠 The Pancake Bakery €€

A sure-fire winner with children and adults alike: more than 75 sweet and savoury varieties of pancake and omelettes are served here, amid the flagstone floors and exposed brick walls of an old canal house. Pick from the international-themed options such as the Egyptian lamb and paprika or red Thai curry fillings, or stick to favourites like ham and cheese or cherries with whipped cream. The pancakes, though more expensive than you might expect, are enormous and memorable.

➕ 203 D2 ✉ Prinsengracht 191
☎ 020 6 25 13 33; www.pancake.nl
🕐 Daily noon–9:30

Toscanini €€/€€€

One of the best Italian restaurants in Amsterdam; the ingredients are organic, the pasta is home-made and the bread is baked on the premises. You won't find pizza here, but instead there are regional dishes and specials such as *orecchiette* with octopus. The restaurant is always bustling and it can be quite noisy. Reservations are a must!

➕ 203 D3 ✉ Lindengracht 75
☎ 020 6 23 28 12; www.restauranttoscanini.nl
🕐 Mon–Sat 6–10:30

Van Puffelen €€

This friendly, canalside establishment is both a classic brown café (➤ 31) and a fully fledged restaurant with a beautiful, panelled dining room. The hearty menu is chiefly French, but includes multi-ethnic forays into such dishes as carpaccio of beef with artichoke salsa and Pangasius with red curry.

➕ 204 B5 ✉ Prinsengracht 375–377
☎ 020 6 24 62 70; www.restaurantvanpuffelen.com 🕐 Mon–Thu 3pm–1am, Fri 1pm–2:30am, Sat noon–2:30am, Sun noon–1am

Insider Tip

Werck €/€€

Enjoy views of both the canal and the Westerkerk next door from the terrace of this trendy but comfortable restaurant/café/bar that was once the church's coach house. The menu has several pub-style favourites such as burgers, but also more stylish fusion dishes. Werck becomes a club with DJs and events on Thursday–Saturday evenings.

➕ 204 B5 ✉ Prinsengracht 277
☎ 020 627 4079; www.werck.nl
🕐 Mon–Thu 11am–1am, Fri 11am–3am, Sat 10am–3am, Sun 10am–1am

Where to...
Shop

The western canal ring and the Jordaan district encapsulate what is best about shopping in Amsterdam. You'll find dozens of endearing, one-off shops over-

looking the canals and in the tiny backstreets, along with art galleries, antiques and flower shops. Individualism rules. Just go on a window-gazing stroll that ties in a visit to the Jordaan's covered markets. Note that many shops don't open on Monday.

9 STRAATJES

The Nine Streets (www.de9 straatjes.nl) are the virtually car-free radial lanes crossing the canals between the Singel and Prinsengracht, and Leidsegracht and Raadhuisstraat. Their houses, once occupied by servants who worked in the grander canalfront homes, are now a treasure trove of whimsical shops.

Working north to south, at No 7 Gasthuismolensteeg you'll find **Brillenwinkel** a shop/museum devoted to spectacles (Wed–Fri 11:30–5:30, Sat 11:30–5, www. brilmuseumamsterdam.nl). In the shop you can buy fun retro specs and antique opera glasses. The upper floors host the museum, where you can admire pince-nez, 19th-century safety goggles and glasses shaped like TV sets.

Across the street the shoe shop at No 16, **Antonia** (www. depantoffelwinkel.nl) specializes in slippers, wellingtons, and flip-flops. At No 28 Hartenstraat, check out **BLGK** (www.blgk.nl) – the jewellery here is more creative than anything you'll find in the city's diamond factories.

Head on to Reestraat. At No 5, **Fifties-Sixties** (www.fifties-sixties.nl) is filled with objects from the 1930s to 1970s. **E Kramer** (Nos 18–20, tel: 020 6 26 52 74) sells candles and all things spiritual.

JAN (Wolvenstraat 9) sells stylish gifts and household products. **Laura Dols** (No 7, www.lauradols.nl) offers vintage 1940s and 1950s clothing, while at Nos 9–11, **Kerkhof Passementen** has the Netherlands' – if not Europe's – largest selection of furnishing trimmings. On Berenstraat, **De Beeldenwinkel** (No 29, tel: 020 6 76 49 03) displays exquisite modern sculpture by local artists.

Insider Tip

Now head to **Pompadour** (No 12 Huidenstraat, tel: 020 6 23 95 54) for a break. You can eat incredibly rich chocolates and cakes on the premises in its tiny Louis XVI-style *salon de thé*.

Runstraat is the street to find top- class bakeries and cheese shops. **De Kaaskamer,** "The Cheese Room", (No 7, www.kaaskamer.nl) is one such a place, with hundreds of cheeses on offer. To experience a Dutch speciality, try Old Amsterdam, a mature Gouda that is wonderfully sharp and has plenty of bite.

Insider Tip

Next door is the quirky **De Witte TandenWinkel** (No 5, www.dewitte tandenwinkel.nl). "The White Teeth Shop", has been selling a dizzying selection of toothbrushes and other dental accoutrements for 20 years.

JORDAAN

The tiny cross-streets in the Jordaan south of Westerstraat have lots of quirky little shops, worth snooping around for things such as second-hand records, film posters and interesting clothes.

Rozengracht is the area's least charming street, but on it you'll find **Wegewijs** (No 32, www.wegewijs. nl), another of the city's best cheese shops, founded in 1884. South on Hazenstraat, **Olivaria** (No 2a, tel: 020 6 38 35 52) sells olive oil products.

For cat lovers, just along the street at No 26 is **Cats & Things** (www.catsandthings.nl), which concentrates on feline-themed gifts, such as tea cosies, playing cards and cute, cuddly toy cats.

PRINSENGRACHT AND HAARLEMMERSTRAAT

The shops along the lovely stretch of Prinsengracht that borders the Jordaan range from smart antiques emporia to appealing gift shops devoted to the likes of comics and candles. Heading south from Noordermarkt, on the western side of the canal, you might want to stop off at **Galleria d'Arte Rinascimento** (No 170, www.delft-art-gallery. com) which is piled high with an excellent range of old and new Delftware.

Further along, gorgeous aromas waft out of **Simon Levelt** (No 180, www.simonlevelt.com), which has been selling tea and coffee since 1817; you can also buy chocolates in the shape of Amsterdam's landmark bollards.

Van Hier tot Tokio (No 262, www. vanhiertottokio.com) specializes in highly desirable Japanese antiques, such as beautiful crafted cabinets from the 1920s and 1930s.

With time to spare, you might also want to venture north of Brouwersgracht to up-and-coming Haarlemmerstraat, which has several good delicatessens and intriguing art galleries among its less salubrious coffeeshops (► 32).

LEIDSESTRAAT AND AROUND

Leidsestraat is a popular shoe shopping street that is lined with one shoe shop after another, including branches of Dutch chains such as **Van Dalen** and **Sacha**, international brands such as **Camper**, but also the exclusive designer shops **Shoebaloo** (No 8) and Paul **Warmer** (No 41).

Heinen, a lovely canal house, just off Leidsestraat at Prinsengracht 440, sells modern Delftware and high-quality pottery painted in Delft style on the premises.

MARKETS

On Mondays (9–1), **Noordermarkt** hosts a flea market selling clothes, records and books, along with more arcane stuff, ranging from flags and rusting tools to classical statuary. Though not as large or diverse as Waterlooplein's market (➤ 81), it's much prettier.

On Saturdays (9–4) the square is taken over by the **Boerenmarkt,** which specializes in organic food, including cheeses, breads and wholefood produce.

Part of the tradition of visiting either market is to pop in to **Café Winkel** for a slice of apple pie (on the corner of the square at Noordermarkt 43).

Lapjesmarkt (Mon 8–1), from the Noordermarkt to Westerstraat, is a bustling locals' market devoted to fabrics and cheap clothes.

De Looier Kunst en Antiekcentrum (Elandsgracht 111, www.looier.nl; Sat–Thu 11–5) is a civilized, laby-rinthine indoor antiques-and-curios centre whose 80-plus stands display such items as china, glass, tele-scopes, military memorabilia and toy cars. Search out the "table market", where anyone can rent a table to sell their own antiques and curios.

Where to…
Go Out

With dozens of restaurants and cafés, nightclubs, cinemas and theatres, Leidseplein and its sur-rounding streets form the epicentre for most kinds of entertainment. For a less noisy, more tranquil, romantic evening, take a stroll through the Jordaan and along Prinsengracht, admiring the lights outlining the bridges and stopping off at a brown café (➤ 31) or two. North of the

Jordaan, the Westergasfabriek, Amsterdam's former gasworks, is the city's most intriguing cultural centre.

THE LEIDSEPLEIN AND AROUND

Leidseplein may be no beauty, and it's certainly not somewhere to come for a quiet drink, but its vivacity can be invigorating. Cafés filled with tourists watching football on satellite TV ring the square. In summer, their tables and chairs smother half of the square, and enthusiastic street musicians entertain the drinkers.

If you want a ringside, people-watching seat, head for the **Café Américain** (➤ 107). Other inter-esting drinking haunts near by are the **Grand Café Stanislavski** (Leidseplein 26, www.stanislavski. nl) in the ground floor of the Stadsschouwburg theatre, and **Lux** (Marnixstraat 403, tel: 020 6422 1412), a late-night bar deco-rated with giant photos of naked women and a DJ most nights.

Several atmospheric bars lay on spirited live jazz every night. See what's playing at **Café Alto** (Korte Leidsedwarsstraat 115, www.jazz-café-alto.nl) and **Bourbon Street** (Leidsekruisstraat 6, www.bourbon street.nl); the cover charge at each is small or non-existent.

If you want to smoke, the obvious choice is the large, heavily com-mercialized **Bulldog** (www.thebull dog.com) coffeeshop (the com-plex includes a separate bar and souvenir shop) right on Leidseplein. However, a much more exotic place is **De Rokerij** (Lange Leidsedwarsstraat 41, ➤ 33).

Amsterdam's casino, **Holland Casino** (Max Euweplein 62, tel: 020 5 21 11 11, www.hollandcasino. nl, daily noon–3am), is a garish affair. You must pay a small entrance fee (free to I amsterdam City Card holders), be over 18 and present your passport, but there is no strict dress code.

Canal Ring – West

Just off Leidseplein is **Melkweg** (Lijnbaansgracht 234a, tel: 020 5 31 81 81, www.melkweg.nl), to the northwest, and **Paradiso** (Weteringschans 6–8, tel: 020 6 26 45 21, www.paradiso.nl), to the southeast, the former converted from a dairy (and translating as the "Milky Way"), the latter from a church. These multifaceted venues were focal points for love, peace and hashish in Amsterdam's hippie era in the 1960s and 1970s.

The Melkweg has evolved into a multimedia cultural centre. The emphasis is on giving new Dutch bands a break and promoting world music at its two intimate concert halls; on weekend nights, they turn into nightclubs. The centre also contains a cinema, theatre, art gallery and café.

At the weekends, clubbers also head to Paradiso – a wonderful, ecclesiastical space – for techno, funk, disco and soul. Often referred to as "the temple of pop", it also hosts rock bands, jazz groups and classical concerts.

The **Nachttheater Sugar Factory** (Lijnbaansgracht 238, tel: 020 6 26 50 06, www.sugarfactory.nl) is an intriguing alternative nightclub. As well as varied music and DJ sets, there's an electic mix of entertainment from live bands, slam poetry to cabaret.

Pathé City Theater is a cinema in an art deco red-brick building close to the Leidseplein. Its seven screens offer a range of art-house films (Kleine-Gartmanplantsoen 15–19, tel: 0900 14 58, www.pathe.nl/city). The **Cinecenter** – tucked away in the alley behind the Stadsschouwburg theatre – is more intimate than the City and also has a pleasant bar (Lijnbaansgracht 236, tel: 020 6 23 66 15, www.cinecenter.nl).

THE JORDAAN

As well as its traditional brown cafés, there are two Jordaan cafés/bars where singing, as much as drinking, is the focus of activity.

At the kitsch and lurid **Café Nol** (Westerstraat 109, tel: 020 6 24 53 80, www.cafenolamsterdam.nl), locals sing along to taped folksy Dutch music.

More intimate **Twee Zwaantjes** (Prinsengracht 114, at Egelantiersgracht, tel: 020 6 25 27 29, www. cafedetweezwaantjes.nl) is often populated by inebriated Amsterdammers accompanying live accordion music.

Boom Chicago (Rozengracht 117, tel: 020 2 17 04 00, www. boomchicago.nl) is an American comedy troupe that performs improvisational comedy.

WESTERGASFABRIEK

In the mid-1990s, the city's former gasworks, **Westergasfabriek** (Haarlemmerweg 8–10, tel: 020 5 86 07 10, www.westergasfabriek. nl), became a venue for illegal rave parties, but now the development of this huge site is funded by the council. Large-scale events – pop concerts, opera, equine ballets, even conferences – are held here. Other buildings are used as film and theatre studios, a cinema (the **Ketelhuis**; www.ketelhuis.nl), and a funky café-restaurant, **Pacific Parc** (www.pacificparc.nl), which is the heart and soul of the complex, filling one of the warehouses. Open every evening, there are DJs each night and often live bands. Pacific Parc is the only part of the complex where you might consider turning up on spec; otherwise, check what's on before heading out. You could tie it in with a visit to the highly recommended **Café-Restaurant Amsterdam** (► 109). A taxi from the city centre costs around €20; otherwise, it's a short walk from tram 10's final stop just across the square.

Insider Tip

Museum Quarter

 **Little Treats**

Garden Culture

In between the boxwood hedges of the **Rijksmuseum's** (➤ 120) historic garden is a fine collection of sculptures.

Explore the city on skates

Join the free **Friday Night Skate Tour** around Amsterdam. Tours set off from the northeast section of **Vondelpark** (➤ 130).

For fish connoisseurs

The **Seafood Bar** (Van Baerlestraat 5, near **Museumplein**) is the ideal spot to enjoy some delicious crab croquettes or smoked eel.

Getting Your Bearings

Amsterdam reaches its artistic climax in a district set apart from the city's core, to the south of Singelgracht. The Museum Quarter contains the big green lung of Vondelpark and is studded with museums – some of them world class.

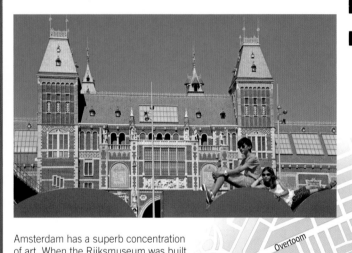

Amsterdam has a superb concentration of art. When the Rijksmuseum was built to house the national collection in 1885, its location marked the edge of the city. The museum spent its infancy in splendid isolation but, a decade later, the Stedelijk Museum of Modern Art opened, and 83 years after his death in 1890, the artist Vincent Van Gogh was honoured

Above: The grand exterior of the Rijksmuseum shows Romanesque and Gothic influences

Left: The entrance area of the newly renovated Stedelijk Museum

by the museum that bears his name. The museums are clustered together in Museumplein and both the Rijksmuseum and the Stedelijk Museum have been recently renovated – the Stedelijk addition takes the form of a futuristic new white "bathtub" wing. The nearby Vondelpark, central Amsterdam's largest open space, surrounded with handsome housing and scattered with eclectic decoration, provides the perfect breath of fresh air while you contemplate the culture.

The Museum Quarter is not merely the city's focus for art; some of the city's best cafés and restaurants can also be found here.

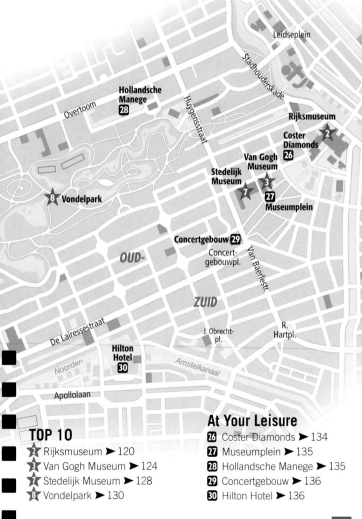

TOP 10

⭐ Rijksmuseum ➤ 120
⭐ Van Gogh Museum ➤ 124
⭐ Stedelijk Museum ➤ 128
⭐ Vondelpark ➤ 130

At Your Leisure

Perfect Days in ...

The Perfect Day

Get to know Amsterdam's cultural attractions and visit world-famous museums such as the Rijksmuseum and the Van Gogh Museum. This itinerary takes in the highlights of the Museum Quarter in one enjoyable day out. For more information see the main entries (► 120–136).

🕘 9:00am

Be first in line at the ⭐**Rijksmuseum** (► 120) and go straight to the Gallery of Honour which houses *The Night Watch*. At this time of the morning there is less of a crowd.

🕓 11:00am

Pop into the museum and workshops at **26 Coster Diamonds** (➤ 128).

🕓 12:00noon

If you don't feel like another museum café then head for the chic Cobra restaurant in the middle of **27 Museumplein** (left, ➤ 135) – or, on a fine day, enjoy a picnic in ⭐ **Vondelpark** (➤ 130).

🕓 1:00pm

Window-shop among the designer stores lining PC Hooftstraat; visit the opulent stables at the **28 Hollandsche Manege** (below, ➤ 135); or stroll down to the **30 Hilton Hotel** (➤ 136). All are within easy reach of the main museums.

🕓 2:30pm

Make your way over to the newly renovated ⭐ **Stedelijk Museum** (➤ 128).

🕓 4:00pm

Back on Museumplein, the crowds at the superb ⭐ **Van Gogh Museum** (above, ➤ 124) are beginning to dwindle, which makes this an ideal time to immerse yourself in the light and shade of the 19th-century genius.

🕓 6:00pm

Follow the cultural tide to Van Baerlestraat to unwind and reflect over a glass of beer at **Welling** (➤ 138), or take an early supper in Mediterranean serenity at **Bark** (➤ 138).

🕓 8:00pm

Take in a performance at the **29 Concertgebouw** (➤ 136).

⭐2 Rijksmuseum

The Rijksmuseum is one of Europe's greatest art centres and the building itself represents the height of 19th-century Dutch ambition. The museum reopened in 2013 after a 10-year renovation and expansion project, and has now once again been restored to its historic grandeur.

The red-brick Rijksmuseum dominates the southwest quarter of Amsterdam. Even among newer, taller buildings, it maintains a certain sense of majesty. The architect, PJH Cuypers – who also designed Centraal Station – took a sombre and formal Romanesque basic design and enlivened it with Gothic flourishes (his combination of Gothic and Renaissance styles proved rather controversial). The ensemble is unmistakably Dutch, though the friezes and reliefs that decorate it could be strays from a German or French cathedral. Envy was the principal motive for the instigation of the national collection. A hoard of 200 paintings had been amassed by Prince William V, who took them to London when he fled in 1795 from the revolutionary French army. Within a few years, envoys from the Dutch government had managed to confiscate the works, and initially housed them at The Hague. In 1808, Louis Napoleon (the French emperor's brother) was crowned king of Holland. He grew jealous of his sibling's collection at the Louvre and determined to match it. The collection was moved out of the palace and housed in the city at the Trippenhuis, but this proved too small for a rapidly growing number of paintings, etchings and sculptures.

The famous Rijksmuseum, seen from the Spiegelgracht

Origins of the Museum
A competition to design a new gallery on the fringe of the city was won by a German, but this was not felt to be

suitable, so a messy compromise was found whereby Cuypers was drafted in to create a replacement. His design drew protest and criticism from Protestant circles who felt that its Gothic style represented Catholic values. Shortly before the opening in 1885, the Dutch King William III commented that he would 'never set foot in that cloister'.

Seeing the Rijksmuseum

Following renovation work, the entrances to the Rijksmuseum were moved to the bicycle tunnel which runs through the museum. Revolving doors lead visitors into a large underground foyer, which is located in two glass-roofed former internal courtyards. The entrance to the **Medieval Collection** is also on this level. Since the reorganization of the museum, paintings and art works are shown alongside historical artefacts in this and all other halls. The highlights include *St Elizabeth's Day Flood*, a 1490 painting by an anonymous master that depicts the

The foyer of the Rijksmuseum

Museum Quarter

1421 storm tide that breached a dyke. After leaving the Medieval Collection, one reaches the newly built **Asian Pavilion**. The collection of Asian art may not be especially large but it is exquisite, and it is an oasis of calm tranquillity. The statues of two grim-looking Japanese temple guards from the 14th century are particularly noteworthy.

However, most visitors leave the foyer, pass through the entrance hall hung with spectacular paintings, and go directly to the second floor Gallery of Honour. Here, there is an almost endless row of masterworks from the Dutch Golden Age ranging from Jan Vermeer's intimate depictions of a milkmaid and a woman reading a letter, to the portraits Frans Hals painted with gossamer brushstrokes, to the hearty genre scenes Jan Steen specialised in. But of course, the absolute highlights are the works by Rembrandt Harmenszoon van Rijn.

The first is a self-portrait of the artist as a young man; in stark contrast is the self-portrait he made in 1661, aged 55, in which he is cloaked as the Apostle Paul. His genius at conveying emotion is evident in *The Jewish Bride*, which shows the passion between Isaac and Rebecca that gave them away in the biblical story.

Rembrandt (► 22) was principally a painter of commissioned portraits. His picture of the ageing Protestant minister Johannes Wtenbogaert proclaims the wisdom of age. *The Syndics* was a trickier matter: the customers all demanded

The Gallery of Honour is the highlight of the museum

INSIDER INFO

- The Rijksmuseum is at its **most crowded on summer weekends**. If you can, visit between Monday and Thursday; if not, arrive a few minutes ahead of opening at 9am. Alternatively, try after 3pm, when there is also less of a crowd. If you purchase **your ticket online in advance**, or if you have a *Museumkaart*, you can avoid the queue and go straight to the entrance doors.
- Take a look at the absolutely **magnificent library**. The balcony is accessible from hall from 1:13 (closed Mon).
- The **historical gardens** that surround the Rijksmuseum are well worth a visit. They are beautifully landscaped and include some sculpture exhibitions.

Insider Tip

that they should be depicted on the same level so they all had equal status; to inject energy he shows one figure half-rising, while the eyes of the ensemble hold the gaze and seem to pierce the viewer. His most celebrated work is *The Night Watch*, commissioned by the Kloveniers' Guild. In the 17th century, it was usual for professions to club together for a painting that would immortalize them. The standard portrait was stiff and formal, but Rembrandt broke with tradition to inject a sense of theatre, vitality and fun at odds with the serious purpose of the militiamen. Two guards were lopped off so that the painting would fit its previous location.

There are countless other works from the Golden Age to be admired in the neighbouring halls on the second floor – as well as three incredibly detailed doll's houses created for the wives of well-to-do merchants in the 17th century. Works from the 18th and 19th centuries are displayed on the first floor and there is also a – still rather small – collection of 20th century art on the third floor.

TAKING A BREAK

Sama Sebo (PC Hooftstraat 27, tel: 020 6 62 81 46, www.samasebo. nl, Mon–Sat 9am–1pm (café), noon–3 (lunch), 5–10 (dinner), just 150m (165 yards) along Hobbemastraat, serves good Indonesian food.

➕ 204 C2
✉ Museumstraat 1
☎ 020 6 74 70 00; www.rijksmuseum.nl
🕐 Daily 9–5 🚊 2, 5, 6, 7, 10, 12
💶 €15; children under 18 free (➤ 41); ICOM Card and I amsterdam City Card holders free

⭐3 Van Gogh Museum

He died by his own hand, after selling just two paintings during a brief and troubled career as an artist, yet today Vincent Van Gogh's art is sold for record sums. And the place that holds the best collection of his work is the most visited museum in Amsterdam and a must-see for art lovers.

Forever Change

Van Gogh began to draw and paint in 1880, after an unpromising career in teaching and preaching in Britain. In the next decade he produced 800 paintings, of which the museum contains a quarter. It also has 500 of his drawings and 700 letters (though because of their fragility these are rarely displayed), and 400 Japanese prints, from which Van Gogh drew inspiration and solace.

The extension to the museum has provided stylish, much-needed space

After his death in July 1890, his works passed to his younger brother, Theo, who survived him by only six months, and Theo's widow, Johanna. Her son, Willem Van Gogh, sold the collection to the Vincent Van Gogh Stichting (Foundation) in 1962.

The Van Gogh Museum opened in 1973. Gerrit Rietveld's austere, rectangular design stands in stark contrast with its conservative redbrick neighbours on Museumplein, but it does make the artist's work seem all the more vivid.

Early Work

The museum includes works by Van Gogh's contemporaries, who were much more illustrious at the time. The **ground floor** (numbered 0) establishes the context from 1850, when Van Gogh was inspired by works such

Sunflowers, Vincent
Van Gogh, 1889

as Léon-Augustin
Lhermitte's *Haymaking*.
He later said it was "As
if made by a peasant
who could paint."
Upstairs on the **first
floor**, you're confronted
first by a sombre self-
portrait, the only one
featuring an easel.
Historical sources sug-
gest this is the closest
likeness of all his self-
portraits. The large
number of self-portraits
is not a sign of vanity:
Van Gogh could not
afford to pay models,
and therefore practised
using himself.

The exhibition runs clockwise and chronologically,
beginning in Antwerp and moving to The Hague. A
brief spell spent in the northeast of Holland in the last
quarter of 1883 proved unproductive, and Van Gogh
was soon back with his parents in the town of Nuenen,
a few miles northeast of Eindhoven. His reverence for
the integrity of manual labour is depicted in *The Potato
Eaters* (1885), which is the first painting that he signed.

THE EXTENSION

Amid great ceremony, the much-needed extension to the Van Gogh Museum, by the
Japanese architect Kisho Kurokawa, was opened in 1999. Its plan is an oval, its exterior clad in titanium and disrupted by wayward cubes, in welcome contrast to the
severity of Gerrit Rietveld's original. To view it most favourably, climb the stairs in the
main building to the third floor. You reach the extension on an escalator that whisks
you below ground from the main foyer, into the "Knot" – the link between old and new.
At the foot, glass surrounds a shallow oval pond. On the far side are the galleries, used
for temporary exhibitions.

Museum Quarter

Near by, *Still Life with Quinces and Lemons* (1887) shows an unusual levity in the way that the image spills out on to the frame.

In the spring of 1886, Van Gogh moved to the Montmartre quarter of Paris, where he stayed with his art-dealer brother, Theo. It was here that he began to draw influence from the Impressionists. His restlessness drove him on to Arles, in the south of France in May 1888, where he hoped to set up an artists' colony in the Yellow House that he rented. Paul Gauguin arrived in October for a brief, unhappy stay. It was during this stormy visit that Van Gogh's mental health deteriorated, demonstrated by the self-mutilation of his left earlobe.

Posthumous fame: today Van Gogh's art is sold for record sums

Wheatfield with crows, c.1890

Van Gogh's Last Years

After Gauguin returned to Paris, Van Gogh suffered a breakdown and was admitted to an asylum at St-Remy in April 1889. Here, he produced some of his greatest work, including *Irises* (1890). Unable to work with models, he resorted to prints of the Old Masters for inspiration: *The Raising of Lazarus* (1890), after Rembrandt, is a bold embellishment in which the sun replaces Jesus, and Lazarus bears an uncanny resemblance to Van Gogh himself. *Wheatfield with a Reaper* (1889) is the portentous view from Van Gogh's room at St-Remy; the artist wrote that he saw in him "the image of death".

In May 1890, he moved north to Auvers-sur-Oise, near Paris. Two months later he shot himself in a wheatfield; he took two days to die from the wounds. The first-floor exhibition closes with three powerful land-scapes showing his brushwork at its most expressive: *Wheatfield with Crows* (1890) was painted just two weeks before his death, aged 37, on 29 July 1890. His last words were "La tristesse durera toujours" ("Sadness will last forever").

The **second floor** is devoted to a shifting collection of prints and drawings, while the **third floor** returns to the 19th-century, with works by Whistler, Monet, Cézanne and Gauguin.

TAKING A BREAK

The museum café serves coffee and more substantial meals. On a sunny day, sit out on the terrace of the **Cobra** restaurant (➤ 137), or pick up a picnic at the Albert Heijn supermarket under the southwest corner of Museumplein.

✚ 208 E2
✉ Paulus Potterstraat 7 ☎ 020 5 70 52 00; www.vangoghmuseum.nl
🕐 Sat–Thu 10–5, Fri 10–10 🍴 Museum café (€) daily 10–5:30
🚊 2, 5 💶 €15; children under 18 free; ICOM Card and I amsterdam City Card holders free

INSIDER INFO

- The queue for the Van Gogh Museum is frustratingly long at times. Even if you arrive early to miss the crowds, you're likely to find large numbers of visitors trying to do the same. However, you can avoid having to queue for a ticket by buying one ahead of your visit via the museum's website.
- Alternatively, **dodge the crowds** by visiting at midday or Monday morning or, if you can manage, after 4pm, when the museum tends to be much quieter.
- Audio tours for adults and children cost extra, but add considerably to the experience. There is also a fun kids' treasure hunt.
- On **Friday evenings**, when the museum stays open until 10pm, there is always some additional entertainment – perhaps live music, or a DJ from 6 to 10pm.

Insider Tip

⭐7 Stedelijk Museum

The Old Masters of the Rijksmuseum and the 19th-century angst of Van Gogh do not have an artistic monopoly in Amsterdam: the Stedelijk, the city's main repository for modern art, brings art lovers up to date with some of Europe's most exciting and challenging work. The Stedelijk was reopened in 2013 after years of renovation, it has been expanded with the addition of a distinctive new white wing on the Museumplein.

Dutch aristocrat Sophia de Bruijn-Suasso bequeathed hundreds of clocks, pieces of jewellery and oddments to the city. Faced at the same time with calls for a contemporary arts venue, the city decided to combine the two under the same roof, and the Stedelijk was built in 1895, to a design by AW Weissmann. Modern art gained the upper hand, and the de Bruijn-Suasso collection was gradually dispersed to other collections. After World War II, Willem Sandberg became curator and placed Amsterdam in general, and the Stedelijk in particular, in the vanguard of modernism. The collection includes works by Matisse, Picasso, Mondrian and Chagall, plus those associated with the Danish CoBrA group and the Dutch De Stijl tradition.

Showcasing the Collection

The renovations have included a major extension, adding over 50 per cent more space to the existing building – space that was desperately needed to house and proudly showcase the museum's massive collection. Part of the new extension includes a covered entrance on Museumplein. This futuristic white "bathtub" building, as it's locally referred to, is made of material used in the aviation industry. The designers are the Benthem Crouwel architects, who are also responsible for the airy Schiphol Plaza and the extension of the Anne Frank Huis. Also new to the museum are various

Entrance to the Stedelijk, popularly known as the "bathtub"

The museum specialises primarily in modern art

outdoor exhibits, a huge library, a subterranean exhibition hall and a museum shop. Along with the renovations, the museum has also digitalized all its historical archives that date back as far as the 19th century. The archives consisted of over 1,500,000 paper documents and state-of-the-art software was created for this enormous project. The museum can now fully utilize the content of its archives and ex-hibitions, and frequently offers programmes that include lectures, performances and film presentations. Visit their website to check the current list of events.

TAKING A BREAK

The museum has a large new **terraced café,** designed by Gilian Schrofer. Located on the first floor of the old building is a bright little **coffee shop,** also designed by Schrofer. Another option is to head for the cafés and restaurants around the Museumplein.

🚹 208 E3
✉ Museumplein 10 ☎ 020 573 2911; www.stedelijk.nl
🕐 Tue–Sun 10–5, Thu 10–10 🍴 Cafés (€/€€)
🚌 2, 5, 12
✋ €15; Museumkaart and I amsterdam City Card holders free

INSIDER INFO

- The museum's **new entrance** is on the glass facade section that faces the Museumplein. Here, visitors enter the dramatic new extension, which houses temporary exhibitions, the shop and a restaurant.
- During major exhibitions the queue can be long so avoid the wait and **purchase your ticket online**. If you have a *Museumkaart* you need to first collect a free ticket from a vending machine or at the museum checkout. Hold onto your ticket as you can reuse and enter the museum as often as you wish on the day.
- One curiosity is the **Appelbar** – a coffee bar that was adorned with murals in 1951 by the Dutch artist Karel Appel.

⭐8 Vondelpark

Even in a green city such as Amsterdam, with no less than 30 parks, Vondelpark stands out. This 45ha (110 acre) area attracts 10 million visitors each year. Locals and tourists alike flock to the large green "lung" to relax and to enjoy its many recreational facilities, which include a theatre, rose garden and a welcome sprinkling of cafés.

Like much of Amsterdam, Vondelpark lies on a limb of reclaimed land situated below sea level. Within the canal ring, there is no room for a substantial open space, so the long, narrow patch of green appears on the map in the shape of a cricket bat, with its handle pressed up against Singelgracht and the other end resting on Amstelveenseweg, nearly 2km (1.25 miles) away.

Another side of Amsterdam – the wide open spaces of Vondelpark

It is a robustly urban park, in which you will find a microcosm of Amsterdam life: families picnicking while rollerbladers race by, and prim dowagers walking poodles past a haze of dope-smokers, though these days you are unlikely to find hippies camping. But this is more than a study in people-watching: you can walk through a rose garden, splash around in the wading pool or enjoy an open-air concert.

English-style Design
British visitors may feel particularly at home, because the layout is similar to many UK city parks. LD Zocher

deliberately imposed this fairly plain style, augmented with plenty of ponds, in his plans for a "horseback riding and strolling park". When Vondelpark opened in 1865, as a public area for horseback riding and strolling, three of its sides faced open countryside. Soon, though, rich residents moved out to enjoy the fresher air: Vondelpark is conveniently southwest of the city centre, the direction from which the prevailing wind blows.

A Walk in the Park

The best way to get to Vondelpark is through the entrance that faces Singelgracht. It is most easily approached from Max Euweplein, the modern complex just south of Leidseplein. There is a bicycle path cutting through it, past the giant chess set, and over a bridge. Cross the busy Stadhouderskade, and you are at the original iron gates at the narrow end of the park.

About 400m in, **Eerste Constantijn Huygensstraat** (the name is nearly as long as the street) leaps across the neck of the Vondelpark. Just before the bridge, on the right (north), is the city's main official **youth hostel** (➤ 43), which was born from the gaunt skeleton of an old school building. Directly opposite, across the park, stands the **Flying Pig,** a newer and more liberal competitor. Beyond the bridge, the park broadens, and the first water feature appears: a serpentine **pond** that snakes for 400m to the heart of the park.

Museum Quarter

Bear right for the Vondelpark **Pavilion**, the elegant, unmistakable building designed by PJ Hamer and his son W Hamer in Italian Renaissance style in 1881. The pavilion has a large elevated veranda and three gracefully decorated dining rooms, which include a French Room in Louis XIV style and a Japanese Room. Embellishments such as the wide-eyed maidens flanking the stairways are Hamer's, but the "new" interior was part of the art deco fixtures that had been taken out of the Cinema Parisien, which had originally opened in 1910. When Amsterdam's first movie house faced demolition in the 1980s, as much as could feasibly be resurrected was reassembled within the pavilion, then home to the Filmmuseum (now part of the EYE Film Instituut Nederland and located on the northern bank of the IJ River).

Honouring a Playwright and Poet

Of all the many citizens whose names could be applied to Amsterdam's most ambitious park, it is telling that the one chosen was the poet Joost van den Vondel. He was a contemporary of Rembrandt, who is commemorated in the smaller and tackier Rembrandtplein. Vondel was writing plays at the same time as Shakespeare, though with considerably less success and durability. Nevertheless, a grand **statue** has him presiding over his park, on the tongue of land opposite the pavilion.

Joost van den Vondel was a Dutch national poet, unusually known for his satires of Calvinism, the state religion

Threading through the centre of the park, the obvious refreshment stop is the **'t Blauwe Theehuis** (The Blue Tea House ➤ 137), a café-turned-flying saucer that has fallen to earth opposite the bandstand. Next door, the **Openluchttheater** (Open-Air Theatre, ➤ 140) has a busy summer programme of free performances. A second refreshment stop, the **Melkhuis**, has both a large terrace overlooking the water and a brasserie and self-service section; the latter has less style but better coffee and cakes than the Blue Tea House.

Stay on the south side of the park, and make your way to the 🚻 **wading pool**, in the summer it is usually full of children splashing around. Just beyond it is the **Rose Garden.** The succession of hexagonal flowerbeds looks superb in summer, although it is disappointingly drab in winter.

Continue in a westerly direction, and you pass the closest thing Vondelpark has to a waterfall: a sculpture called *Cascade,* with water washing over some rocks. There is much ongoing restoration work at the western end of the park: this is being allowed to grow wilder, with hopes that the sorts of creatures that inhabited the original marshland will return. Information displays explain the steps being taken, and the aspirations of the project.

Another sculpture of interest is *The Fish* (1965), by Pablo Picasso, donated for the park's centennial in 1965 by the Spanish artist. The large stone piece stands in a field in the middle of the park, appropriately called the Picasso Meadow, it makes for a perfect location for picnics and people-watching on a warm sunny day.

There is one last opportunity for refreshment at the **Vondeltuin** (Vondelpark 7, tel: 06 27 56 55 76, April–Oct daily 9–6), a thatched café at the southwest corner, before you emerge on to Amstelveenseweg – or the other way around, and head back towards the city centre.

TAKING A BREAK

If you don't want to stop at Vondeltuin or 't Blauwe Theehuis, put together a picnic; there are several branches of Albert Heijn around the park, the closest two on Overtoom.

✚ 208 B2

INSIDER INFO

- Given the size of the Vondelpark, you may wish to **rent a bicycle** (➤ 28), there is a branch of Mac Bike (macbike.nl) nearby at Weteringschans.
- Trams 2 and 5 stop outside the park's **eastern entrance**; tram 2 stops outside the **southwestern entrance**.
- Vondelpark is excellent for **bird-watching**. Look out for herons, cormorants, swans, and even a colony of parrots camouflaged among the trees.

At Your Leisure

26 Coster Diamonds

One of Amsterdam's leading diamond-polishing factories sits snugly next to the Rijksmuseum and along the road from the Van Gogh Museum, and operates regular 45-minute tours devoted to the hardest mineral in the world.

The experience begins in an exhibition space that includes replicas of some of the world's most celebrated diamonds, such as the Koh-i-Noor and the Cullinan. The most interesting part of the tour is seeing the diamond cutters: you can peer right over their lathes to watch the intricate process as they grind each facet.

Each tour group is then ushered into one of·the "private rooms" for an explanation of the way that diamonds are assessed and graded. Trays of rings are brought out for inspection. It's an opportunity for you to ask questions – and for the guide to sell.

Coster Diamonds has opened a museum, the Diamant Museum Amsterdam, at Paulus Potterstraat 8. It explains how diamonds are made, where they are found, and the four Cs that determine their quality – carat, clarity, colour and cut. There are also fun touches:

an interactive screen allows you to crown yourself, and inside a room-sized diamond you are bombarded with images selling the glamour of diamonds.

➕ 204 B2
✉ Paulus Potterstraat 2–8
☎ 020 3 05 55 55;
www.diamantmuseumamsterdam.nl
◷ Tours and museum: daily 9–5
🚊 2, 5 💶 €7.50

An expert examines a diamond at Coster Diamonds

DIAMOND LIFE

Most of the world's diamonds are mined in equatorial regions, or well inside the southern hemisphere, but trade in the gems is largely controlled by the London office of De Beers. When the first diamonds from India arrived in Europe in the 15th century, they were cut in Bruges, but with that city's decline the industry moved to Antwerp – where the centre of the trade remains today. Amsterdam became significant after the Habsburg Spanish took Antwerp in 1589 and thousands of Protestant and Jewish merchants fled north. Even when Antwerp's diamond trade was re-established, enough traders stayed in Amsterdam for there to develop a considerable industry. For a time, the diamond trade was one of the few businesses open to Jewish people in the Netherlands. Today, the city is a distant second to Antwerp – now in competition, too, with India, source of many of the rough diamonds, and also developing a trading role.

27 Museumplein

The name means "Museum Square" but it is actually more of a park, thanks partly to a complete redesign in 2000. The apron of green that spreads out southwest from the Rijksmuseum is more than just a patch of open space with museums scattered around – and much more than it was in the early 1990s, when a wide, fast road sped straight down the middle of the park on the axis of the Rijksmuseum tunnel. Much to the relief of locals and tourists, the road has been replaced with a long, narrow pond (providing splendid photographic reflections of the Rijksmuseum on sunny afternoons) and plenty of lawn.

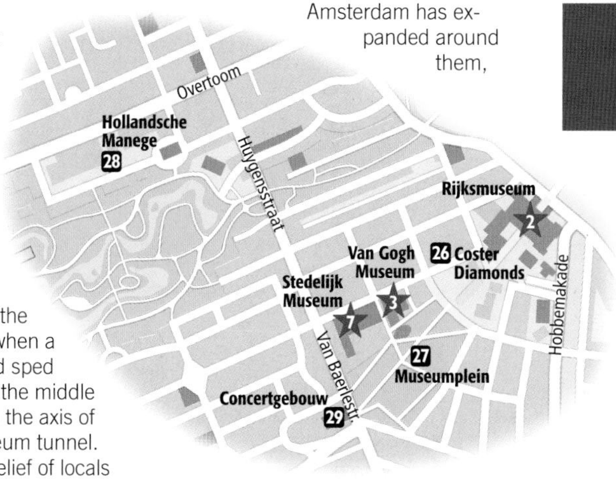

➕ 204 B1
🚊 2, 5 (northern corner); 16 (southern corner); 3, 5, 12 (Van Baerlestraat, on southwest edge)

28 Hollandsche Manege

The design of these fine stables, by AL Van Gendt, was heavily influenced by the Spanish Riding School in Vienna. They were built in 1882, when the location was positively rural; gradually Amsterdam has expanded around them,

A grassy vista of Museumplein, with the Rijksmuseum in the background

but their character has remained intact.

From the street, the entrance looks rather forbidding, but you can wander in and 👥 survey the arena from the balcony; and you can also watch the horses from the comfort of the opulent café.

➕ 208 off D1
✉ Vondelstraat 140
☎ 020 6 18 09 42; www.dehollandschemanege.nl
🕐 Daily 9–5 🍴 Café (€)
🚊 1 (Overtoom, one block north) ♿ €8

Map labels: Overtoom · Hollandsche Manege 28 · Huygensstraat · Rijksmuseum · Van Gogh Museum · 26 Coster Diamonds · Stedelijk Museum · Hobbemakade · Van Baerlestraat · 27 Museumplein · Concertgebouw 29

Museum Quarter

29 Concertgebouw

Amsterdam has always had a problem with monuments – or, rather, the lack of them. Towards the end of the 19th century efforts were made to add grandeur to the city: the Rijksmuseum and Centraal Station were two results, and another was the Concertgebouw, the city's first substantial performance venue.

PJH Cuypers, who built the first two icons, also chaired the design committee for the Concertgebouw, which explains why the design of the architect, AL Van Gendt, complements that of the Rijksmuseum.

On Wednesday lunchtimes, there is a short free concert. The performances are laid on in both the Grote Zaal (Great Hall), which has superb acoustics, and the Kleine Zaal (Recital Hall).

✚ 202 D2 ✉ Concertgebouwplein 2–6
☎ 020 6 71 83 45; www.concertgebouw.nl
🚋 3, 5, 12, 16

30 Hilton Hotel

Like other properties in the Hilton hotel chain, Amsterdam's version is visually uninspiring: a 1960s block awkwardly parked on a bend of the Noorder Amstelkanaal. The plan of the hotel mirrors the kink in the canal.

People do not come here to look at the architecture, however. They are here either to stay in one of the 271 rooms, or to make a pilgrimage to an important venue

Concertgebouw concert hall lit up at night

on the Lennon trail. Here, in March 1969, John Lennon and Yoko Ono checked into what is now room 702, and arranged for all the furniture except the bed to be removed. They then invited the world's media to witness their "bed-in for peace". The event was later immortalized in The Beatles' hit *The Ballad of John and Yoko*; the lyrics were written here.

Yoko revisited in 1991 and the bedroom was given a hippy-chic makeover. The bed has been left where it was, but the rest has been turned into something of a shrine, with drawings on the ceiling supposedly inspired by the lyrics to Imagine. To see it, you need to book it – at €1,000 or so per night.

✚ 208 C1 ✉ Apollolaan 138
☎ 020 7 10 60 00; www.hilton.com
🚋 16 (De Lairessestraat, two blocks north)

Where to...
Eat and Drink

Prices
Expect to pay per person for a three-course meal, excluding drinks and service:
€ under €20   €€ €20–€40   €€€ over €40

CAFÉS AND BARS

't Blauwe Theehuis €
This 1930s blue-and-white, pagoda-like structure is in the heart of Vondelpark, surrounded by mature trees and waterways. The interior is quite small with most of the seating outdoors, either on the large ground floor terrace or on the balcony upstairs. There are self-service sandwiches, muffins and snacks.

🔳 208 B2
✉ Vondelpark 5
☎ 020 6 62 02 54; www.blauwetheehuis.nl
🕔 Mon–Fri 9–6, Sat, Sun 9–8

Bakkerswinkel €
The "bakery", one of several in Amsterdam, has comfortable chairs and an inviting atmosphere. During lunch they serve sandwiches, salads and soups, while the afternoon selection includes delicious cheesecake, scones and other tasty home-made treats. Try the *karnejus* drink, a blend of buttermilk and fresh orange juice.

🔳 208 E3
✉ Roelof Hartstraat 68
☎ 020 6 62 35 94; www.bakkerswinkel.nl
🕔 Tue–Sat 7:30–5, Sun 9–4

Café Loetje €
This popular *eetcafé* (➤ 32) is serving some of Amsterdam's best steaks. During the summer the large outdoor patio is packed with professionals and hungry students. Inside is cosy and lively and although the menu is in Dutch, written daily on a chalkboard on the wall, the staff will be happy to translate it and make recommendations for you.

🔳 208 E3
✉ Johannes Vermeerstraat 52
☎ 020 6 62 81 73; www.cafeloetje.nl
🕔 Mon–Fri 11am–midnight, Sat 5pm–midnight

Caffepc €€
An ultra-modern café on Amsterdam's smartest shopping street, Caffepc is just the place for a state-of-the-art sandwich or salad washed down with champagne. Enjoy tapas, nibble a delicious cake or tuck in to some more substantial fare while sitting in a leather booth surrounded by wood panelling. Mellow music plays in the background.

🔳 204 A2
✉ Pieter Cornelisz Hooftstraat 87
☎ 020 6 73 47 52; www.unlimitedlabel.com
🕔 Sun–Mon 10–7, Tue–Wed 8:30–7, Thu 8:30–10, Fri–Sat 8:30–8

Cobra €€
This modern café on Museumplein takes its name from a late-1940s expressionist art movement in which painters from Copenhagen, Brussels and Amsterdam (CoBrA) played a leading role. Everything from the pattern on the floor to the crockery on the tables is inspired by the movement. However, if the weather's fine you may prefer to sit outside.

🔳 204 C1
✉ Hobbemastraat 18
☎ 020 4 70 01 11; www.cobracafe.nl
🕔 Daily 10–3

👥 Kinderkookkafé €

This unique children's café is housed in a converted cowshed on the northern side of Vondelpark. It has a big outdoor terrace and play area. You can pop into the café with the family for a snack – the children prepare and decorate their own food, such as pizzas, sandwiches and cakes.

Alternatively, with children aged eight or older, call ahead and see if you can book them into a children's cookery class. Here they prepare a full lunch in the morning, which they then serve to their parents – surely, this has to be a good thing?

✚ 208 C1
✉ Vondelpark 6B at Kattenlaan
☎ 020 6 25 32 57; www.kinderkookkafe.nl
🕓 Daily 10–5

Welling €

This is one of the few traditional drinking spots in this part of the city. Welling delights in being a slightly genteel brown corner café that is behind, and derives much of its trade from, the Concertgebouw.

✚ 208 E2
✉ JW Brouwersstraat 32
☎ 020 6 62 01 55; www.cafewelling.nl
🕓 Sun–Thu 4–1, Fri–Sat 3–2

Wildschut €/€€

This off-the-tourist-track art deco grand café (► 33) is a five-minute walk south of the Concertgebouw. Its long, curved front forms part of a 1920s Amsterdam School of architecture square that you can admire from a large outdoor terrace (although there is usually a considerable amount of traffic on Roelof Hartplein). Lunches concentrate on good sandwiches, while more substantial dishes, such as steak, are on offer in the evening. Extensive snacks options are available all day.

✚ 208 E3 ✉ Roelof Hartplein 1–3
☎ 020 6 76 82 20; www.cafewildschut.nl
🕓 Mon–Fri 9am–1am, Sat, Sun 10am –1am

RESTAURANTS

Bark €€/€€€

A busy fish bistro close to the Concertgebouw that delivers swift service and takes orders later than usual. Choose from oysters or a platter of *fruits de mer* or try a more creative dish such as duck with apple syrup. Its more meat-oriented sister, De Knijp, at No 134 (tel: 020 6 71 4248), is similar in style.

✚ 208 E2
✉ Van Baerlestraat 120
☎ 020 6 75 02 10; www.bark.nl
🕓 Mon–Fri noon–3, 5:30–12:30, Sat, Sun noon–12:30am

Blue Pepper €€€

At one of Amsterdam's best Indonesian restaurants, diners face something of an assault on their senses: bright blue walls, elaborate plates, white orchids and excellent, innovative cuisine. Make the staff aware of your spice requirements and follow their advice – and try not to miss the sticky rice ice cream with coconut pancakes.

✚ 204 A3
✉ Nassaukade 366 ☎ 020 489 7039; www.restaurantbluepepper.com
🕓 Daily 6pm–10pm

Café De Toog €/€€

Off the tourist path (take Gerard Brandtstraat going away from Vondelpark, turn right on to Eerste Helmersstraat), this lively, informal restaurant is housed in a traditional building dating from 1890. The global menu might include warm Thai beef salad or venison steak with cranberry sauce. There are three eating areas. Big windows ensure that the lower levels are kept bright.

✚ 208 C1
✉ Nicolaas Beetsstraat 142
☎ 020 6 18 50 17; www.cafedetoog.com
🕓 Mon–Thu 3pm–1am, Fri 3–3, Sat noon–3am, Sun noon–1am

Le Garage €€€

Once a backstreet garage near Vondelpark, this is one of the city's most glamorous restaurants. Behind an open-plan kitchen and sleek bar lies a dining area of mirrored walls and red banquettes. Most dishes, such as *fruits de mer* and *rôtisserie* meats, are French. Other international dishes also appear, such as Dutch chicory with smoked eel and Thai salad. Book well ahead and dress to impress.

✚ 208 C3
✉ Ruysdaelstraat 54–56
☎ 020 6 79 71 76; www.restaurantlegarage.nl
◉ Mon–Fri noon–11, Sat, Sun 6–11

Momo €€

Billed as a Pan-Asian restaurant, Momo is more eclectic than that. Start with South American *ceviche,* Alaskan King crab or Japanese sushi, all accompanied with delicious sauces. Although the interior and diners can be showy, the waiting staff are friendly.

✚ 204 B2
✉ Hobbemastraat 1
☎ 020 6 71 74 74; www.momo-amsterdam.com
◉ Daily 10am–1am (bar); 12pm–2:30pm (lunch), 6pm–10:30pm (dinner)

Where to…
Shop

The Museum Quarter not only has priceless objects to look at. It is *the* place to spend a fortune, or to watch others spend theirs, in exclusive boutiques dedicated to the creations of Dutch and international fashion designers, or at Coster Diamonds (➤ 134).

PC HOOFTSTRAAT

Amsterdam's smartest shopping area, named after the 17th-century poet Pieter Cornelisz Hooft, fills the three compact blocks between Hobbemastraat and Van Baerlestraat. You may consider the boutiques to be too intimidating to enter, but their window displays are often as striking, and their goods almost as costly, as the art on show in the museums just round the corner, so it's fun to have a look.

Gucci (Nos 56–58, tel: 020 6 62 51 84, www.gucci.com) often has eye-catching displays. Others worth a peek on this (north) side of the street include **Shoebaloo** (No 80, tel: 020 6 71 22 10, www.shoebaloo.nl), for head-turning footwear in a futuristic interior; **Anne Fontaine** (No 92) for a huge selection of her signature white women's blouses.

On the south side, check out: **Emporio Armani** (No 39) for classic design; **Oger** (No 81, www.oger.nl), for ultra-conservative menswear; and **Supertrash** (No 31, www.supertrash.com) for trendy, affordable women's fashion with a hint of glamour. And if you are after something other than clothing, visit **Schaap & Citroen** (No 40, www.schaapcitroen.nl) one of the leading Dutch jewellers.

Lifestyle (No 116, tel: 020 4 70 99 13, www.lifestyle94.com) is specializing in furniture and interior decorations.

Just off the top of PC Hooftstraat, **Romeo Vetro** (Hobbemastraat No 11, tel: 020 4 70 27 05, www.romeovetro.com) has outlandish glassware blown into the shape of musical instruments, dolphins and boats. Off the western end of PC Hooftstraat, on Van Baerlestraat, are more trendy clothes boutiques, such as **Sissy Boy** (No 15, tel: 020 6 71 51 74, www.sissy-boy.nl).

CORNELIS SCHUYTSTRAAT

Well off the tourist path, this street caters for well-heeled locals.

Museum Quarter

Among the artistic flower shops and chic boutiques are several cafés with outdoor seating to show off your latest buys. Put together a great picnic at the organic **Food for You** (No 26, tel: 020 3 79 51 95, www.organicfoodfor you.nl) and the classy pâtisserie, **Van Avezaath** (No 36, tel: 020 6 62 08 91, www.vanavezaath-beune.nl), to take to Vondelpark at the end of the street.

Insider Tip

MUSEUM SHOPS

The big museums all have good shops. The **Van Gogh Museum** offers a good selection of posters and items such as lunch-boxes with sunflowers and watches decorated with Van Gogh land-scapes. A one-stop tourist shop on Museumplein also does a good line in Rembrandt and Van Gogh jigsaws, umbrellas and fridge magnets.

Inside the **Rijksmuseum,** the shop on the first floor sells good reproduction works of Rembrandt, Vermeer, and other artists. They also have books, DVDs, jewellery and toys.

Where to...
Go Out

The Museum Quarter has a lack of atmospheric cafés and, after dark, is sedate and dull, without the appeal of the city's more central districts. However, on fine days, Vondelpark and the Museumplein, the grassy square backing on to the museums, are pleasant places to spend time in; street musicians usually provide some entertainment.

The area's main cultural attraction is the **Concertgebouw**

(Concertgebouwplein 2–6, tel: 020 6 71 83 45, www.concert gebouw.nl, ► 136), the most important venue for classical music in Amsterdam, which also has a full programme of jazz and world music performance. Home to the Royal Concertgebouw Orchestra, the grand neoclassical building lords it over the south-western side of Museumplein. As well as evening performances, there are Sunday morning con-certs (and a backstage tour for which you pay a small extra charge).

Thanks in no small part to the presence of the Concertgebouw, **Van Baerlestraat** has several good restaurants, and is the Museum Quarter's liveliest street at night.

One late-night option along Van Baerlestraat, at No 128, is **Café Lusthof** (tel: 020 6 62 82 89, www.cafelusthof.nl), which is a rather modest looking, but friendly brown café (► 30), that's popular with locals and tourists alike and stays open till at least 1am. Simple, hearty food and snacks are served all day.

Another option for nightlife, a little further away is **En Pluche** (Ruysdaelstraat 48, 020 4 71 46 95, www.enpluche.nl). This lounge bar is the perfect venue to spot local celebrities. Come here for cocktails, and nibble on Asian-inspired streetfood, burgers or fish and chips.

Many Amsterdammers hang out in Vondelpark on summer evenings. From the end of May to late August, the **Openluchttheater**, the open-air theatre (www.open luchttheater.nl), lays on free evening performances, includ-ing jazz, rock and classical music, children's theatre and stand-up comedy. On Friday nights in summer, DJs appear at **'t Blauwe Theehuis** (► 137) in Vondelpark.

Canal Ring – East

 **Little Treats**

Concerts by candlelight
The **Portuguese Synagogue** (► 157) regularly hosts atmospheric concerts by candlelight, a truly memorable experience.

Sumptuous cinema experience
Treat yourself and your sweetheart to a box with love seat in the magnificent art deco **Tuschinski Theater** (► 166).

Summer sunsets
One of the best places to enjoy the last rays of the setting sun is from the **Muziekgebouw aan 't IJ** (► 178) café terrace.

Getting Your Bearings

The eastern side of Amsterdam offers real urban diversity. It encompasses the wealthy Plantage neighbourhood, the multi-cultural De Pijp district, the trendy Eastern Docklands – and it also has some fascinating museums.

Hermitage Amsterdam and the recently revamped Het Scheepvaart Museum have really put this part of town on the map. But there are also some smaller, more unusual museums on offer, such as the Museum of Bags and Purses and the Museum of the Canals, the latter housed in a stately canalside mansion. Here you'll also find the city zoo, the Botanical Gardens and the beautiful Portuguese Synagogue.

Amstel

**Tassenmuseum
Hendrikje** 37

35 **Museum
Van Loon**

Vijzelstraat

Wetering-
circuit

31 **Heineken
Experience**

View of the Het
Scheepvaart
Museum
and the *De
Amsterdam*

The New Guinea
Gallery at the
Tropenmuseum

The Perfect Day

If you're not quite sure where to begin your travels, this itinerary recommends a practical and enjoyable day out in the eastern canal ring taking in some of the best places to see. For more information see the main entries (➤ 146–160).

🕘 9:00am

Wander through the quiet streets of the eastern canal ring to the Amstel River, to see the prosaic sluice gates and the pretty **36 Magere Brug** ("Skinny Bridge", above, ➤ 156).

🕙 10:00am

Be among the first visitors at the splendid **32 Hermitage Amsterdam** (➤ 150).

🕐 1:00pm

Have lunch at the brasserie of the **Amstel Intercontinental** (➤ 162). You might consider returning here for afternoon tea under the chandeliers in the glass conservatory.

🕝 2:30pm

Walk along the Amstel River and then turn into **Nieuwe Herengracht** (➤ 183)

🕝 2:30pm

Take a break to explore the collections of greenhouses and rare and exotic flora at the **34 Hortus Botanicus** gardens (right, ➤ 154) or the fauna at **Artis Zoo** (➤ 154).

🕐 5:00pm

Have some light-hearted fun at the **③① Heineken Experience** (➤148) with an introduction to the art and science of brewing, and perhaps a glass of beer.

🕐 7:00pm

Splash out on a Michelin-starred meal at one of two restaurants in the **Okura Hotel** – either traditional Japanese at Yamazato (➤164) next to a garden, or French haute cuisine at Ciel Bleu on the top floor, where you can also enjoy a magnificent view over Amsterdam (➤163).

Joods Historisch Museum
Portugees Israëlietische Synagoge
Tassenmuseum Hendrikje
ARCAM ④② 🌟 **Scheepvaart Museum**
④① **Entrepotdok**
④⓪ **Verzetsmuseum**
③③ ③⑧
③⑦ ③⑨ ③②
③④ **Hortus Botanicus**
Hermitage Amsterdam
Museum Van Loon ③⑤
③⑥
④③ **Tropen-museum**
Magere Brug
Museum Willet-Holthuysen
③① **Heineken Experience**

🕐 9:00pm

Soak up the views over the water near the **Eastern Docklands** (➤178), then sit back and let the sounds of some jazz at the Bimhuis (➤166) or classical music at the **Muziekgebouw aan 't IJ** (➤178) wash over you.

⭐ Het Scheepvaart Museum

Formerly a naval storehouse dating back to 1656, the superb National Maritime Museum's extensive collection of maritime memorabilia tells how Amsterdam became the world's most important port: the hub of a merchant fleet that instigated and controlled a large proportion of global trade.

The museum building itself is most attractive, and is worth admiring from science center NEMO (►73) to appreciate the simplicity and symmetry of the former naval arsenal.

The Het Scheepvaart Museum was once a naval arsenal

History of Shipping and Trade

In terms of the collection, much is made of 17th- and 18th-century shipping, the golden age of Amsterdam's merchant fleet as well as its cultural life. There are several paintings of famous Dutch naval victories. Among the more compelling exhibits is a map of the world drawn in 1648 with evidence that the Dutch knew about Australia long before Captain Cook. It appears on the map marked *"Hollandia Nova, detecta 1644"*. There are also impressive models of ships – plus some real ones, including an 18th-century barge in fine condition.

By the 19th century, commerce and technology were racing ahead. There were highly effective workaday sailing vessels, nicknamed "butter boxes", in action, and techniques for high-speed, wind-powered shipping were being perfected.

For about half a century, the clipper enjoyed its own golden age. The steamship was in development, but was proving slower. The completion of the Suez Canal in 1869 changed all the rules, and soon sank, in commercial terms, the clipper fleets.

The Netherlands re-emerged rapidly as a maritime force with the development of shipping companies such as the Holland-America Line. A network of routes sprang up: some of them linked the Dutch colonies with the mother country, while others exploited gaps in the global market for links between other nations. All these developments and more are detailed in interactive and static displays, with many of the newer exhibits being aimed squarely at children.

🎎 De Amsterdam

A full-size replica of *De Amsterdam*, a tall ship belonging to the Dutch East India Company, is moored outside the museum. You can crawl all over the bridge, the hold and the living quarters. The original 18th-century ship was built to transport weapons, silver and gold coins, and building materials to trade with in the East Indies. The maiden voyage commenced in late 1748 but the ship never made it past the English Channel due to a severe storm. She still rests in the mud, with much of the cargo still on board. The wreck site is currently protected with hopes for excavation in the future.

TAKING A BREAK

The museum's **Restaurant Stalpaert** offers simple but good sandwiches, soups and salads. The restaurant has a sunny terrace overlooking the water for warmer days.

🚩 207 D3
✉ Kattenburgerplein 1
☎ 020 5 23 22 22; www.hetscheepvaartmuseum.nl
🕐 Daily 9–5
🚌 22, 42, 43 🚉 Centraal Station is a brisk 15-minute walk away
💶 €15; Museumkaart and I amsterdam City Card holders free

INSIDER INFO

- During the summer actors in **period costume** perform on aboard *De Amsterdam*.
- Aboard the ship, **mind your head** on the low beams unless you are under 1m (3 feet 4 inches) tall.
- During the 2011 renovation the museum's inner courtyard was covered by a glass and steel lattice roof. The structure itself is quite remarkable as the **delicate design** is based on the compass rose shown on old nautical charts. For purposes of conservation it was only allowed to touch the original building at four points.

31 Heineken Experience

From outside, little suggests that the interior of this former brewery on the Stadhouderskade – owned by the leading Dutch beer maker – has been gutted and turned into one of Amsterdam's more offbeat, but undeniably popular, tourist attractions. While beer is no longer brewed here, the interactive tour of the old brewery will give you all the information you need to know about beer.

In December 1864, Gerard Adriaan Heineken bought a decrepit 16th-century brewery called De Hooiberg (the Haystack), which stood behind the Royal Palace. Over the next four years, he moved production to a new site which was, at the time, in open fields south of the centre. Besides introducing the Czech technique of bottom fermentation and overseeing the development of a robust strain of yeast, Mr Heineken established rigorous quality control and innovative marketing techniques – not least the red star logo – that created the conditions for successful mass production. Today, the main Heineken brewery can produce a bottle of beer for Amsterdam's whole population every 45 minutes.

The (former) brewery *(brouwerij)* is the unpretentious old red-brick building that dominates the corner of Stadhouderskade and Ferdinand Bolstraat. Heineken lager was brewed here until 1988, when production moved out and replaced with an interactive exhibition about beer production.

Entertaining and interactive: the Heineken Experience

INSIDER INFO

- Your admission charge includes coupons for a Heineken or two (or soft drinks, if you're not here just for the free beer). To avoid queuing, book online in advance.
- It's well worth combining a visit to the Heineken Experience with a **canal cruise.** These cruises start from just across Stadhouderskade, opposite the main entrance (► 88).
- The "Stable Walk" on level 2 takes visitors into the secret world of the working stables. Meet the **magnificent shire horses** up close that still deliver Heineken beer to some parts of the Netherlands.

Part of the original complex was demolished, and the redesigned "visitor experience" brewery was opened to the public in 1991. It was further refurbished and upgraded in 2001 and again in 2008. Some of the original equipment, such as malt silos and mash coppers, was incorporated into the development, but most of the Heineken Experience has been specifically created for visitors.

The Exhibition

The entrance fee includes two drinks – either Heineken or a soft drink – at one of the two bars. At the entrance level, visitors are shown some of the **history of the brand** and can even bottle their own, featuring their message on the label. A shop on this level is full of Heineken products of all descriptions. Level 1 features a gallery of **advertising past and present** as well as some of the company's sporting sponsors. Don't miss the chance to make you very own **music video** on level 2, where the historic brewing room is found, along with the **"Innovation Station",** showing the development of the beer and brand. The highlight is **"Brew U"** on level 3, where you experience the brewing process from the point of view of a bottle. This interactive journey seems to put a smile on everyone's face.

TAKING A BREAK

The **World Bar,** with photographs of panoramic views from around the world, is on the ground floor and there is a tasting bar on level 3 where you can use your free drinks tokens (see above). As both bars are part of the "Experience", neither serve food but the surrounding area of De Pijp is full of cheap eateries.

✚ 205 D1
✉ Stadhouderskade 78
☎ 020 5 23 94 35; www.heinekenexperience.com
🕐 Mon–Thu 11–7:30, Fri–Sun until 8:30
🚊 16, 24, 25
💶 €18

32 Hermitage Amsterdam

The first satellite of St Petersburg's Hermitage State Museum outside of Russia opened in Amsterdam on the banks of the Amstel River in 2009. On display are prestigious exhibitions of masterpieces from the main museum. And the building itself is also worth a visit.

Housed in the historic Amstelhof, built in the 17th century as a nursing home, the new museum is part of the Hermitage's commitment to show its dazzling collections around the globe. Peter the Great (1672–1725) visited Amsterdam in 1697, then the wealthiest city in the world, and was so impressed by its cultural aspects that he began his art collection.

World-class art collections are now exhibited in what was originally a shelter for the elderly

Touring Exhibitions

The Hermitage Amsterdam exhibitions change twice a year. Past exhibitions have included masterpieces by Gauguin, Bonnard and Denis as well as arts and crafts from the Russian court. There are usually also some additional smaller exhibitions.

Amstelhof

The exhibitions are not the only attraction; the historic Amstelhof – a square building around a large inner courtyard – is worth seeing on its own. In the exhibition

The Hermitage stages two temporary exhibitions each year

area there is little to indicate that the building originated in the 17th century, it has been refurbished in a very modern minimalistic style. Those who want to learn more about the Amstelhof's history will have to go to the west wing facing the river. That is the site of the former chapel, which was once one of the largest halls in Amsterdam and can now be used for formal receptions. As soon as one sees the spectacular view of the river, it is clear why it is such a popular venue. There are exhibitions dealing with the history of the Amstelhof, as well as Russian-Dutch relations, in the smaller, neighbouring rooms. And, don't forget to visit the old kitchen downstairs!

TAKING A BREAK

The stylish **Neva** restaurant (tel: 020 5 30 74 83, www.neva.nl, Tue–Sat 10am–1am, Sun–Mon 10–6) in the East wing offers a Russian-influenced menu. Otherwise, have a coffee or a glass of wine with a panoramic view of the museum courtyard.

➕ 206 B2 ✉ Amstel 51
☎ 020 5 30 74 88; www.hermitage.nl
🕐 Daily 10–5 🚌 4, 9, 14
🎫 €15; free to I amsterdam City Card holders

INSIDER INFO

- The restaurant is worth visiting even if you haven't been to the museum (daily 10–6).
- The **entrance** is located at the front of the building, at Ossenpoort (ox gate), the former tradesman's entrance on the Amstel River.
- **Concerts and lectures** are often held in the Church Hall.
- The courtyard that had been closed for centuries has been restored as a **green oasis** for all to enjoy. The peaceful garden was designed by landscape architect Michael van Gessel and now visitors can relax on seats, or on the stone perimeter around the lawn, and admire the 200-year-old chestnut trees.

㉝ Joods Historisch Museum

Steel and glass have been used to combine four neighbouring Ashkenazi synagogues – dating from 1670 to 1778 – into the Jewish Historical Museum, which does everything from explaining the tenets of Judaism to outlining the importance of Jewish people to the thriving business life in Amsterdam. The motto of the museum is taken from the Babylonian Talmud: "Seeing leads to remembering, remembering leads to the doing."

Pause outside on Nieuwe Amstelstraat to take in the fine structures that go to make up the museum. Outside, two large, yellow triangles have been hoisted high on a frame. Their shapes combine to form a golden Star of David, the symbol that Jewish people were obliged to wear by the occupying Nazis in World War II.

Founded in 1932, the museum was originally housed in *De Waag,* the old weigh house on Nieuwmarkt, which is now a café (➤ 75). The museum was closed during the German occupation and was only reopened in 1955. It moved to its current location in 1987.

The Great Synagogue

The centrepiece of the complex is the 18th-century **Great Synagogue,** which contains an introduction to Judaism and Jewish tradition. A permanent exhibition here explains the religion and its symbols. In a side room of the Great Synagogue, a bath is on display to explain the tradition of ritual purity for

The Holy Ark in the Great Synagogue is central to Jewish heritage in the city

The Star of David, the religious emblem of Judaism, stands tall outside the museum

women after menstruation or childbirth. It also explains how the bath was used as part of a ceremony for conversion to Judaism.

In the **galleries** on the upper level, the life of Jews in Amsterdam between 1600 and 1900 is revealed: even in this tolerant city, Jews often encountered anti-Semitism (► Jewish Amsterdam, 20–21).

The New Synagogue

The **New Synagogue** was built in 1752 to replicate what was believed to be the design of the Second Temple in Jerusalem, and the glorious dome was restored in 2000. The galleries here continue the story of Jewish life in the Netherlands from 1900 onwards. A ground-floor shop stocks Judaica and, upstairs, a new floor was added to house a purpose-built Print Room for fragile writings and drawings.

Dating from 1685 and originally used by less affluent worshippers, the **🔓 Obbene Shul** now houses a Children's Museum, geared to 8- to 12-year-olds.

The museum also looks at the growth of the Zionist movement, which began in the 19th century, calling for a permanent Jewish homeland in Israel.

TAKING A BREAK

The **Museum Café** has a reading table with Jewish magazines and cookbooks, and internet terminals linked to sites of Jewish interest.

🕂 206 B2
✉ Nieuwe Amstelstraat 1
☎ 020 5 31 03 80; www.jhm.nl
🕐 Daily 11–5. Closed Yom Kippur and Rosh Hashanah
🚇 Waterlooplein
🚌 9 and 14. The Canal Bus stops adjacent to the Blue Bridge, 200m west of the museum
✋ €12; free to under-13s and I amsterdam City Card holders

INSIDER INFO

- Beyond the cash desk, you can pick up a device for a **free audio tour**; this will add greatly to the experience.
- To find out more about the Jewish community in Amsterdam, you are free to use the **Resource Centre**, Monday to Friday 1 to 5pm.

㉞ Hortus Botanicus

The calm of the garden, coupled with the intensely pleasurable smell, will lift you gently out of the city. This is one of the oldest botanical gardens in the world, with more than 4,000 plant species.

The city's Botanical Garden began as a herbal collection – the *Hortus Medicus* – for pharmaceutical purposes, in 1638, and moved to its present location in 1682, expanding rapidly when the Dutch East India Company brought flora from expeditions across the globe.

The Modern Collection
The collection is divided into an outdoor garden, occupied by temperate or Arctic plants, and a series of greenhouses. On your left as you go in is a reconstruction of the original *Hortus Medicus* itself, containing all the plants listed in the first garden catalogue, written in 1646. Just beyond it is the **Mexican/Californian Desert House,** a nursery for **orchids** and a **butterfly house.** Just south, an elegant 17th-century semi-circular plot ripples out from the administration building.

Heading clockwise, you reach the beautiful **Palm House,** whose highlight is a 300-year-old cycad, still producing cones.

On the far side, the **Three Climates Greenhouse** is a late 20th-century addition, expertly constructed to allow you to weave between different climatic zones (tropical, subtropical and desert), on a sequence of paths. A highlight of the desert section is the *Welwitschia mirabilis,* the plant known as the "living fossil" because it can live for 2,000 years yet produces only two leaves in its entire life. The tropical section displays a Wardian case, an airtight wood-and-glass frame invented in 1829 by Englishman Nathaniel Bagshaw Ward to enhance the survival of rare tropical plants. Before its introduction, most plants died on the long sea journey to Amsterdam; afterwards, the survival rate increased to 99 per cent.

For a different view of the garden, follow the splendid walkway 5m (16ft) above the ground to explore the re-created rainforest canopy.

🐾 ARTIS ZOO
The curious name of Amsterdam's zoo derives from the Latin "Natura Artis Magistra", meaning "Nature is the teacher of art". Artis, as it is locally known, has a large butterfly pavilion, an attractive old aquarium, a planetarium, a geology museum, and an insectarium. Highlights include the sea lion training and feeding sessions, the Predator Gallery and the penguin enclosure. Highlights include the training and feeding of the sea lions, the penguin enclosure and the lemur island, where the lemurs jump around freely and almost eat out of your hand. In June, July and August there are often open-air concerts on Saturdays. ➕ 207 D2 ✉ Plantage Kerklaan 38–40 ☎ www.artis.nl 🕐 Mar–Oct 9–6, Nov–Feb until 5 🚊 9, 10, 14 💶 €19.50

The large and ornate palm house was built in 1912

TAKING A BREAK

Escape the heat of the greenhouses at the lovely **Orangery**, an airy, outdoor café dating back to 1875 and surrounded by rare and exotic plants. The café serves locally sourced, organic lunches, snacks and drinks.

➕ 206 C2 ✉ Plantage Middenlaan 2
☎ 020 6 25 90 21; www.dehortus.nl
⏱ Daily10–7 🍴 Orangery café (€)
🚊 9, 10, 14 💶 €8.50

INSIDER INFO

- The **garden entrance** is difficult to spot: it's concealed behind a gatehouse on the corner of Plantage Middenlaan and Dr D M Sluyspad, opposite the Nieuwe Herengracht.
- **Pick up a plan** in English at the door when you go in; labelling is mostly in Dutch and Latin.
- On Sundays there is a **tour at 2pm,** for which you pay a small extra charge.
- Summer weekends are very busy. The **early morning** is usually quieter, though the plants are not at their best on a hot summer's day.

At Your Leisure

35 Museum Van Loon

The beautifully preserved interior and exterior of this museum forms an important piece of Amsterdam's history. Designed by Adriaen Dortsman and built in 1672, this historic, double-fronted canal house became the home of the Van Loons in the 19th century. The family, who still own the house, were an influential lot, counting mayors, members of the Dutch East India Company. Don't miss the interesting video by one of the Van Loons, who wanders the house describing the various rooms (some are closed to the public) and relating tales of his relatives.

🔲 205 D3
✉ Keizersgracht 672
☎ 020 6 24 52 55; www.museumvanloon.nl
🕐 Wed–Mon 11–5 🚊 16, 24, 25
💶 €8; under-6s, Museumkaart and I amsterdam City Card holders free

36 Magere Brug

The "Skinny Bridge" is the most photographed bridge in Amsterdam. According to local legend, it was built for two sisters who were reluctant to take a circuitous route

The peaceful, formal garden at the Museum Van Loon

from their home on Kerkstraat, the west end of the present bridge, to the stables on the far bank of the Amstel River. One story says their surname was Mager, which means "skinny", after which the bridge is named; another attributes the title to the original design.

Either way, the first "Skinny Bridge" on this site was a simple wooden drawbridge. It was torn down in 1929 and was replaced by a replica based on the original design. From the south side, you

can look along the river to the sluice gates that are an essential part of the water management system in Amsterdam. These allow the canal network to be regularly flushed out.

⊞ 206 B1

🚊 4 to Utrechtsestraat, one block west

⅙7 Tassenmuseum Hendrikje

The Museum of Bags and Purses, housed in this grand canal house, is an extraordinary collection of Western bags from the Middle Ages through to now. There are 16th-century gaming purses, 17th-century chatelaines – chains on which well-to-do ladies hung their keys and bible – and an eye-popping array of 20th-century designs: look for ones shaped as magazines, phones and clocks.

Insider Tip

⊞ 205 E3

✉ Herengracht 573

☎ 020 5 24 64 52; www.tassenmuseum.nl

🕐 Daily 10–5 🍴 Museum café (€)

🚊 4, 9, 16, 24, 25 💶 €9

⅙8 Portugees Israëlietische Synagoge

The year 1492 was a highly significant one for Spain – not simply because Christopher Columbus, sailing on behalf of the Spanish Crown, landed in the New World, but because the country expelled its Jewish population. Some became Maranos ("crypto-Jews"), which allowed them to stay, but many of the Sephardic victims of the Inquisition moved to neighbouring Portugal.

When increased persecution forced Jewish people from both Iberian countries to seek sanctuary in Amsterdam, they called themselves "Portuguese Jews" – Spain was at war with the Netherlands at the time. Hence their new place of worship was called the "Portuguese Synagogue".

The designer was Elias Bouwman, who also built the Great Synagogue, now one of the components of the Jewish Historical Museum (➤ 152), which stands opposite. Unlike the museum, the Portuguese Synagogue is a functioning place of worship. There is tight security, and male visitors must wear a *yarmulke* – one can be borrowed from the cash desk.

Begin with the film in the introduction area which explains the growth of the Sephardic community in Amsterdam (in English and Dutch), visitors can then explore the treasure chambers before entering the main synagogue.

In spite of the Nazi occupation of Amsterdam, the synagogue miraculously survived

Canal Ring – East

When it was completed in 1675, it was the largest in Europe. Its wooden roof is supported by four massive columns; candles on large brass chandeliers provide the lighting. The Holy Ark is made from Brazilian jacaranda wood.

🕂 206 B2

✉ Mr Visserplein 3

☎ 020 6 24 53 51; www.portugesesynagoge.nl

🕓 Apr–Oct Sun–Thu 10–5, Fri until 4; Nov–March Sun–Thu 10–4, Fri until 2. Closed on Jewish holidays

🚇 Waterlooplein 🚋 9, 14

💳 €12; under 13s, Museumkaart and I amsterdam City Card holders free

39 Museum Willet-Holthuysen

Abraham Willet (1825–88) grew up in a wealthy family and became an avid art collector – he was so interested in art that he even dropped out of law school to devote him time to collecting art. In 1861 he married Louisa Holthuysen, a merchant's daughter, and together they decorated their 17th century house on Herengracht in the latest French fashion. In 1895 Holthuysen bequeathed the house to the city and it today you can admire the sumptuous residence in all its historic splendour. Particularly beautiful are the ballroom, and the ladies and gentlemen's salon

on the first floor, but also the small manicured garden.

🕂 206 A2 ✉ Herengracht 605

☎ 020 5 23 18 22; www.willetholthuysen.nl

🕓 Mon–Fri 10–5, Sat, Sun 11–5

💳 €8, Museumkaart and I amsterdam City Card holders free

40 Verzetsmuseum

The Nazi occupation of the Netherlands lasted five days short of five years, a traumatic time for Dutch people. Amsterdam, with easily the largest population of Jewish people, was the city that saw the most suffering – and the greatest resistance against the German forces. The Resistance

The Verzetsmuseum recalls Amsterdammers' fight against Nazi occupation, 1940–45

Museum's central purpose is to deal with the fight against the Nazi occupation from 1940 to 1945, but it encompasses much more, including the very great suffering in the Dutch East Indies under the Japanese reign of terror.

The museum is housed in the Plancius Building, built in 1876 as a social club for the Oefening Baart Kunst, a Jewish choral society. As well as temporary exhibitions, the permanent collection takes you back in time to the streets and houses of the war years.

The museum is an important complement to the Anne Frank House (➤ 96), describing the wider context of the grim game of hide-and-seek that took place during the occupation. Thousands of Jewish people were hidden by fellow citizens, while others were spirited out of the country or given false identities. The stirring events of February 1941, when a general strike was called in protest against a Nazi crackdown on Jewish people, are covered – as are the terrible "Hunger Winter" of 1944–45 and the incentives given to the Dutch who collaborated with the occupation force. Revealing a hiding place earned a reward of 7 guilders per person apprehended, a substantial sum in wartime Amsterdam.

➕ 207 D2

✉ Plantage Kerklaan 61

☎ 020 6 20 25 35; www.verzetsmuseum.org

🕐 Tue–Fri 10–5, Sat–Mon and public holidays 11–5. Closed 1 Jan, 26 April and 25 Dec

🚋 9 and 14 stop just outside Artis Zoo, diagonally across the road

💶 €8; Museumkaart and I amsterdam City Card holders free

🔢 Entrepotdok

In addition to the Eastern Docklands (➤ 178), other former docks are now being reclaimed as cafés, artists' studios and luxury housing. The Entrepotdok was Amsterdam's own "free port",

Many buildings at Entrepotdok have been preserved and are now highly sought after

a zone beyond the reach of the Custom authorities, where goods could be shipped in and out as long as they were not actually "landed" on Dutch territory. During the 19th century it became the richest dock in the city. With a southwest-facing waterfront, it is especially pleasant on summer afternoons.

➕ 201 D3

🚌 6 stops just outside Artis Zoo (➤ 154); from the opposite direction, the closest stop is on Plantage Middenlaan, one block south of the zoo entrance

💶 Free

🔢 ARCAM

To see the future face of Amsterdam, call in at this splendid Architecture Centre by the water overlooking Oosterdok. The startling, shiny building (finished in zinc-clad aluminium) rises from the water like a fragment of the much larger NEMO building (➤ 73) – which, indeed, is exactly how it started. The pavilion was originally used as the NEMO ticket office. After a major refurbishment, the Architecture Centre was opened in 2003.

Besides experiencing the space itself, you can also find out about the exciting developments taking place in and around the capital. To help you explore, the centre offers a booklet containing several walks around the rejuvenated Eastern Docklands (➤ 178).

⊕ 207 D3 ⊠ Prins Hendrikkade 600
☎ 020 6 20 48 78; www.arcam.nl
⊙ Tue–Sat 1–5 💷 Free 🚍 22

🔢 Tropenmuseum

Tucked away beyond Singelgracht, in the southeastern suburbs, this grand edifice is easily missed, despite its ornamented facade. The building is an eclectic, early 20th-century structure by J J and M A van Nieukerken, with the Gothic overtones seen in Centraal Station and the Rijksmuseum. It

opened in 1910 as home to the Vereeniging Koloniaal Instituut, now the Royal Tropical Institute. One of its duties is to run the most politically correct museum in Amsterdam. Its ethnographic collection – including modern and traditional visual arts and photography – is divided into several permanent displays. A free audio tour (available in English) talks you through the highlights of the collection.

Although much of the exhibition is grouped by geographical region – focusing largely, but by no means exclusively, on former Dutch colonies – it begins on the ground floor with a display on Man and Environment, with the emphasis on the destruction of the rainforest. The first floor, reached by a sweeping staircase, concentrates on Asia and Oceania, in particular India and its neighbours, and Indonesia. From the second floor, the museum's striking design is evident, with an arc of glass sweeping over the hall. This floor has exhibits on Latin America (especially the Caribbean and Suriname) and Africa. The Kartini wing houses 🔢 **Tropenmuseum Junior**, aimed at 6- to 12-year-olds.

⊕ 207 E1 ⊠ Linnaeusstraat 2
☎ 020 5 68 82 00; www.tropenmuseum.nl
⊙ Tue–Sun 10–5 🍴 Ekeko Restaurant (10–5)
🚍 3, 7, 9, 10, 14 💶 €12; Museumkaart and I amsterdam City Card holders free

The Tropenmuseum displays a wealth of cultural exhibits from around the world

Where to...
Eat and Drink

Prices
Expect to pay per person for a three-course meal, excluding drinks and service:
€ under €20   €€ €20–€40   €€€ over €40

CAFÉS AND BARS

Bagels & Beans €
This popular daytime café is a successful franchise, with outlets throughout the city. It's an ideal spot for breakfast or lunch if you're visiting the Albert Cuyp market, just across the road. Its superb bagels come with cream cheese, Dutch cheese or combinations such as banana and maple syrup. Other specialities of the house include muffins, coffee and heavenly fruit juices including forest fruits or kiwi. There is a outdoor terrace.

➕ 205 off D1
✉ Ferdinand Bolstraat 70
☎ 020 6 72 16 10; www.bagelsbeans.nl
🕐 Daily 8–6

Bloem Eten & Drinken €
Housed in one of the old warehouses on Entrepotdock, this small café-restaurant is right opposite Artis Zoo. In summer you can sit at one of the few outside tables and admire the beautiful scenery. During the day they serve a variety of organic sandwiches and in the evening it is salads and meat dishes.

➕ 207 D3
✉ Entrepotdok 36
☎ 020 3 30 09 29, www.bloem36.nl
🕐 Daily 11am–midnight

Brouwerij 't IJ €
The windmill, a short walk from the Het Scheepvaartmuseum and close to the Tropenmuseum, is worth paying a visit. The in-house brewery has at least four beers on tap, ranging from five to nine per cent in strength. The basic beer hall has a no-frills bar, a few wooden benches, and a view of the giant beer kettle at the rear. Snacks are limited to peanuts but the café next door does tapas.

➕ 207 F2
✉ Funenkade 7
☎ 020 6 22 83 25; www.brouwerijhetij.nl
🕐 Daily 2–8

Café Brecht €
This inviting living room café is inspired by Berlin's alternative bar scene – complete with grandmother's furniture. There are a variety of German beers on tap along with bratwursts and pretzels, although the casual menu also includes freshly made cakes and paninis and the ingredients are generally locally sourced and organic. Every last Sunday of the month is open mic night for poets.

➕ 204 C2
✉ Weteringschans 157
☎ 020 6 27 22 11; www.cafebrecht.nl
🕐 Daily noon–1am

De Druif €
"The Grape" brown café has been here since 1631: the mustard walls, tiers of old liqueur barrels and antique *jenever* (gin) pump on the bar all indicate its age. It's very much a locals' haunt. The café overlooks the Entrepotdok's entrance.

➕ 205 C3
✉ Rapenburgerplein 83
☎ 020 6 24 45 30
🕐 Sun–Thu noon–1am, Fri–Sat noon–2am

Canal Ring – East

De Kroon €/€€

Adding a welcome touch of sophistication to Rembrandtplein, this is one of the city's trendiest grand cafés. Situated on the first floor, it has a glassed-in balcony terrace overlooking the square below. The decor takes the form of modern paintings by local artists, bold lighting fixtures and natural history artefacts around the bar. The eclectic menu features a fair sprinkling of Italian favourites, although the food is decent rather than outstanding.

🞣 205 E3
✉ Rembrandtplein 17
☎ 020 6 25 20 11; www.dekroon.nl
🕓 Sun–Thu 11am–1am, Fri–Sat 11am–3am

Oosterling €

The Oosterling's pedigree is indisputable: it occupies a building dating from 1735 that was once owned by the Dutch East India Company, and the Oosterling family has been selling drinks here since 1879. Old barrels are used for table tops, others are racked up behind the long granite-topped bar. Unusually, the café doubles as a retail outlet.

🞣 205 E2
✉ Utrechtsestraat 140
☎ 020 6 23 41 40
🕓 Mon–Sat noon–1am, Sun 1pm–8pm

Patisserie Kuyt €€

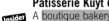

A boutique bakery and deli that is known for its apple pie. Visible in perfect rows behind the long glass counter are delectable pastries, cookies, cakes and quiches. Have lunch or afternoon tea seated in a modern little space next door and take some dessert with you on your way out to enjoy again later.

🞣 205 E2 ✉ Utrechtsestraat 109–111
☎ 020 6 23 48 33; www.patisseriekuyt.nl
🕓 Mon–Sat 8–5:30

De Wetering €

A cosy old brown corner café (► 30) full of slightly bohemian locals, despite the fact that it is just round the corner from the smart antiques shops of the Spiegelkwartier and the Rijksmuseum. Downstairs is standing room only; on the upper level, sand covers the floorboards, and a log fire burns in winter.

🞣 204 C2
✉ Weteringstraat 37
☎ 020 6 22 96 76
🕓 Daily 4–1

Xtracold €€

This is the Netherlands' first ice bar. In return for €19.50, you're lent a coat and gloves, and ushered into a bar made out of 60 tonnes of ice. The tables, fireplace and windows are all constructed from ice, and tulips are set in ice blocks. The fee includes a beer or vodka cocktail plus a 20-minute 3D movie experience..

🞣 205 E3
✉ Amstel 194–196
☎ 020 3 20 57 00; www.xtracold.com
🕓 Daily 11:30am–midnight

RESTAURANTS

Amstel Intercontinental €€€

One of Amsterdam's smartest hotels is a little too far from the centre to be a convenient base to stay at, but it's just the place to live it up for a couple of hours. Choose between a substantial afternoon tea with delicious sandwiches and pastries in its conservatory lounge, a meal in the less welcoming, library-styled Amstel Bar & Brasserie or a table at its smart restaurant, La Rive (you'll need to wear a jacket). This restaurant has the feel of a dining room of a grand country-house hotel.

🞣 206 off B1
✉ Prof Tulpplein 1
☎ 020 6 22 60 60, La Rive: 020 5 20 32 64; www.amsterdam.intercontinental.com
🕓 Afternoon tea: daily 1–3, 4–6.
Amstel Brasserie: daily noon–midnight.
La Rive: Mon–Sat 6:30pm–8, Sun 5–9

Artist Libanees Restaurant €/€€

This Lebanese restaurant, run by Simon, a former cabaret artist, and his son Ralph, offers authentic Lebanese cooking at reasonable prices. If you come with four guests, you can make a meal of the *mezes* (warm and cold appetizers), which smaller parties need to order à la carte. You can choose from several variations of lamb and even okra. Don't miss the *baba ghanouj,* a delicious garlicy purée made from aubergine, onions and tomatoes that is eaten with warm pitta.

➕ 205 E1
✉ Tweede Jan Steenstraat 1
☎ 020 6 71 42 64; www.libanees-artist.nl
🕐 Daily noon–1am

Bazar €/€€

In a former church, the owners of a popular Rotterdam hotel now run this Middle-Eastern themed café/bar/restaurant. The food is reliable with favourites such as falafels, hummus and kebabs, but the richly patterned, cheerful setting is the main draw. Sit upstairs on the pretty mezzanine balcony if possible.

➕ 205 D1
✉ Albert Cuypstraat 182
☎ 020 6 75 05 44; www.bazaramsterdam.nl
🕐 Mon–Thu 11am–midnight, Fri 11am–1am, Sat 9am–1am, Sun 9am–midnight

Ciel Bleu €€€

Make reservations as far in advance as possible for this French restaurant boasting two Michelin stars. On the 23rd floor of the Okura Hotel, diners can enjoy panoramic views of the city or book themselves in at the "Chef's Table", adjoining the kitchen for an eight-course feast created in front of them. The menu, which focuses on regional and seasonal produce, changes four times a year.

➕ 205 off D1 ✉ Ferdinand Bolstraat 333
☎ 020 6 78 74 50; www.cielbleu.nl
🕐 Daily 6:30pm–10:30pm

Cous Cous Club €

The relaxed Cous Cous Club restaurant offers just three couscous dishes: vegetarian, the house special and the "Royal" (with Merguez sausages). Pair the meal with a glass of the Tunisian house wine and you have the making of a convivial and reasonably priced evening.

➕ 205 off D1
✉ Ceintuurbaan 346
☎ 020 6 73 35 39, www.couscousclub.nl
🕐 Tue–Sun 5–11

Dynasty €€/€€€

This seductive, stylish southeast Asian restaurant fills the ground floor of an old gabled house on a street well known for its gay bars. You dine, by candlelight, under a ceiling entirely covered in upturned paper umbrellas, or, weather permitting, in the pretty garden at the rear. The kitchen's repertoire covers Thai, Vietnamese and Chinese dishes.

➕ 205 D3
✉ Reguliersdwarsstraat 30
☎ 020 6 26 84 00
🕐 Wed–Mon 5:30–11

Fifteen Amsterdam €€

At this Dutch version of British chef Jamie Oliver's Fifteen, much of the cooking is done by trainee chefs. Enjoy modern Italian food made from fresh, seasonal ingredients in a warehouse decorated with corrugated-iron walls and graffiti art. Alternatively you can just come along for a drink.

➕ 207 E5
✉ Jollemanhof 9, Eastern Docklands
☎ 020 5 09 50 15; www.fifteen.nl
🕐 Mon– Sat noon–3, 5:30–1, Sun 5:30–1

Tempo Doeloe €€

If asked to pick one Indonesian restaurant, many Amsterdammers would choose this intimate, smart yet informal establishment whose name translates as "the old days". Its only drawback is its popularity:

it's invariably full, and consequently service can be stretched to the limit. You will need to ring the doorbell to be admitted. The cuisine is authentic (dishes marked "*pedis*" will almost blow your head off if you're not used to spicy food), and the *rijsttafels* (rice dishes, ➤ 46) are generous and varied.

➕ 205 E2
✉ Utrechtsestraat 75 ☎ 020 6 25 67 18; www.tempodoeloerestaurant.nl
🕐 Daily 6–11:30

Warung Marlon €

De Pijp is the area to go for down-to-earth ethnic eating, and on Eerste Van der Helststraat nowhere is less pretentious than this spartan yet lively little Surinamese place. Although Suriname is in South America, there are numerous Asian dishes on the menu; the reason is that most restaurants in Suriname are Asian-run. For lunch, you will probably find that one of the large soups, served with a boiled egg, rice and beansprouts, is a meal in itself.

➕ 205 D1
✉ 1e Van der Helststraat 55
☎ 020 6 71 15 26
🕐 Wed–Mon 11–8

Yamazato €€€

Found in the Okura Hotel, this is the only traditional Japanese restaurant in Europe that has a Michelin star. Yamazato provides a wonderfully authentic experi-ence, overlooking a peaceful Japanese garden and a carp-filled lake, complete with a sake bar and smiling waitresses in kimonos. The lunch box is highly recom-mended as a way to sample a variety of dishes, finished off with green tea ice cream; there is also a full sushi menu. Reservations are essential!

➕ 205 off D1
✉ Ferdinand Bolstraat 333
☎ 020 6 78 83 51; www.yamazato.nl
🕐 Daily noon–2, 6–9:30

Le Zinc...et les autres €€

This restaurant in an old canalfront warehouse is an engaging pastiche of rural France with candlelight, wooden floors and original beams. Sit downstairs by the lovely zinc-topped bar, or in the brighter, larger room upstairs. With a strong regional French influence, it is not surprising that much is made of the wine selection – and the cheeses. Chef Edwin van Westrop's varied menu changes monthly, but starters might include Norwegian scallops or wild sea bass, with at least one fish dish and perhaps roast goose breast or loin of veal among the main courses.

➕ 205 D2
✉ Prinsengracht 999
☎ 020 6 22 90 44; www.lezinc.nl
🕐 Mon–Sat 5:30–11

Where to...
Shop

The essential shopping highlights in this part of the city are the art and antiques of the Spiegelkwartier, the touristy but colourful Flower Market and the Albert Cuypmarkt, which has something of the flavour of a street market in London's East End.

SPIEGELKWARTIER

The 100 shops of Amsterdam's premier fine art and antiques district deal in everything from Old Masters to antiquities, and from Russian icons to Chinese prints. At its heart is Nieuwe Spiegelstraat, perhaps the city's prettiest canal-free thoroughfare, and ideal for a spend-free wander and browse.

Starting at the Herengracht end. **Umbria** (No 20, tel 020 4 20 41 08, www.umbriaantiques.com) deals in such things as antique ceramic urns, modern sculptures and old photographs. While jewellers **Schilling** (No 23) have everything from earrings to mirrors. You'll find classic 17th- and 18th-century Delftware pieces at **Aronson Antiquairs** (No 39; tel: 020 6 23 31 03, www.aronson.nl), and **Eduard Kramer** (No 64, tel: 020 6 23 08 32, www.antique-tileshop.nl) has a vast selection of old Delft tiles, most of which have been salvaged from kitchens in canal houses, as well as trinkets and jewellery.

Meulendijks & Schuil (on the corner with Kerkstraat; www.staetshuysantiques.com) is stocked with model planes, telescopes and globes.

At No 72, **Vanderdonk Fine Chocolates** (www.vanderdonkchocolates.nl) sells chic handmade bonbons and truffles crafted from fair trade and organic chocolate. Chocolatiers Pimm and Marcel van der Donk also happily sell sweets such as French marshmallows and caramels.

Nieuwe Spiegelstraat runs into Spiegelgracht, where you'll find many of the quarter's modern art galleries, and also, at No 10, 🔢 **Tinker Bell** (www.tinkerbelltoys.nl), an excellent children's toy shop.

More intriguing shops can be found just off Spiegelgracht and Nieuwe Spiegelstraat on the streets facing or parallel to the canals.

Ria Jong (Prinsengracht 574, tel: 020 6 25 23 55) has an interesting antique collection.

Anton Heyboer (Prinsengracht 578, www.antonheyboerwinkel.nl) deals in antique toys, such as scooters, dolls and rocking horses; while **Thom & Lenny Nelis** (Keizersgracht 541, www.nelisantiques.com) is devoted to antique pharmaceutical paraphernalia.

OTHER SHOPPING STREETS

The shops on the section of the Singel alongside the Flower Market sell amusing souvenirs, such as singing Father Christmases and ties decorated with cows and windmills. **Marañon** (Singel 488–490, www.maranon.nl) has a colourful collection of hammocks.

Utrechtsestraat, with its old-fashioned delis, and its flower and herring stalls on the bridges that cross it, is one of Amsterdam's more chic shopping streets, with several stylish boutiques and art galleries.

Worth a look are the retro fashions at **Twice As Nice** (No 47), and **Concerto** (Nos 52–60, www.concerto.nl), a music store with second-hand collections. *Insider Tip*

On Vijzelgracht, look for **Holtkamp** at No 15 (www.patisserieholtkamp.nl), which, with its handmade chocolates and swan-shaped meringues, understandably bills itself as a luxury bakery.

Peter Doeswijk, (www.petersdoeswijk.nl) two doors down at No 11, sells telephones and lavatory seats painted with one-off designs.

MARKETS

Bloemenmarkt (Mon–Sat 9:30–5, Sun noon–5): the Flower Market projects out over the Singel, but don't take the often-quoted "floating" description literally. Growers once used to sell flowers from boats, but the stalls and garden shops are now fixed. It's a good place to buy bulbs and wooden tulips.

Albert Cuypmarkt (Albert Cuypstraat, Mon–Sat 9–6): the lifeblood of De Pijp district is the city's biggest and best general market, running from Ferdinand Bolstraat to Van Woustraat with 350 stalls. Fruit and vegetables, herring and eels, cheese and olives, underwear and jeans, and every item under the heading of general bric-a-brac that you can imagine are on offer. As interesting are all the multicultural shops and cafés along the street: for more salubrious-looking eating and drinking options, head for **1e Van der Helststraat.**

Where to...
Go Out

Rembrandtplein and its nearby streets are a nocturnal focal point. Named after a 19th-century statue of Rembrandt, the tacky, sometimes rowdy, square is lit by neon at night, and surrounded by mostly second-rate cafés and restaurants (➤ 161 for recommendations). But if you sit on their large outdoor terraces, street musicians and passing trams provide free entertainment. It's a little more stylish in the Grand Café L'Opéra with its crystal chandeliers and art deco furniture.

To the west, Reguliersdwarsstraat (beyond Vijzelstraat) is a focal point for Amsterdam's happening gay scene, with explicit sex shops, gay clubs, restaurants and cafés. One of the most civilized cafés is Ludwig II (No 37); though you could say that it still performs its original role as a working men's club as the night progresses, at other times it's not at all cruisy.

NIGHTCLUBS

One of the hip clubs on the square is **AIR** (Amstelstraat 16, tel: 020 3 62 41 50, www.air.nl) which features international DJs from Thursday to Sundays. **Escape** (Rembrandtplein 11, tel: 020 6 22 11 11, www.escape. nl), is the largest club in town. Its big night, called Framebusters, is

on Saturdays: be ready to queue and dress smartly. Well-established **Vivelavie** (Amstelstraat 7, www. vivelavie.net) is a male-friendly lesbian bar, while the **Hotel Arena** (s-Gravesandestraat 51; tel: 020 8 50 24 00), a designer hotel housed in a former orphanage, has their own **club** inside the old orphanage chapel. The club has different areas, one that plays hits from the 80s and 90s and another that plays hip-hop.

CINEMA

If you decide to go to the cinema, be sure to make it the **Tuschinski Theater** (Reguliersbreestraat 26–28; www.pathe.nl). Built in 1921 in the most over-the-top art deco style, Amsterdam's showcase cinema would look more at home in Los Angeles. The cinema's original gaudy fittings have been restored. Have a peek at them in the lobby, but better still buy a ticket for whatever is showing in Screen 1, the main (giant) auditorium. The priciest tickets are for double seats, and include a free glass of champagne. Occasionally, guided tours are offered – contact the cinema for times and dates. Expect queues at weekends if you haven't booked in advance.

THEATRE AND CHAMBER MUSIC

Down by the Amstel, the **Koninklijk Theater Carré** (Amstel 115–125, www.theatercarre.nl), built in the 19th century as a circus, now hosts large-scale musicals, along with opera and ballet.

Near the Passenger Terminal in the Eastern Docklands, the **Muziek-gebouw aan 't IJ** (➤ 178) is one of the city's leading live music venues.

The adjoining **Bimhuis** (Piet Heinkade 3, tel: 020 788 2188, www.bimhuis.nl), is Amsterdam's top venue for jazz, with over 300 concerts annually.

Excursions

Excursions

Excursions

One great advantage of the Netherlands is that almost anywhere in the country is quick and easy to reach from Amsterdam. In just a few minutes the free ferry north across the IJ River will deposit you on the edge of Waterland – the start of a tranquil region steeped in tradition.

Just east of the city's medieval centre is a very different world – the **Oostelijk Havengebied** (Eastern Docklands) that has undergone a radical transformation. Heading west instead, within 15 minutes you can exchange the bustle of Holland's biggest city for the much calmer and more manageable town of **Haarlem** – and, on a hot summer's day, join the Amsterdammers at play on the beach at **Zandvoort.**

To the south, the ancient capital of **Utrecht** is only 30 minutes away. Although it has long since relinquished political power to Amsterdam, it retains a certain majesty. The core of the city, carved through by a unique pair of "sunken canals", is one of the most alluring in Europe. Go southwest to **Leiden**, and, at the right time of year, you drift through swathes of colour as you pass the country's famous tulip fields. The university city of Leiden is both handsome and historic, with traces of the Pilgrim Fathers, who sought religious freedom here before crossing the Atlantic aboard the *Mayflower.*

Noord-Holland

Noord-Holland (North Holland) is the name for the piece of land poking north from Amsterdam, with the North Sea on one side and the IJsselmeer (created by damming the Zuiderzee) on the other.

This semi-rural region is dotted with lovely villages and pockets of history. The countryside looks and feels very different to the busy land- and cityscapes further south. In blustery, grey weather, the windswept fields can epitomize the bleakness depicted by Van Gogh – but on sunny days, they resemble his most optimistic landscapes. The coast and waterways still bear evidence of the ocean-going tradition that ended when the Afsluitdijk cut off the Zuiderzee from the North Sea. At weekends, the area is a playground for Amsterdammers and is also a sanctuary for bird life.

Trains will take you to some of the places of interest, and buses fill in many of the gaps: 111 runs from Amsterdam's Centraal Station to the **island of Marken,** 110, 112 and 116 go to **Volendam** and 114 and 116 to **Edam.** But this is one part of the country where your own transport, whether on two or four wheels, can be a real advantage, conferring the freedom to create your own circuit. If you're on foot or cycling, a good way to begin is with a free ferry across the IJ from behind Amsterdam's Centraal Station; there are three ferries that cross the IJ from Centraal Station, each arriving at a different location. All three depart every few minutes all day long, and one runs 24 hours. On the northern bank, there are buses and cycle paths to take you through the undistinguished suburbs of Amsterdam-Noord to the charming and picture-perfect village of **Broek-in-Waterland,** well signposted for motorists emerging from the tunnel under the IJ.

Wooden slat houses at Marken

Broek-in-Waterland
A pretty patchwork of cottages, amid a tapestry of serene waterways, Broek-in-Waterland sets the tone for the region. A 17th-century church stands primly at the heart of the village.

Marken
A minor road northeast takes you to the causeway leading to Marken, an island with this single tenuous road connection. Cars and buses

Excursions

are obliged to halt at the south end of the settlement. The quiet and relative isolation makes this the loveliest of all North Holland's villages, with its quaint collection of wooden houses linked by venerable bridges.

For a while, it was one of the busiest ports in the region, thanks to the fishing and whaling fleet; now its main industry is tourism, and there are plenty of cafés and restaurants on the waterfront. From here, there are regular ferries shuttling across to the lively port of Volendam.

Cyclists may decide to turn around and head for home after Marken, while motorists must first retrace their steps to continue further north, hugging a coastline that is protected by a formidable dyke.

Volendam and Edam

The road along the shore passes through Monnickendam, then winds around the coast to Volendam, whose waterfront is a frenetic collusion of boats painted in primary colours, cafés and souvenir shops. The "real" town that lies immediately behind it has considerable charm.

Volendam merges with Edam, a place much less bland than the cheese that shares its name. When the tourist coaches have gone for the day, usually by around 4pm, it is a delight to wander around the quiet streets, heavy with history (and cheese shops). Bus 114 or 116, a fast main road, or a handy cycle path, will take you directly back to Amsterdam from Edam. But to complete a circuit, you could head west to take in a couple of extra sights.

Zaanse Schans

The Zaan River has, like others in the area, become a commercial backwater. During the 17th and 18th centuries, however, the town of **Zaandam** was an important ship-building centre. Most visitors to Zaandam these

Boats in the harbour in Volendam

days come to see **Zaanse Schans,** a collection of historic merchant houses and windmills to the north of the town. The mills that parade along the east bank of the Zaan are the survivors of around 600 that used to dominate the horizon. Six can be found at Zaanse Schans.

The most interesting is the **Verfmolen De Kat** (www.verf molendekat.com), the Paint Mill. Wood, plants and roots were ground here for textile dyes, and chalk was crushed for paints. The mill still earns its keep, supplying naturally made colours to artists.

Windmills are a delightful sight at Zaanse Schans

Peter the Great's home

It's a long mental leap from this placid part of Holland to the Winter Palace in St Petersburg, but the origins of Russia's finest city can be traced to the town of **Zaandam**. Early in his reign, Peter the Great toured Western Europe to study the techniques that would enable him to modern-ise the then-primitive Russian Empire. He came to Holland at the tail end of the 17th century to study the latest maritime technology, meeting accomplished ship-builders and cartographers. His home, **Czaar Peterhuisje** (Czar Peter House), in the town, is now a museum: you may be surprised at the modest scale of the small wooden house, now enclosed in a more permanent stone building. The museum describes ship-building on the Zaan, and the life of the Czar. It has become a place of pilgrimage for Russian visitors.

While based here, the Czar also learned about land reclamation, which proved invaluable when creating his new capital, St Petersburg, from the marshland fringing the Baltic.

Zaanse Schans

✉ Zaandam ☎ 075 6 81 00 00; www.zaanseschans.nl
🕐 Times and days vary from site to site
🍴 De Hoop Op d'Swarte Walvis restaurant
(Kalverringdijk 15; tel: 075 6 16 56 29; www.dewalvis.eu),
Tue–Sun noon–10. Reservations required at weekends (€€€)
🚉 Koog-Zaandijk, four trains each hour
🎟 Site: free; Zaanse Schans Card: 10 €

Czaar Peterhuisje

✉ Krimp 23, Zaandam ☎ 075 6 81 00 00; www.zaanseschans.nl
🕐 Tue–Sun 10–5
🚉 Zaandam (four trains an hour from Centraal Station)
🎟 €3

Haarlem and Zandvoort

On a sunny day, this handsome town with excellent restaurants and lively beach resort of Zaandvoort make a great combination to visit, as both are easily accessible from Amsterdam.

Haarlem

Just 15 minutes from Amsterdam, Haarlem is the perfect antidote for anyone who feels overwhelmed by the city. Small, manageable and friendly, this town has an authentic Dutch feel and a strong historical and cultural character of its own.

Begin you tour at the splendid 1908 art nouveau **railway station.** In the main ticket hall, there is a pair of large tiled murals designed to inspire the working classes: one showing a ploughman, the other two blacksmiths. Start walking south, directly away from the VVV, on Kruisweg, which turns into Kruisstraat halfway along. You will pass **Steedehuys Antiek** (Kruisstraat 11), one of Haarlem's many antiques shops. Continue down Kruisstraat and almost directly opposite is the **Hofje van Oorschot;** this particular almshouse is unusual in that it is open to the street.

Continuing south along Barteljorisstraat, you pass on your left the **Corrie ten Boomhuis.** The ten Boom family were evangelists who played an important part in the Resistance during World War II, providing shelter for Jewish people.

A few metres further on, the **Grote Markt** opens up – a broad and beautiful jumble of buildings. The market square is dominated by **Sint Bavokerk,** also known as the Grote Kerk or Great Church. This 15th-century late Gothic brute

Haarlem's Grote Kerk was technically a cathedral for only 19 years (1559–78)

exceeds, in sheer bulk, anything in Amsterdam. It has been under repair for several years, but has remained open – the entrance is hidden around the back on Oude Groenmarkt. Inside, the highlight is the extravagant baroque organ, installed in 1738 and later played by 10-year-old Mozart. Head south along Warmoesstraat. This turns into Schagchelstraat and **Groot Heiligland,** a street endowed with some lovely houses. Near the end is the **Frans Hals Museum,** commemorating and displaying works by the 17th-century Haarlem artist and his contemporaries.

Zandvoort

Amsterdam's local beach Zandvoort (www.zandvoort.nl), is tending to attract young families. The original settlement was a fishing village, established at a gap in the dunes that run along the North Sea shore west of Haarlem. It's been transformed into a strip of hotels and apartment blocks, though there is still some evidence of the old port. A few kilometres north is Zandvoort's more stylish sibling, **Bloemendaal**, which is said to be the richest place in Holland. In summer many trains continue through Haarlem direct to the resort.

Corrie ten Boomhuis

⊠ Barteljorisstraat 19 ☎ 023 5 31 08 23; www.corrietenboom.com
🕓 Apr–Oct Tue–Sat 10–4 (last tour 3:30); Nov–March Tue–Sat 11–3 (last tour 2:30). Visits are by guided tour 🖐 Free; donations appreciated

Sint Bavokerk

⊠ Grote Markt ☎ 023 5 53 20 40; www.bavo.nl
🕓 Mon–Sat 10–4 (summer till 5) 🖐 €2.50

Frans Hals Museum

Visitors in the Frans Hals Museum

⊠ Groot Heiligland 62, Haarlem ☎ 023 5 11 57 75; www.franshalsmuseum.nl
🕓 Tue–Sat 11–5, Sun and public holidays noon–5
🖐 €10; Museumkaart and I amsterdam City Card holders free

Utrecht

With a distinctive cathedral, interesting history, and a museum dedicated to Dick Bruna, the creator of the much-loved *Miffy* books, this attractive city, within easy reach of Amsterdam, makes a pleasant day trip.

The Rhine once flowed through this part of the Netherlands, and the Romans established an important crossing here. By the time the river shifted its course south of the city, Utrecht was an important political base, its bishop one of the most influential figures in the Low Countries. His grant of a charter to the young settlement of Amsterdam in 1300 is often taken as the date of that city's founding. Although power ebbed away, Utrecht's university has provided a dynamic edge, and the central location attracts plenty of business.

Five trains run each hour from Amsterdam, taking 30 minutes. Follow the signs for "Centrum" through the shopping centre next to the station and you should emerge on Lange Elisabethstraat; any of the side streets opposite should take you to the main canal, **Oudegracht.** Located next to the Dom Tower, the tourist office (www.utrecht.nl) is well signposted.

Oudegracht to Nieuwegracht

A great trench has been dug for the **Oudegracht** and the **Nieuwegracht,** which runs parallel. Each is flanked by paths below street level, and several cafés, restaurants, studios and galleries have sprung up in the cellars that line the canals. Oudegracht temporarily narrows in the area of the **Stadhuis,** an imposing structure with a modern annexe, then reappears to head south. A 20-minute walk south along the east bank is a good way to acquaint yourself with the city. Stay at street level: you'll see more.

Just after the street becomes **Twijnstraat** and separates from the canal, you will be at the corner of Nicolaasstraat:

The Oudegracht is an old canal system running through the old city

turn left along it to visit the **Centraal Museum,** a sumptuous collection, covering the origins of the city, the Golden Age and contemporary art.

The Dom Tower, built between 1321 and 1382, is the tallest church tower in the Netherlands

Near by, along **Agnietenstraat,** is the **Dick Bruna Huis,** home of Dick Bruna (b.1927), who brought Miffy (Nijntje is the original Dutch name), the now world-famous rabbit, to life in 1955. On display are 1,200 of his works, including picture books and original sketches. Turn up Lange Nieuwstraat to the **Catharijne Convent.** This is one of the most imaginatively created museums in the country, a collection of religious art – including works by Frans Hals and Rembrandt – threading through the old convent and into St Catharijnekerk, behind it.

Utrecht Cathedral

Continuing north, you pass through a calm and beautiful quarter to reach the **Dom** (Cathedral of St Martin), one of Holland's strangest sights. Construction began in 1254 and it was completed in 1517, but in 1674 a thunderstorm caused part of it to collapse.

Since then, all that remains is the choir, transept and a fine 112m (367ft) tower (tours hourly 11–4) with an agreeable carillon (heard on the hour and half-hour). On the south side, an ancient boulder brought here with great difficulty from Jutland (mainland Denmark) dates from the 10th century and bears runes devoted to King Harald.

Centraal Museum
✉ Nicolaaskerkhof 10 ☎ 030 2 36 23 62; www.centraalmuseum.nl 🕐 Tue–Sun 11–5 👜 €11; Museumkaart holders free

Dick Bruna Huis
✉ Agnietenstraat 2
☎ 030 2 36 23 53; www.dickbrunahuis.com
🕐 Tues–Sun 11–5
👜 €11; under-12s and Museumkaart holders free

Catharijne Convent
✉ Lange Nieuwstraat 38
☎ 030 2 31 38 35; www.catharijneconvent.nl
🕐 Tue–Fri 10–5, Sat, Sun and public holidays 11–5. Closed 1 Jan, 26 April
🍴 Café (€€)
👜 €12.50; Museumkaart holders: €2.50

Leiden and the Bulbfields

The historic and picturesque university town of Leiden has a very appealing atmosphere with lovely canalside walks, narrow medieval lanes, attractive cottages and first-rate museums, as well as the world's largest bulb display. And there is no shortage of places to eat, drink and relax.

From the railway station, take Stationsweg, and you can begin sightseeing almost at once. The **Museum Volkenkunde** (National Museum of Ethnology, Steenstraat 1, tel: 071 5 16 88 00, www.volkenkunde.nl, Tue–Sun 10–5, €11), is a huge old 19th-century hospital, filled with the gatherings of Dutch explorers. The best exhibits are those from Asia, particularly Java and Japan, though there is also a fine collection of Peruvian ceramics.

Follow the canal past the museum to the florid **Morspoort,** one of the original city gates. This opens on to a street filled with restaurants, and takes you along to one of the most-photographed sites in the city, the chunky bridge that spans the **Oude Vest** waterway. Immediately to your right is another bridge across the Rhine – or at least the course cut by that great river long ago, when it used to flow through Leiden after Utrecht. Now it is known as the **Oude Rijn,** or Old Rhine.

There are many charming windmills to see in the area around Leiden

The Beauty of Leiden

The walk south along Rapenburg takes you to the loveliest part of the city. On the left (east) is the **Rijksmuseum van Oudheden** (National Museum of Antiquities, Rapenburg 28, tel: 071 5 16 31 63, www.rmo.nl, Tue–Sun 10–5, €9.50).

Close to the **Botanical Gardens** (Rapenburg 73, tel: 071 5 27 72 49, www.hortusleiden.nl, April–Oct daily 10–6, Nov–March Tue–Sun 10–4, €7), the mighty **Pieterskerk** dominates this area. Inside, near the north entrance, is a mummified body from the early 18th century, discovered under the pulpit. An

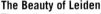

alcove in the southwest corner is devoted to the Pilgrim Fathers, the puritanical English Calvinists from Scrooby, Nottinghamshire, who stayed in Leiden for 11 years, before deciding the Dutch were not pious enough and sailing to America.

Immediately west, you will find **Pieterskerk-Choorsteeg**, with plenty of eating possibilities plus, on the left (north), a sign at the start of **William Brewster Steeg** noting that this was the site of the Pilgrim's Press.

Beyond it is the **Stadhuis** (town hall), with a richly decorated stairway, and behind that an artificial mound – the citadel – with views across the city. If you look towards the northwest, you should see the windmill museum, **Molenmuseum De Valk** (2e Binnenvestgracht 1, tel: 071 5 16 53 53, molendevalk.leiden.nl, Tue–Sat 10–5, Sun 1–5, €4).

The Tulips of Keukenhof

For a couple of months each spring, the fields between Leiden and the small town of Heemstede dazzle with colour. This is the centre of tulip cultivation in Holland, and at its heart is **Keukenhof**, near the village of Lisse.

Keukenhof means "kitchen garden" as the location was used for market gardening. Today, it forms the largest flower garden in the world.

Keukenhof

✉ Stationsweg 166a, Lisse

☎ 025 2 46 55 55; www.keukenhof.nl

🕐 Spring Garden: mid-March to mid-May daily 8–7:30 (last ticket 6pm)

🍴 Refreshment facilities (€€)

🚌 Leiden; sign at main exit directs you to the adjacent bus station, from which the "Keukenhof Express" runs direct

💶 €15

Keukenhof gardens offer 80 acres of tulips, daffodils and hyacinths

Oostelijk Havengebied

Created in the 19th and early 20th centuries, the man-made peninsulas and islands of the Oostelijk Havengebied (Eastern Docklands), began to fall into disuse in the 1950s. Desolate by the late 1980s, they now boast cutting-edge design and eye-catching housing and shops.

From Centraal Station, head east down Piet Heinkade, past the city's new waterfront concert hall, the **Muziekgebouw aan 't IJ** (➤ 166), and the wave-shaped cruise ship passenger terminal. Pass under the De Zwijger warehouse and across the bridge to Java-eiland. Here, the bicycle lane crosses canals lined with 21st-century versions of 17th-century canal houses. Java-eiland merges into KNSM-eiland, which is dominated by large apartment complexes – or "superblocks", as the Dutch call them. The Barcelona complex, on the Levantkade, has a courtyard designed like the interior of an opera house, with the apartments' balconies as theatre boxes.

From the Levantkade, you get a perfect view of the oddest superblock, The Whale on Sporenburg, covered in grey zinc and rearing asymmetrically into the skyline. Cross the red Python Bridge at the east end of Sporenburg on to Scheepstimmermanstraat, on Borneo-eiland. The owners on one side of Scheepstimmermanstraat were allowed to create their own designs. Many are eye-catching: No 120 has been constructed around a tree.

From here, head up to Oostelijke Handelskade, to the **Lloyd Hotel** (➤ 45), built in 1921 as a boarding house for Eastern European emigrants on their way to the Americas.

➕ 207 E5

Muziekgebouw aan 't IJ
➕ 207 D5 ✉ Piet Heinkade 1 ☎ 020 7 88 20 10; www.muziekgebouw.nl

The Muziekgebouw aan 't IJ concert hall in the Eastern Docklands

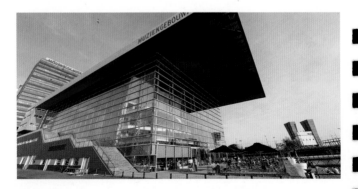

Walks

Walks

1 BREWER'S CANAL TO NEMO

> **DISTANCE** 4km (2.5 miles) **TIME** 2–3 hours **START POINT** Café
> Papeneiland (corner of Brouwersgracht and Prinsengracht)
> ✚ 203 D3 **END POINT** science center NEMO ✚ 207 D4

There are many candidates for the loveliest canal in Amsterdam. But for a fascinating and fun introduction to the city, the walk around Herengracht is hard to beat. Preceding it with Brouwersgracht and ending with Nieuwe Herengracht gives an ideal, balanced walk; or, if you are feeling fit, this walk can easily be combined with Walk 2 (➤ 184), to provide a complete circuit of the city centre.

❶–❷

Begin at the southern side of **Brouwersgracht** ("Brewer's Canal", named for the breweries that lined it in the 17th and 18th centuries) at its junction with Prinsengracht. Start with a coffee at the charming

Café Papeneiland (➤ 107), on the upper floor if you can get a seat. Housed in a magnificent, 17th-century gabled building, with an impressive Delft-tiled bar, this is one of Amsterdam's oldest brown cafés. Take in the view down Prinsengracht, or "Princes' Canal", one

Leliegracht

Westerkerk

Bartolotti Huis

Raadhuisstraat

Prinsengracht

Herengracht

Bijbels Museum

Leidsegracht

of the city's liveliest waterways. There is a tunnel beneath it that took Catholics to worship – an illegal act in the 17th century – in the church opposite. It is the origin of the café's name, "Popes' Island". Continue and cross **Keizersgracht** ("Emperor's Canal").

The Bartolotti Huis

At the start of Herengracht, pause to take in a definitive Amsterdam scene of water, trees and crowds of buildings. Cross Brouwersgracht and walk east to the next bridge, near several gabled houses. This is the dainty pedestrians-only bridge, **Melkmeisjesbrug**. It deposits you

TAKING A BREAK

At Rembrandtplein, you can make a short detour to Utrechtsestraat and the popular **Patisserie Kuyt** (➤ 162) to enjoy a delicious fruit tart (their apple pie won the "The Best Pie in Amsterdam" award) or a tasty quiche.

at No 1 **Herengracht.** Herengracht translates as "Gentleman's Canal" or "Lord's Canal" and was traditionally where Amsterdam's wealthiest visitors lived. Their mansions have largely been taken

Brouwersgracht
2 Melkmeisjesbrug
Centraal Station

0 250 m
0 200 yd

Prins Hendrikkade
Wissenschaftszentrum NEMO 9
Osterdok

Koninklijk Paleis

IJ-Tunnel

Scheepvaart Museum

Volkenburgerstraat
Schippersgracht
Entrepotdok

Wertheim Park

Amstel
Blauwbrug
Walter Susskindbrug
Hortus Botanicus 8

Thorbeckeplein
7
Herengracht
Amstelhof (Hermitage Amsterdam)

6
De Bazel

Vijzelstraat

Magere Brug

over by banks and other financial institutions. It is punctuated by scenic humpback bridges and dotted with colourful houseboats. Almost anywhere you look along Herengracht, there is something to delight the eye. Even where

Walks

the 20th century intervenes, as in the new building at Nos 105–107, the addition is sympathetic, with careful details such as a decorative tablet on an otherwise plain wall.

2–3

Walk on and, at the point where **Leliegracht** sets off to the right

Keizersgracht looking west from Nieuwe Spiegelstraat

(west), there is a rare opportunity to see a canal along its length from close to water level while still on dry land. Stay on the east side of Herengracht and admire the **Bartolotti Huis**, a particularly fine mansion, from afar. The 20th century intrudes at the intersection with Raadhuisstraat, "Town Hall Street", which runs to the Royal Palace – formerly the town hall. In the other direction, an elegant early 20th-century terrace draws the eye towards **Westerkerk** (► 101).

3–4

At Oude Spiegelstraat, you enter the area known as **9 Straatjes**

(► 105–106). Wijde Heisteeg marks its end. Cross Herengracht, to continue south on the other bank.

4–5

Just past the **Bijbels Museum** (Herengracht 366–368, tel: 020 6 24 24 36, www.bijbels museum.nl, Mon–Sat 10–5, Sun and holidays 11–5, €8), with its intricate stonework, is the **Netherlands Institute for War Documentation**.

5–6

Soon Herengracht swerves to the left while, **Leidsegracht** sets off to the right. This stretch of the canal is busy with tour boats, people and vehicles, but is quieter once you cross Leidsestraat on to the **Golden Bend** (Gouden Bocht), the most fashionable and desirable stretch of Herengracht (hence the "golden"). It is now occupied by business and foreign consulates. The bend itself takes place at the start of Nieuwe Spiegelstraat, lined with art and antiques shops.

6–7

Vijzelstraat marks the end of the Golden Bend. The **De Bazel building**, at the corner with Herengracht, has a fascinating display of documents and photos from the city's archive in its ornate basement – follow the signs for the Schatkamer. Beyond is **Thorbeckeplein,** facing you where Reguliersgracht begins. Tour boats pause here to give their passengers the chance to gaze at the Seven Bridges (only properly visible at water level). This is also the point where you cross Walk 3 (► 187). The calm resumes for the last 300m (330 yards) of Herengracht. Just before you cross Utrechtsestraat, a flamboyant St George appears on the Italian consulate on the opposite (north) side – the patron saint of England originally patronized Genoa. Just ahead is the Amstel River, and to the right the **Magere Brug,** the "Skinny Bridge" (➤ 156). The walk heads left (north) to the **Blauwbrug** (Blue Bridge), constructed in cast iron in 1874. There has been a crossing here for centuries, and from here you can gaze at the scene as Rembrandt did – he lived 200m away.

🏿-🏿

The Blue Bridge marks the end of the Herengracht proper. You can finish the walk here – trams 9 and 14 cross the bridge, and Waterlooplein metro station is 200m (220 yards) northeast. Otherwise, turn right across the Blue Bridge along the east bank of the Amstel. Cross the first bridge and turn left on to Nieuwe Herengracht. The bridge, a replica of the Magere Brug, is named **Walter Süskindbrug** after the German who helped hundreds of Dutch children escape the Nazis during World War II. Alongside is the neat terracing of the **Amstelhof,** the first of the city's refuges for older people and now the location

of the **Hermitage Amsterdam** (➤ 150). Head along the south bank of Nieuwe Herengracht, which cuts through part of the old Jewish quarter and skirts Three Climates Greenhouse of the **Hortus Botanicus** (➤ 154).

🏿-🏿

Across bustling Plantage Middenlaan, you enter **Wertheim Park**, with a memorial at the far end to the thousands of Dutch people of Jewish descent who died in the Nazi death camp at Auschwitz-Birkenau in Poland. Cross the canal to reach Anne Frankstraat; once across, turn right down the path. Look across the **Entrepotdok** (➤ 159), one of the original free ports. The very last stretch of canal – which is no longer than 200m (220 yards) – is called **Schippersgracht**. Cross Prins Hendrikkade to reach the statue of Neptune. From here, skirt the edge of the entrance to the IJ tunnel as you aim for **NEMO** (➤ 73). Once you reach it, just keep walking – up the building. Usually the stairway to the crest of the science and technology centre is open, and provides a wonderful view of the old town.

The Auschwitz memorial commemorates the Dutch Jews who were killed at Auschwitz, in Poland

2 ALONG THE WATERFRONT

DISTANCE 2km (1.25 miles)   **TIME** 1 hour
START POINT Scheepvaartmuseum ✚ 207 D3
END POINT Haarlemmerplein ✚ 203 D4

Amsterdam's old waterfront is full of maritime history, from the Het Scheepvaartmuseum that celebrates the history of the Dutch East India Company to the headquarters of the Dutch West India Company and beyond. This walk begins near the end of Walk 1 (➤ 180–183) and can be easily combined to form a kind of circuit. Alternatively, it places you close to the start of Walk 4 (➤ 190–192).

🔟–2

The **Het Scheepvaartmuseum** (➤ 146) can give you some sense of how the Oosterdok must have looked from outside the entrance. Keep on the north side across the Nieuwevaart and Schippersgracht

TAKING A BREAK

Highlights along the route include the **Café VOC Schreierstoren** (www.schreier-storen.nl; Mon–Thu 10–10, Fri–Sun 10am–1am).

canals, passing the statue of Neptune down to the right. Visit the **ARCAM** (➤ 159) if open. At the next bridge, admire the **science center NEMO** (➤ 73). Cross the road and look along **Oudeschans** – *schans* means "fortress" – this was one of the city's defences. The tower on the right, **Montelbaanstoren,** was part of the fortifications.

2–3

Stay on the landward side of Prins Hendrikkade. At **No 131,** a plaque marks the home of the Dutch naval hero Admiral de Ruyter. Further on is the **Scheepvaarthuis** (➤ 72), which once organized a global fleet

Café VOC with the dome of St Nicolaaskerk behind

but is now the luxury Grand Hotel Amrâth (➤44).

3–4

The next stretch of water along on the left is the Waalseilands-gracht; the street that leads off along its western edge is named Kromme Waal, and No 9 has a fine example of a step gable. Rounding the next bend to the left suddenly

reveals a splendid vista, from the easternmost turret of the Centraal Station ensemble to **St Nicolaaskerk**, and in the middle of it, the **Schreierstoren**, where, it's said, women gathered to give their menfolk a tearful fare-well. These days the tower is home to the Café VOC. A plaque relates how English navigator Henry Hudson (c.1550–1611) set sail from here on 4 April 1609, aboard the *Half Moon*, to discover the harbour of what is now New York and the river that bears his name.

4–5

Keep to the landward side of Prins Hendrikkade (and watch out for traffic, especially bicycles). St Nicholas is the patron saint

Walks

of sailors, and his church, to the left, was the last many mariners saw of the city as they set off on their voyages. These days, the city is cut off from the water by **Centraal Station** (➤ 72), and the church bids farewell to rail travellers. Past the tour boats moored in **Damrak**, the **Park Plaza Victoria Hotel** is ahead. On its north side directly facing the station, two 17th-century houses seem to have been embedded in the facade. The story is that the hotel wanted to demolish a string of houses to allow it to expand west along Prins Hendrikkade, but the adjacent landlords refused to sell out. The expansion went ahead, but had to detour around the back of the two awkward abodes.

5–**6**

If you look towards the train station, you will now see the **Fietsflat**, a large floating bicycle garage with room for 2,500 bikes. When the road crosses Singel, just ahead, you get a superb view straight ahead: on the right, the flourishing, French Renaissance-style **Hogeschool**

van Amsterdam (Amsterdam High School); in the centre, the lopsided **Café Kobalt**; and on the left, a warehouse topped with a blue **Angel Gabriel** standing on a globe. At ground level, a ship's propellor donated by a shipping company is fixed to a brick plinth.

6–**7**

Aim for the warehouse with Gabriel on top, and a cheese shop below, and turn right here on to Haarlemmerstraat. From the **West Indisch Huis** (West India House), the well-proportioned mansion along on the left, Dutch maritime activities in the Caribbean and South America were controlled; it now houses media companies.

7–**8**

After a slight kink in the road, two chimneys appear in the distance, while in the foreground you can enjoy an impressive array of gables. There is a good canal view south from the bridge over **Korte Prinsengracht,** where Haarlemmerstraat turns into Haarlemmerdijk. Three blocks later, at the intersection with Binnen Dommersstraat, two foghorns are on display, while diagonally across there is a modern tablet showing a decorator's brush. The walk ends where Haarlemmerdijk broadens out into **Haarlemmerplein**. On the far side of the square is the closest Amsterdam has to a triumphal arch, the **Haarlemmer Poort,** which provides a view of the primary-coloured sculpture that marks the entrance to Westerpark. From Haarlemmerplein, you can take tram 3 back to the centre, commence Walk 1 (➤ 180), go a short distance east to the start of Walk 4 (➤ 190–192), wander around the Jordaan (➤ 92–95) or enter the Westerpark (➤ 106).

West India House used to rule half an empire

3 FROM CENTRAAL STATION TO THE RIJKSMUSEUM

DISTANCE 3km (2 miles) **TIME** 1 hour 30 minutes at a gentle pace
START POINT NH Barbizon Palace Hotel, southeast of Centraal Station
➕ 203 F3 **END POINT** Rijksmuseum ➕ 204 C2

Almost any walk in Amsterdam that takes you around the city's arc of canals is bound to be enjoyable. The same cannot be said, though, for those that cut against the watery grain – for example, finding a pretty way to cover the ground from Centraal Station to the Rijksmuseum is tricky. This itinerary is the most pleasant way to walk between two of the city's nodes, taking in some lovely spots – both historic and scenic – along the way.

1–2

Begin just southeast of Centraal Station, where Zeedijk branches from Prins Hendrikkade. The name **Zeedijk,** "sea dyke", was correct when it was first built: it provided protection when the Zuiderzee was open water and Amsterdam was thus connected to the North Sea. On your right, **Sint Olofskapel** has an alarming tablet above the door, of a skeleton reclining among skulls. Built in c.1445, it served as the city's stock exchange in the 16th century. You will shortly see a fine view as Zeedijk crosses the water, with the narrow finger of **Oudezijds Kolk** to the left and the broader expanse of **Oudezijds Voorburgwal** to the right.

2–3

Zeedijk once had a seedy, even dangerous reputation but the street is now monitored by surveillance cameras and is recovering some of its old respectability: among

> **TAKING A BREAK**
> Options are **Bird** (Zeedijk 77, ➤ 77), **In de Waag** (➤ 75), in the middle of Nieuwmarkt, or, for something more substantial try, **Le Zinc...et les autres** at Prinsengracht 999 (➤ 164).

the garish snackbars are excellent places to eat and drink. Still, it's hard to forget that this is the eastern boundary of the red-light district (➤ 56). The southern portion also borders Amsterdam's modest **Chinatown,** where many signs appear in both Dutch and Chinese. Further on Zeedijk expands into Nieuwmarkt, dominated by the large **Waag** (➤ 75). On the north side of the marketplace is a sculpture of a man forcing a kiss on a woman; on the north, wood-and-ceramic street furniture allows people (mainly all-day drinkers) to sit and reflect on the canal ahead.

3–4

Take the right (west) side of Kloveniersburgwal. A short way along the canal you can look across to the **Trippenhuis,** the original location for the collection now hanging in the Rijksmuseum. The headquarters of the **Oost Indisch Huis** (East India House), around the corner on Oude Hoogstraat, is now part of the University of Amsterdam; on weekdays you can admire the beautifully proportioned courtyard.

Walks

4–5

Heading south, you are moving into accommodation territory: across the canal is one of the city's downtown **youth hostels**. Near the end of Kloveniersburgwal, reach the Balmoral "Scottish Pub", part of the Doelen Hotel. Unless you are desperate for one of the extensive range of malt whiskies that it sells, cross the structure to your left: the first lifting bridge to be built in the city.

5–6

Continue south along Kloveniersburgwal; the waterway opens up into a broad basin, the Binnenamstel. Cross it on Halvemaansbrug, and continue across the road into the short pedestrian street named Halvemaansteeg. This takes you over a busy tram line into **Rembrandtplein**, a square that is now largely devoted to serving tourists with food and beer. Rembrandt occupies a plinth in the middle, surrounded by 22 bronze statues of people who are in his painting The Night Watch.

Rembrandt presides over the square named after him

6–7

This open space comprises two discrete squares. The southern one, **Thorbeckeplein**, named after the statesman Johan Rudolph Thorbecke, whose statue stands on the southern side, facing on to Herengracht. With a bandstand in the middle, the square is the closest Amsterdam gets to a Parisian feel.

Look due south along **Reguliersgracht**, which begins here, and you will see the first of the **Seven Bridges** that are only properly visible from the water at this point. Stay on the left (east) bank and continue south, looking out for fine woodwork on a bay window poking out of No 57 Reguliersgracht. You reach Kerkstraat immediately, named after the beautiful 17th-century, wooden **Amstelkerk**, now a concert venue, on the left-hand side, also occupied by the NEL restaurant (tel: 020 6 26 11 99, www.nelamstelveld.nl).

7–8

Cross bridge five, heading west along the south side of **Prinsengracht**, the outer canal of the three concentric arcs. Just before you start along it, look for the stork planted above the door of the

Rijksmuseum
Coster Diamonds
Van Gogh Museum
Stedelijk Museum
Weteringschans
Stadhouderskade
Spiegelgracht
Spiegelgracht
Hobbemakade

0   250 m
0   250 yd

Spiegelstraat. If you have an hour or two to spare, browse among the art and antiques shops down on the right (north). The walk heads left (south) over Prinsengracht, to one of the prettiest and liveliest intersections in the city.

8–9
Head along **Spiegelgracht,** towards the twin towers of the Rijksmuseum rising ahead. Pause on the bridge over the Lijnbaansgracht for a tranquil canal view. After negotiating the busy Weteringschans and Singelgracht, you approach the **Rijksmuseum** (➤ 120) as the architect intended: square on to the handsome facade. If you're heading for the **Van Gogh Museum** (➤ 124–127) or **Stedelijk Museum** (➤ 128), continue straight on underneath one of the four arches, building works permitting. This is also the way to the Rijksmuseum entrance, which is located in the museum underpass.

architect's office on the corner. There are a few houseboats strung out along here, but the main attractions are the houses and their elaborate gables. Cross the busy **Vijzelgracht**; calm is restored as you continue to the next crossing along, Nieuwe

The Stedelijk Museum entrance

Walks

4 THE WESTERN ISLES

DISTANCE 2km (1.25 miles)
TIME 1 hour
START POINT/END POINT South end of Grote Bickersstraat 🕂 203 E4

Nowhere on this short walk are you more than 1.5km (1 mile) from Centraal Station, yet it takes you to a part of Amsterdam that feels very different from the rest of the city: a series of small islands that have something of the atmosphere of provincial Holland.

❶–❷

Going west from Centraal Station, the railway line marks what was the northern shore of the IJ – until a succession of islands was created in the shallow river by enterprising merchants of the 17th century. The walk begins on the north side of the tracks, at the foot of Grote Bickersstraat, where it meets the busy Haarlemmer Houttuinen, at **Hendrik Jonkerplein.** A good

landmark is the Blaauw Hooft Café at No 1 (www.blaauwhooft. nl). From here, head right (east) for a short distance along **Blokmakerstraat**, named after the craftsmen who made the pulleys that helped keep the mercantile fleet moving. Nowadays, the Westelijke Eilanden (Western Isles) are residential, with modern apartment blocks and charming old warehouses.

❷–❸

Turn left (north) along the Hollandse Tuin, flanked by some 1970s housing, and admire the sailing barges and well-kept houseboats moored across on the far side of **Westerdok**; you pass Zeilmakerstraat to your left. Bear left and head along Touwslagerstraat; take the first right from here on Grote Bickersstraat. You soon reach a typical **lifting canal bridge**, over Realengracht; on the far side, you can see the first striking pair of warehouses converted into apartments, **De Lepelaar.**

❸–❹

Continue over the bridge and straight on along **Zandhoek**. Three houses proclaim their loyalties – No 3, De Eendracht, is guarded by the image of a fierce lion; No 4 features Noah's Ark; and No 6 has

The Western Isles of Amsterdam offer an interesting mix of the traditional and modern

TAKING A BREAK

Open overlooks the water and serves food all day, every day (Westerdoksplein 20, tel: 020 6 20 10 10, www.open.nl, Mon–Sat 5pm–10pm). The building is a clever, redevelopment of a railway bridge – this modern reinvention being typical of the area. If you're taking an evening stroll, you could call in at the wonderful **Marius** at Barentszstraat 243 (tel: 020 4 22 78 80, Tue–Sat 6–10). Serving modern French cuisine fresh from the market, some say it is one of Amsterdam's best restaurants.

Otherwise, settle for one of the cafés of the Jordaan, across on the south side of the tracks, at any time, though on a fine evening the light on the islands is particularly appealing.

Insider Tip

a white horse. Further on, at No 14, stands De Gouden Reael (tel: 020 6 23 38 83, www.goudenreael.nl, daily 4–midnight, dinner from 6pm), a café-restaurant with huge picture windows. It specializes in French regional cuisine and is named after the "golden real", a Spanish coin. Across another bridge, over Zoutkeetsgracht, you reach an island devoted to **Willem Barentsz**, the ill-fated Dutch

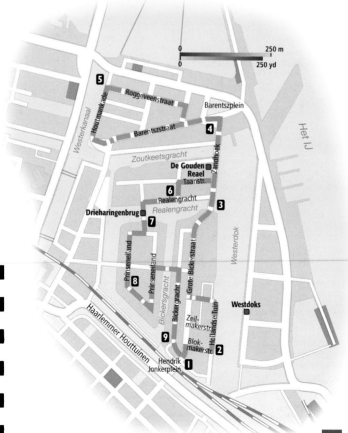

Walks

explorer who sought a Northeast Passage between Europe and Asia in the 16th century. He reached the island of Novaya Zemlya, in the sea that now bears his name, but perished in the Arctic winter.

❹–❺

Turn left at **Barentszplein** along Barentszstraat, past a coffeeshop named after the explorer. Barentszstraat ends at the **Westerkanaal,** one of the main maritime gateways to the web of canals in Amsterdam, and a sharp right turn on to Houtmankade. Continue until turning right on to Roggeveenstraat.

❺–❻

Roggeveenstraat, a pedestrianized street with an imposing school building on the left and handsome 19th-century housing on the right. At the end, skirt around Barentszsplein and go south back over the bridge to Realeneiland. Turn right along Taandwarsstraat, and left past modern residential developments – including two converted warehouses.

❻–❼

Turn right along **Realengracht** (the name of the canal and the waterside street) to **Drieharingenbrug,** one of Amsterdam's loveliest – and youngest – bridges. The

Realengracht is a quiet, prosperous and friendly area, where houseboats line the canal

present structure replaced the 18th-century original in 1983, and is wide enough for two bicycles. The "three herrings" of its name are carved above a door on the north side of the bridge.

❼–❽

On the south side of the bridge, you are on **Prinseneiland** – the smallest of the Western Isles. Bear right past a particularly fine house, built in 1629, and proceed to circumnavigate counterclockwise along the street that wraps around the isle. The line of buildings on the western flank have their shutters painted with mercantile slogans such as *D'Korenbeurs en D'Schelvis*. At the bend in the road, look for Nos 24A and 24B, just two of the many studios used by the artist George Breitner (1857–1923).

❽–❾

Follow Prinseneiland around through an interesting mix of new and old housing to the bridge over Bickersgracht. Cross it, and turn right down the street of the same name. There's a lovely garden at No 29, and across the canal from here, summer houses stand where ships were once launched. A short way south, towards the main railway line that marks the abrupt conclusion of the Western Isles, you soon reach **Hendrik Jonkerplein**, the starting and finishing point of the walk.

Practicalities

Practicalities

WHAT YOU NEED

● Required ○ Suggested ▲ Not required	Some countries require a passport to remain valid for a minimum period beyond the date of entry – contact their consulate or embassy for details	UK	USA	Canada	Australia	Germany	Ireland	Netherlands	Spain
Passport/National Identity Card		●	▲	●	●	●	●	●	●
Visa (regulations can change – check before you travel)		▲	▲	▲	▲	▲	▲	▲	▲
Onward or Return Ticket		▲	▲	▲	▲	▲	▲	▲	▲
Health Inoculations		▲	▲	▲	▲	▲	▲	▲	▲
Health Documentation (▶ 198, Health)		▲	▲	▲	▲	▲	▲	▲	▲
Travel Insurance		○	○	○	○	○	○	○	○
Driving Licence (national)		●	●	●	●	●	●	●	●
Car Insurance Certificate		○	n/a	n/a	n/a	○	○	○	○
Car Registration Document		●	n/a	n/a	n/a	●	●	●	●

WHEN TO GO

High season   Low Season

JAN	FEB	MAR	APRIL	MAY	JUNE	JULY	AUG	SEP	OCT	NOV	DEC
5°C	6°C	10°C	14°C	18°C	21°C	23°C	23°C	20°C	16°C	10°C	6°C
41°F	43°F	50°F	57°F	64°F	70°F	73°F	73°F	68°F	61°F	50°F	43°F

☼ Sun   Sunshine/Showers   Cloud   Wet

Temperatures are the **average daily maximum** for each month. "Damp and mild" sums up the climate in Amsterdam. The ideal month to visit is May, when both the rain and the crowds are less intense than in June, July and August. September, though wetter, is also a good bet. The weather is often miserable – chilly and drizzly – between October and March, though **the canals rarely freeze**. Strong winds in winter can **increase the chill factor**, and fog can blot out the sunlight for days. During December, Amsterdam is **crowded with Christmas shoppers**, and with foreign visitors spending the festive season in the city. November to March are the coldest months; temperatures start warming up in April.

GETTING ADVANCE INFORMATION

Internet
■ www.iamsterdam.com
The official tourist board website is a useful starting point for research.

■ www.holland.com
The official tourist site for Holland – useful information about out-of-town excursions.

GETTING THERE

By Air Schiphol airport has good flight connections from all over the world. From the UK, there are **non-stop flights** from 20 airports on 10 airlines, notably **British Airways** (www.britishairways.com), **easyJet** (www.easyjet.com) and **KLM** (www.klm.com).

From Ireland, **Aer Lingus** (www.aerlingus.com) has daily departures from Dublin and one flight a day from Cork.

From the US, there are **daily non-stop flights** from Atlanta, Boston, Chicago, Detroit, Houston, Los Angeles, Miami, New York, San Francisco, Seattle and Washington DC.

The Canadian cities with **non-stop links** are Calgary, Montreal, Toronto and Vancouver.

There is no longer a direct flight from Sydney; from this and other Australian and New Zealand cities the best connections are in Singapore, Bangkok, Hong Kong and Los Angeles.

Typical flying times to Amsterdam: UK (1 hour), Dublin (1.5 hours), New York and Toronto (8 hours), Vancouver and Los Angeles (11 hours), Sydney (22 hours).

By Rail Centraal Station has direct connections from major cities in Western Europe, including high-speed Thalys links from Paris, Brussels and Cologne. From Britain, there are connections at Brussels with trains operated by Eurostar (tel: 0843 218 6186; www.eurostar.com), with good-value through-fares to Amsterdam.

By Sea Stena Line (tel: 0844 770 7070; www.stenaline.co.uk) operates a link between Harwich in Essex and Hoek van Holland; crossings take 6 hours 45 minutes. **P&O Ferries** (tel: 0871 664 2121, www.poferries.com) has a nightly service from Hull to Rotterdam. **DFDS Seaways** (tel: 0871 522 9955, www.dfdsseaways.co.uk) sails from Newcastle to IJmuiden, with a bus to Amsterdam.

TIME

Holland is on Central European Time, one hour ahead of GMT in winter, two hours ahead in summer. The clocks change at the end of March and October.

CURRENCY & FOREIGN EXCHANGE

Currency The monetary unit of the Netherlands is the euro (€). Notes are issued in denominations of €5, €10, €20, €50, €100, €200 and €500, and coins in denominations of €1 and €2, and 1, 2, 5, 10, 20 and 50 cents. **Debit cards** Debit cards are the most convenient way to obtain cash – from ATMs throughout the city. **Credit cards** All major credit cards are widely accepted. **Exchange** The cheapest way to obtain euros is to use a debit card in one of the many automatic teller machines (ATMs) outside most banks, at Schiphol airport and at Centraal Station.

NETHERLANDS BOARD OF TOURISM (www.holland.com):

In the UK
PO Box 30783,
London WC2B 6DH
☎ 020 75 39 79 50

In the USA and Canada
215 Park
Avenue South, Suite 2005,
New York, NY 10003
☎ 212 3 70 73 60

Practicalities

NATIONAL HOLIDAYS

1 Jan	New Year's Day
Mar/Apr	Good Friday, Easter Monday
26 Apr	King's Day
5 May	Liberation Day
40 days after Easter	Hemelvaartsdag (Ascension Day)
50 days after Easter	Pinksteren (Whit Sun & Mon)
25 Dec	Christmas Day
26 Dec	Tweede Kerstdag (Boxing Day)

On these days, most businesses close all day, though tourist facilities usually remain open. On 5 December, St Nicholas's Eve, businesses close early.

ELECTRICITY

 Plugs have two round pins, with an optional earth pin, requiring an adaptor for UK, North American, Asian and Australasian appliances. The power supply is 220 volts. Appliances on 110 volts may need a transformer.

OPENING HOURS

○ Shops
● Offices
● Banks
● Post Offices
● Museums/Monuments
● Pharmacies

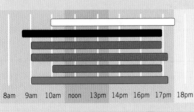

8am 9am 10am noon 13pm 14pm 16pm 17pm 18pm

☐ Day   ☐ Midday   ☐ Evening

Shops On the main shopping streets in the centre, stores typically open Mon 11–6, Tue–Wed and Fri 10–6, Thu 10–9, Sat 9–5 and Sun 12–5.
Museums While the big attractions are usually open from 9 or 10am to 6pm or later, smaller ones may keep shorter hours, such as 11–5, and Sun 1–5. There is no general policy of closing on a Mon, though a few of the minor museums do.

TIPS/GRATUITIES

In restaurants and cafés the custom is to leave a few coins or round up the bill even if the 15% service charge is already included in the bill.

Tour guides	€3–€5
Toilet attendants	€0.50
Taxis	round up fare
Chambermaids	€4
Porters	€3–€5

SMOKING/DRUG LAWS

Smoking tobacco is banned in public indoor spaces. But this does not apply to marijuana, which means you can be arrested for smoking a joint for its tobacco, not its marijuana, content. There are always stiff penalties for possessing "hard" drugs.

TIME DIFFERENCES

Amsterdam (CET)	London (GMT)	New York (EST)	Los Angeles (PST)	Sydney (AEST)
12 noon	← 11am	← 6am	← 3am	→ 9pm

STAYING IN TOUCH

Post Amsterdam's main post office is at Singel 250, at the corner of Raadhuisstraat (Mon–Fri 7:30–6:30, Sat 7:30–5), which is busy, but efficient.
Stamps can be bought in newsagents and souvenir shops, as well as post offices. Postboxes are bright red; for mail outside Amsterdam, use the slot labelled "Overige Postcodes".

Public telephones There are now very few public phones on the streets of Amsterdam. The few that remain are run by a private company and they accept coins or pre-paid cards (available at tobacconists, supermarkets and *bureaux de change*); the most expensive method is from a hotel bedroom.

International Dialling Codes from Amsterdam

UK:	44
USA/Canada:	1
Ireland:	353
Australia:	61
New Zealand:	64

WiFi and internet Many hotels and cafés provide WiFi for free (although some of the more traditional hotels continue to charge a high, hourly rate), but you'll need your own laptop. Internet cafés, with reasonable hourly rates for the use of a computer terminal and internet access, are found throughout the city, most of them serving coffee and other drinks and even snacks.

Mobile providers and services Before you leave, ask your provider about roaming charges and, remember, you will also be charged if you receive calls from home. Texting is usually cheaper. If you are away for more than two weeks, consider buying a SIM card in the Netherlands to cut down on costs.

PERSONAL SAFETY

Violent crime is a rarity in the city, but petty theft is common – particularly on crowded trams and at popular tourist destinations.

■ Take sensible precautions and don't carry large amounts of cash or valuables with you.

■ A recent trend is for thieves to target trains operating between Schiphol airport and Centraal Station, as well as trams. Visitors laden with luggage are distracted by one thief as they are robbed by the other.

■ Take real care locking up bicycles and avoid leaving them out overnight (most hotels have safe areas to store them): Amsterdam has one of the highest rates of bike theft in the world.

■ The whole of the red-light district, De Wallen, is generally to be avoided at night, when it attracts unsavoury types, including drug dealers, although there is a strong police presence after dark here.

POLICE 112 or 0900 8844 for non-emergencies

FIRE 112

AMBULANCE 112

Practicalities

HEALTH

 Insurance EU citizens receive free or re-duced-cost emergency medical treatment with relevant documentation (European Health Insurance Card), but private medical insurance is still advised and is essential for all other visitors.

 Dental Services Emergency treatment is available at reduced cost for EU citizens, but fees can be high. Other visitors should have medical insurance covering dental treatment.

 Weather Amsterdam is farther north than Warsaw and Winnipeg, but the summer sun can still burn. Use sunscreen in June, July and August, and drink plenty of fluids – carry a bottle of mineral water rather than stopping at streetside terraces for a beer.

 Drugs Pharmacies can provide a wide range of remedies over the counter. The recreational narcotics on offer in Amsterdam should not be treated lightly: the effects on mind and body can be severe, and are often exacerbated when mixed with alcohol.

 Safe Water Tap water is safe to drink. Canal water is unpalatable in the extreme, and is also not suitable for swimming. Bottled mineral water, often called by the generic name "spa," is readily available everywhere.

CONCESSIONS

Students/Youths Discounts are offered by some museums and sometimes there are special deals for air travel. On the rare occasions when "student discounts" are advertised, they're usually restricted to people studying in Amsterdam.

Senior Citizens Visitors aged 65 or over qualify for discounts at museums and other tourists attractions. Proof in the form of a passport or identity card may be required.

TRAVELLING WITH A DISABILITY

Positive steps have been taken to make Amsterdam a disability-friendly destina-tion, with lifts and ramps installed in many public buildings, and easy access to public transport. But the unique geography, with cobbled streets, parked cars and awkward canal bridges, can be difficult for wheelchair-users.

CHILDREN

There is no common agree-ment on what age qualifies children for free or reduced-rate entry. Special attrac-tions for kids are marked out with the logo shown above.

LAVATORIES

Men's urinals are easy to find. The more discreet type comprises a wrap-around steel frame but in busy are-as, urinal "pillars" may be used by four men at once. Women can use facilities in cafés.

LOST PROPERTY

Schiphol airport, tel: 09 00 01 41; on trams, buses or the Metro, tel: 09 00 80 11.

EMBASSIES AND CONSULATES

UK	USA	Canada	Australia	New Zealand
☎ 070 427 0427	☎ 070 310 2209	☎ 070 311 1600	☎ 070 310 8200	☎ 070 346 9324
(The Hague)	(The Hague)	(The Hague)	(The Hague)	(The Hague)

Useful Words and Phrases

SURVIVAL PHRASES

Yes/no **Ja/nee**
Hello **Dag/hallo**
Good morning **Goedemorgen**
Good afternoon **Goedemiddag**
Good evening **Goedenavond**
Goodbye **Dag/tot ziens**
How are you? **Hoe gaat het (met u)?**
Fine, thank you **Goed, bedankt**
Please **Alstublieft**
Thank you **Dank u (wel)/bedankt**
Excuse me **Pardon**
Sorry **Het spijt mij/sorry**
Do you have…? **Heeft u…?**
I'd like… **Ik wil (graag)…**
How much is it? **Hoeveel is het?**
Open **Open**
Closed **Gesloten**
To push/pull **Duwen/trekken**
Women's lavatory **Dames**
Men's lavatory **Heren**

DIRECTIONS AND GETTING AROUND

Where is…? **Waar is…?**
  the tram stop **de tramhalte**
  the telephone **de telefoon**
  the bank **de bank**
  (note: bank also means seat)
Turn left/right **Ga naar links/rechts**
Go straight on **Ga rechtdoor**
Here/there **Hier/daar**
North **Noord**
East **Oost**
South **Zuid**
West **West**

TRAVEL

Aeroplane **Vliegtuig**
Airport **Luchthaven**
Bicycle **Fiets**

Bus **Bus**
Taxi **Taxi**
Train **Trein**
Tram **Tram**
Arrivals **Aankomst**
Departures **Vertrek**
Non-smoking **Niet roken**
Platform **Spoor**
Seat **Plaats**
Reserved **Gereserveerd**
Ticket **Kaartje**
Ticket office **Loket**
Timetable **Dienstregeling**
First class **Eerste klas**
Second class **Tweede klas**
Single/return **Enkele reis/retour**

DAYS OF THE WEEK

Monday **Maandag**
Tuesday **Dinsdag**
Wednesday **Woensdag**
Thursday **Donderdag**
Friday **Vrijdag**
Saturday **Zaterdag**
Sunday **Zondag**

OTHER USEFUL WORDS AND PHRASES

Yesterday **Gisteren**
Today **Vandaag**
Tomorrow **Morgen**
I don't understand **Ik begrijp het niet**
Do you speak English? **Spreekt u Engels?**
I need a doctor **Ik heb een arts nodig**
Do you have a vacant room? **Zijn er nog kamers vrij?**
  with bath/shower **met bad/douche**
  with balcony met **balkon**
Single room **Eenpersoonskamer**
Double room **Tweepersoonskamer**
One/two nights **Een/twee nachten**
Rate **Prijs**

NUMBERS

1	een	12	twaalf	30	dertig	102	honderd twee
2	twee	13	dertien	31	eenendertig	200	tweehonderd
3	drie	14	veertien	32	tweeëndertig	300	driehonderd
4	vier	15	vijftien	40	veertig	400	vierhonderd
5	vijf	16	zestien	50	vijftig	500	vijfhonderd
6	zes	17	zeventien	60	zestig	600	zeshonderd
7	zeven	18	achttien	70	zeventig	700	zevenhonderd
8	acht	19	negentien	80	tachtig	800	achthonderd
9	negen	20	twintig	90	negentig	900	negenhonderd
10	tien	21	eenentwintig	100	honderd	1,000	duizend
11	elf	22	tweeëntwintig	101	honderd een		

Useful Words and Phrases

EATING OUT

Have you got a table for two?
Heeft u een tafel voor twee?
I want to reserve a table
Ik wil een tafel reserveren
I am a vegetarian **Ik ben vegetariër**
Could I have the bill, please?
De rekening alstublieft
This is not what I ordered
Dit is niet wat ik besteld heb
Can we sit by the window?
Mogen wij bij het raam?
Is the kitchen still open?
Is de keuken nog open?
What time do you close?
How laat gaat u dicht?
Do you have a highchair?
Heeft u een kinderstoel?
Is this spicy/highly seasoned?
Is dit gerecht pikant/gekruid?
The food is cold **Het eten is koud**
Enjoy your meal! **Eet smakelijk!**
Service included **Bediening inbegrepen**
Service not included **Exclusief bediening**

Bottle/glass **Fles/glas**
Breakfast **Ontbijt**
Café **Café**

Cold **Koud**
Cover charge **Couvert**
Dessert **Nagerecht**
Dinner **Diner/avondeten**
Dish of the day **Dagschotel**
Drink **Drank/drankje**
Dry **Droog**
Fork **Vork**
Fried **Gebakken**
Hot **Warm/heet**
Hot (spicy) **Pikant (scherp)**
Knife **Mes**
Lunch **Lunch/middageten**
Main course **Hoofdgerecht**
Medium **Medium**
Menu **Menukaart**
Rare **Rare**
Restaurant **Restaurant**
Set (prix-fixe) **menu Menu**
Specialities **Specialiteiten**
Spoon **Lepel**
Starter **Voorgerecht**
Table **Tafel**
Waiter **Ober**
Waitress **Serveerster**
Well done **Doorbakken**
Wine list **Wijnkaart**

MENU A–Z

Aardappelen
Potatoes
Ansjovis Anchovies
Appelgebak
(met slagroom)
Apple pie (with
whipped cream)
Azijn Vinegar
Biefstuk Steak
Bier or Pils Beer
Bonen Beans
Boter Butter
Boterham Sandwich
Bouillon Consommé
Brood Bread
Broodje Bun or roll
Carbonade
Pork chop
Champignons
Mushrooms
Chips Crisps
Chocola Chocolate
Citroen Lemon
Eend Duck
Ei Egg

Erwten Peas
Forel Trout
Garnalen Prawns
Hachée Stew
Ham Ham
Hamburger
Hamburger
Haring Herring
Hertenvlees Venison
Honing Honey
Hutspot Hot-pot
Ijs Ice cream
Jenever Gin
Jus Gravy
Kaas Cheese
Kabeljauw Cod
Kalfsvlees Veal
Kalkoen Turkey
Kip Chicken
Knoflook Garlic
Koffie Coffee
Kreeft Lobster
Lamsvlees Lamb
Makreel Mackerel
Melk Milk

Mineraalwater
Mineral water
Mosterd Mustard
Oesters Oysters
Olie Oil
Paling Eel
Pannenkoeken
Pancakes
Patat frites
Chips/french fries
Peper Pepper
Rijst Rice
Rode wijn Red wine
Rookworst Smoked
sausage
Room Cream
Rundvlees Beef
Salade or Sla Salad
Saus Sauce
Schaaldieren
Shellfish
Schelvis Haddock
Schol Plaice
Sinaasappelsap
Orange juice

Soep Soup
Spek Bacon
Stamppot
Sausage stew
Suiker Sugar
Thee Tea
Tong Sole
Tosti Cheese
on toast
Uien Onions
Uitsmijter
Fried egg on
bread with ham
Varkensvlees Pork
Vis Fish
Vlees Meat
Vruchten Fruit
Water Water
Wild Game
Witte wijn
White wine
Worst Sausage
Wortelen Carrots
Zalm Salmon
Zout Salt

Street Atlas

For chapters: see inside front cover

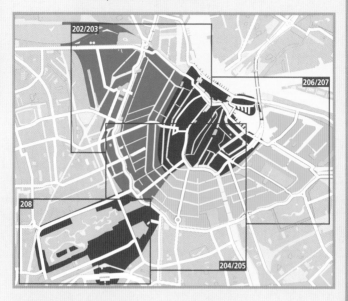

202/203
206/207
208
204/205

Key to Street Atlas

Information		Berth, harbour	
Museum		Youth hostal	
Theatre, opera house		Indor swimming pool	
Windmill		Parking area, car park	
Synagogue		Metro	
Mosque		Canal Bus	
Monuments		Public building / Building of interest	
Church		Pedestrian precinct	
Hospital			
Police station		TOP 10	
Post office		Don't Miss	
		At Your Leisure	

1 : 11.000

0   500   800 m
0   500   800 yd

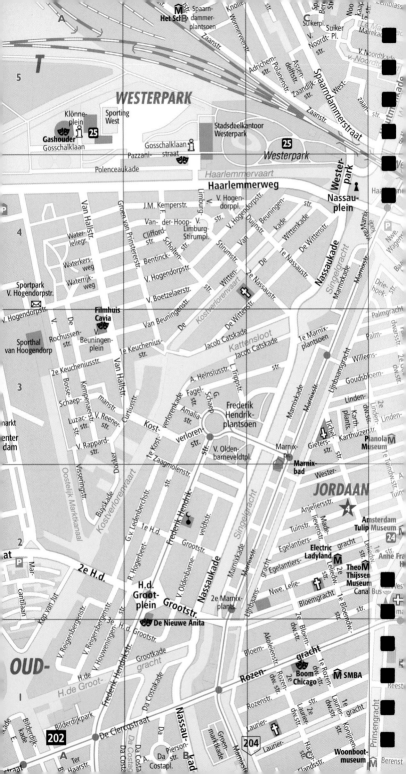

WESTERPARK

Het Sch

Spaarn-
dammer-
plantsoen

Spaarndammerstraat

Sukerpl.

Noordt-Pl.
v. Noordt-
str.

5

Klönne-
plein

Sporting
West

Gashouder
Gosschalklaan

Pazzani-
straat

25

Stadsdeelkantoor
Westerpark

Gosschalk-
laan

Westerpark

25

Westerpark

Polenceaukade

Nassau-
plein

Haarlemmervaart

Haarlemmerweg

V. Hogen-
dorppl.

J.M. Kemperstr.

Limburg

V. Hogendorpstr.

Beuningen-
str.

Nwe.
Wagen-

4

Water-
leliegr.

Van- der-Hoop-
str.

V.
Limburg-
Stirumpl.

Clifford-
str.

Scholten-

Bentinck-
str.

V. Hogendorpstr.

V. Boetzelaerstr.

Van Hallstr.

Groen van Prinstererstr.

V. Hogendorppl.

V. Dulinstr.

Wittenkade

De Wittenstr.

1e Nassaustr.

2e Nassaustr.

Nassaukade

Singelgracht

Marnixkade

Drie-
hoek

Palmgracht

Sportpark
V. Hogendorpstr.

Filmhuis
Cavia

Van Beuningenstr.

Kostverlorenvaart

De Wittenstr.

De

Witten-

str.

De Nassaustr.

Jacob Catskade

Kattensloot

Jacob Catskade

1e Marnix-
plantsoen

Palm-

Willems-

Goudsbloem-

V. Hogendorpstr.

Sporthal
van Hoogendorp

De
Beuningen-
plein

Rochussen-
str.

2e Keucheniusstr.

V. Keucheniusstr.

A. Heinsiusstr.

Limpistr.

Marnixkade

Linden-

Karth.
plants.

Linden-

3

Bosse-
str.

Kempenaerstr.

Fagel-
str.

Marnixstr.

Linden-

Luzac-
str.

V. Reener-
str.

Curtiusstr.

Kost-

verlorenkade

Amalia-
str.

G.
Schaep-
str.

Frederik
Hendrik-
plantsoen

Gietersr.

Tichel-
str.

Karthuizerstr.

Pianola
Museum

V. Rappard-
str.

V. Oldenbarneveldtpl.

Marnix-
pl.

Wester-

Schaep-
str.

2e Tuindwstr.

Oostelijk Marktkanaal

Kostverlorenvaart

Visseringstr.

Donker

1e Kost-

verloren

str.

Zaagmolenstr.

Marnixbad

JORDAAN

Anjeliersstr.

Amsterdam
Tulip
Museum

Buyskade

G.v. Ledenberchstr.

1e H.d.

Frederik Hendrik

veldtstr.

Grootstr.

Singelgracht

Tuinstr.

Made-
lieve-
str.

Egelantiersstr.

Electric
Ladyland

gracht

Anne Fra

24

2

Mar-
canfillaan

Kop van Jut

2e H.d.

R. Hogerbeet-

V. Oldenbarne-

Nassaukade

Marnixkade

Egelantiers-

gracht

Nwe. Lelie-

Bloemgracht

Theo
Thijssen
Museum

1e Bloemdw.

Canal Bus

H. d.
Groot-
plein

Grootstr.

2e Marnix-
plants.

V. Reigersbergenstr.

V. Reigersbergenstr.

V. Houweningen-

H. d. Grootstr.

De Nieuwe Anita

Grootkade

gracht

Bloem-

Akoleienstr.

Bloem-

gracht

Boom
Chicago

SMBA

OUD-

H.de
Groot-

Frederik Hendrikstr.

H. de Groot-
gracht

Da Costakade

Rozen

Rozen

dw.str.

2e
Laurier-

1e

gracht

Prinsengracht

I

Bilderdijk-
kade

Bilderdijkpark

202

De Clercqstraat

Da Costastr.

Nassau-
kad

Rozengr.

Rozenstr.

Laurier-

2e
Laurier-
dw.str.

Laurier-

Woonboot-
museum

Ter
Haarst.

A

Da Costastr.

Da Pierson-
str.
Da Costapl.

B

Groen-
marktkade

Marnixstr.

204

Laurier

Laurierstr.

Konijnen-
str.

Berens

str.

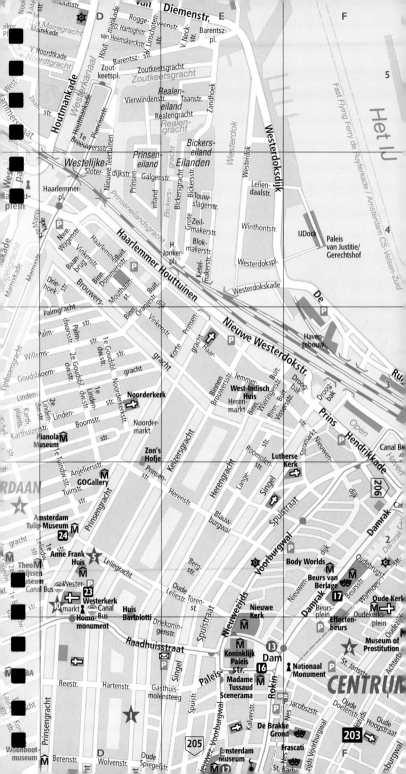

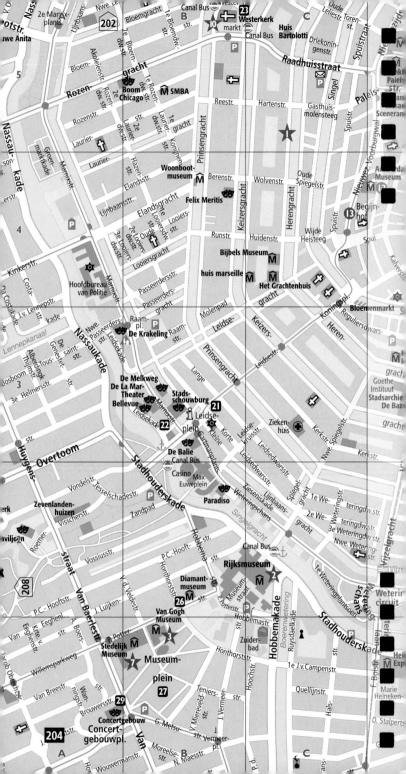

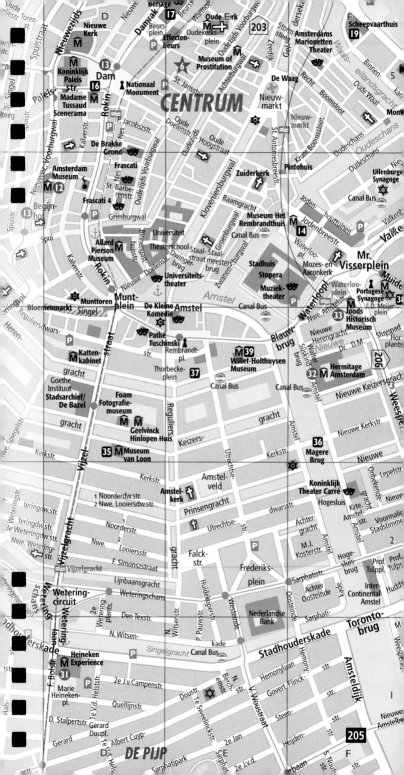

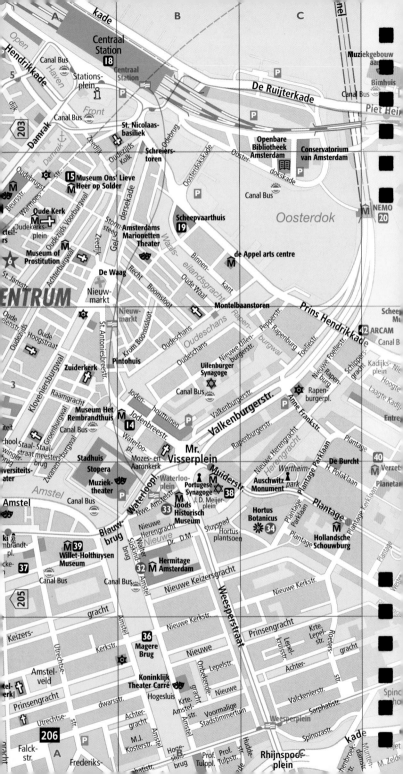

Street Index

Street Index

Street Index

Index

Index

Index

Index

Picture Credits

AA/Alex Kouprianoff: 55, 197 (bottom)

AA/Alex Robinson: 10/11, 29, 30 (centre left), 30 (centre right),
31 (centre left), 31 (centre right), 32, 34, 35, 52, 54, 60, 61, 62, 65, 66, 68,
69, 70, 84 (bottom), 86, 87, 89, 90, 94, 95, 101, 102, 103, 104 (bottom), 118,
119 (top), 119 (bottom), 125 (top), 126 (bottom), 132, 134, 143, 144, 145,
146/147, 152, 153, 155, 156, 157, 160, 169, 170, 171, 172, 174, 175, 176, 177,
182, 183, 185, 186, 188, 190, 192, 197 (top), 197 (centre)

AA/K Paterson: 72

AA/Max Jourdan: 73

Corbis: Fotomaschinist/Westend61 16, Barry Lewis 22, Corbis 24, Massimo
Borchi 63, 104/105, Frans Lemmens 122/123

DuMont Bildarchiv: Rainer Kiedrowski 25, 180, Thomas Linkel 56/57,
84 (top), 91, 96/97, 116 (top), 116 (bottom), 120, 121, 124, 125 (bottom), 128,
129, 130/131, 133, 135, 136, 158, 159, 173, 178, 189, Arthur F. Selbach 67

getty images: Sara Winter 13 (top), Fred Froese 19, Ingolf Pompe 92/93

laif: Gladieu/Le Figaro Magazine 8, Rademaker/Hollandse Hoogte 12,
Reporters 27, Hollandse Hoogte 106, Miquel Gonzalez 148, Wouters/
Hollandse Hoogte 151

LOOK-foto: age fotostock 4, 98, 126/127, Ingolf Pompe 7, 142,
Rainer Mirau 14/15

mauritius images: Alamy 13 (bottom), 26, 105 (bottom), 150, imagebroker 17,
20, United Archives 99 (top)

On the cover: F1online: Robert Harding (top), F1online: Alvaro Leiva (bottom),
Getty Images: sbayram (background)

Credits

1st Edition 2015

Worldwide Distribution: Marco Polo Travel Publishing Ltd
Pinewood, Chineham Business Park
Crockford Lane, Chineham
Basingstoke, Hampshire RG24 8AL, United Kingdom.
© MAIRDUMONT GmbH & Co. KG, Ostfildern

Authors: Simon Calder, Fred Mawer ("Where to…"), Jane Egginton,
Anneke Bokern
Editor: Bintang Buchservice GmbH (Gudrun Raether-Klünker),
www.bintang-berlin.de
Revised editing and translation: Margaret Howie, www.fullproof.co.za
Program supervisor: Birgit Borowski
Chief editor: Rainer Eisenschmid

Cartography: © MAIRDUMONT GmbH & Co. KG, Ostfildern
3D-illustrations: jangled nerves, Stuttgart

Printed in China

Despite all of our authors' thorough research, errors can creep in.
The publishers do not accept any liability for this. Whether you
want to praise, alert us to errors or give us a personal tip –
please don't hesitate to email or post:

MARCO POLO Travel Publishing Ltd
Pinewood, Chineham Business Park
Crockford Lane, Chineham
Basingstoke, Hampshire RG24 8AL
United Kingdom
Email: sales@marcopolouk.com

FSC
www.fsc.org
MIX
Paper from
responsible sources
FSC® C020056

10 REASONS
TO COME BACK AGAIN

1. The **canals** are lovely in all season – in the summer sunshine or festively lit in winter.

2. In no other city is **cycling** is so natural and so pleasant.

3. Dutch *matjes* herrings are tasty treats that just melt in your mouth and smack of the sea.

4. The **Rijksmuseum** is so large that you will discover new artworks every time you visit.

5. The countless **small shops in the old town** offer endless possibilities for rummaging.

6. Amsterdammers are friendly, **open-minded** and incredibly laid back.

7. It takes some time to eat your way through the **cuisines from 55 different nations**.

8. Time and time again, you can experience the *gezelligheid* of the **brown cafés**.

9. The beaches near the city and the **Ijsselmeer coast** lie waiting for you to discover them.

10. The sound of **the Westerkerk's carillon** will warm the cockles of your heart whenever you hear its chimes.